CYBER POP

Routledge Studies in New Media and Cyberculture

Routledge Studies in New Media and Cyberculture is dedicated to further-ing original research in new media and cyberculture studies. International in scope, the series places an emphasis on cutting edge scholarship and interdis-ciplinary methodology. Topics explored in the series will include compara-tive and cultural studies of video games, blogs, online communities, digital music, new media art, cyberactivism, open source, mobile communications technologies, new information technologies, and the myriad intersections of race, gender, ethnicity, nationality, class, and sexuality with cyberculture.

Series Titles

Cyberpop: Digital Lifestyles and Commodity Culture
Sidney Eve Matrix, University of Winnipeg

Forthcoming Titles

The Internet in China: Cyberspace and Civil Society
Zixue Tai, Southern Illinois Univeristy

Racing Cyberculture: Minoritarian Internet Art
Chris McGahan, Yeshiva University

Virtual English: Internet Use, Language, and Global Subjects
Jillana Enteen, Northwestern University

CYBER POP

DIGITAL LIFESTYLES

AND

COMMODITY CULTURE

SIDNEY EVE MATRIX

Routledge
Taylor & Francis Group
New York   London

Routledge is an imprint of the
Taylor & Francis Group, an informa business

Published in 2006 by
Routledge
Taylor & Francis Group
711 Third Avenue
New York, NY 10017

Published in Great Britain by
Routledge
Taylor & Francis Group
2 Park Square
Milton Park, Abingdon
Oxon OX14 4RN

© 2006 by Taylor & Francis Group, LLC
Routledge is an imprint of Taylor & Francis Group
First issued in paperback 2012

ISBN13: 978-0-415-97677-0 (hbk)
ISBN13: 978-0-415-64901-8 (pbk)

Taylor & Francis Group
is the Academic Division of Informa plc.

Visit the Taylor & Francis Web site at
http://www.taylorandfrancis.com

and the Routledge Web site at
http://www.routledge-ny.com

Contents

Acknowledgments

I am grateful to friends and colleagues who provided constructive feedback on chapters including Naomi Scheman, John Mowitt, Amy Kaminsky, Gwendolyn Pough, Linda Wayne, and Jigna Desai.

Financial assistance for this research was provided by the Harold Leonard Memorial Fellowship in Film Studies and the Center for Advanced Feminist Studies at the University of Minnesota.

I would like to thank Matthew Byrnie at Routledge for his expertise, active support, and encouragement of the project from its early days.

The greatest debt of gratitude is owed to my family for their emotional and material support, for their commitment, investment, optimism, and faith. Thank you, Penny, Mike, Shawn, and Martin.

Introduction

This is a theoretical analysis of representational politics in the popular media of cyberculture. It considers the role that films, advertising, and other mass-marketed cyberpop texts play in the formation of digital lifestyles, identities, and subjects. Cyberpop is a category of cultural productions that spans several media forms (including visual, textual, and electronic multimedia) and subgenres, such as cyberpunk novels and film, comic books and graphic novels, interactive computer games and visual art, advertisements for information and computer technologies, Web sites, and digital culture magazines. What makes cyberpop a coherent analytic category is its relationship to recently emergent technologies, models, and metaphors borrowed from what Evelyn Fox Keller calls the "cybersciences"—informatic, computer, and genomic technosciences, but also more experimental sciences such as biocomputing, artificial intelligence, robotics, artificial life, and virtual reality research and development.[1]

As is the case with most popular cultural productions, cyberpop is a form of escapist mass media, "manufactured diversions," and "forms of pure spectacle"; yet it is a mistake to dismiss these popular texts as unworthy of serious consideration or merely trivial.[2] Like much science fiction, cybercultural popular media productions oftentimes promote technoliteracy, serve to popularize a high-tech aesthetic, and transmit a technoscientific imaginary to large public audiences—in other words, cyberpop has a *didactic* function. A book like *Neuromancer* or a film like *GATTACA* performs as an "infomediary" operating between mass culture and the specialized worlds of technoscience, transferring cybernetic paradigms and rhetoric, translating models, inventing metaphors for mass distribution. In the role of infomediary, cyberpop is in a powerful position to shape the public's perception of the place of technoscience in our everyday lives. Inspired by the cybersciences, we know that cyberpop sometimes *inspires* research and development, in a science-culture

1

feedback loop. As Arturo Escobar observed in his early essay, "Welcome to Cyberia: Notes on the Anthropology of Cyberculture":

> The study of cyberculture is particularly concerned with the cultural constructions and reconstructions on which the new technologies are based and which they in turn help to shape. The point of departure of this inquiry is the belief that any technology represents a cultural invention, in the sense that it brings forth a world; it emerges out of particular cultural conditions and in turn helps to create new ones. Anthropologists might be particularly well prepared to understand these processes if they were to open up to the idea that science and technology are crucial arenas for the creation of culture in today's world.[3]

Likewise, Donna Haraway suggests that "how we figure technoscience makes an immense difference" in how we imagine and develop future cultures, epistemologies, technologies, and identities.[4] Finally, in his book *Technoromanticism*, Richard Coyne agrees that "the narratives we construct [about technologies] are consequential in the developments that take place [and] influential in the kinds of products and systems we create and demand."[5] Cyberpop media entertains, inspires, and educates its audiences with high-tech wonders.

An excellent example of this process is the case of author William Gibson who, in 1984 published *Neuromancer*, a novel that established the genre of cyberpunk.[6] Here Gibson coined the phrase *cyberspace* to describe his science-fictional vision of a virtual reality environment wherein users could interface with each other within, as part of, and constituted by the flow of information or *the matrix*. *Neuromancer* was composed the same year that Apple Computer Company launched its Macintosh personal computer, but when Gibson constructed his narrative of computer hackers he had never seen a computer; ironically Gibson used a portable typewriter to produce his award-winning portrait of a digital global capitalist technoculture in the not-too-distant future. Nevertheless, fifteen years after the novel was published, cyberspace was no longer a far-fetched idea from a paperback novel; the term was adopted to describe the vision that computer scientists, programmers, and hardware designers had for the information society they were building. As Sandy Stone observes about *Neuromancer*, Gibson's powerful vision provided "the imaginal public sphere" and discursive framework or network that was the grounding for an e-generation, and the impetus for what we now call cyberculture.[7] Cyberpop texts such as Gibson's resonate with and encode the values of digital capitalism, citing the dominant and hegemonic cultural arrangements therein, while at the same time offering innovative and imaginative, critical and creative representations of the emerging cyberculture and its subjects.

THINK DIFFERENT

Like *Neuromancer*, contemporary cyberpop popularizes, valorizes, and celebrates the latest in computer technologies, simultaneously encouraging the intended audience to develop a mildly skeptical, resistant, or critically self-reflexive relationship to the digitalization of everyday life. In doing so, seemingly very different examples of cyberpop, such as a cyborg comic book *Witchblade,* the SF film *Strange Days,* or a Microsoft advertising campaign for networked environments can, in their employment of science-fiction discourse, achieve what postmodern theorist Fredric Jameson describes as *a critical discourse on the present,* by inventing "multiple mock futures" to "defamiliarize our science fictional lives" and reflect them back to us.[8] This was both the aim and (in the view of many spectators and reviewers) the strength of the cinematic cyberpop trilogy *The Matrix*. In the words of the filmmaker Larry Wachowski:

> We're tired of dumb movies. We like action movies. We like Kung Fu. We like those genre films. But we wanted to make one that was smarter, that was socially and politically relevant, with something that involved more than giving people a good time. The idea of *The Matrix* is that it's very easy to live an unexamined life.[9]

Similarly, in the opinion of film critic Read Schuchardt:

> The Wachowski's seem to have posed themselves this question: How do you speak seriously to a culture reduced to the format of comic books and video games? Answer: You tell them a story from the only oracle they'll listen to: a movie, and you tell the story in the comic-book and video-game format that the culture has become so addicted to. In other words, *The Matrix* is a graduate thesis on consciousness in the sheep's clothing of an action-adventure flick. Whether you're illiterate or have a PhD, there's something in the movie for you.[10]

The radical potential of imaginative forms of cyberpop such as *The Matrix* film lies in its ability to inspire and challenge its audience to "think different"—to adopt a slogan from the advertising campaign used by Apple Computer Company in the 1980s and 1990s—about the technologies that shape our lifestyles and communities, our bodies, and imaginaries. The chapters that follow argue that the representational politics in cyberpop media also invite us to think deeply and differently about the impact of the digital revolution on our identities and lifestyles.

It comes as no great surprise that the most popular cyberpunk and science-fiction texts celebrate and fetishize technology, but they also encourage the intended audience to develop a skeptical, critical, resistant, or at least self-reflexive relationship to emergent technologies and to consider our implication and pleasure in the digitalization of everyday life. As a result, cyberpop is sometimes characterized by a tongue-in-cheek tone, to encourage a kind of hip consumerism—in other words, you can *buy in* (engage and consume technology) without *selling out* (conforming to corporate capitalist computer culture). Thus, what a cyberpop film like *Vanilla Sky* has in common with a trendy advertisement for *Yahoo!* Web services is that both texts can be read as tools for the enculturation of what Scott Bukatman calls "terminal subjects," or what other media commentators have called *Generation D* (digital).[11] Yet, at the same time these cyberpop texts have an *edginess* to them, operating as sometimes subtle but unmistakable examples of sexy social criticism (Bruce Sterling's phrase). The most compelling cyberpop media is "thicker than it first seems," because it contains "multiple bottom lines" (to borrow phrasing from Haraway).[12] In the case of *Vanilla Sky* and ads for *Yahoo!,* both encourage spectators and consumers to forge intimate relationships with computer technologies and digital services, and both feature promises of the extension of human functionality via information and computer technologies. Yet, the representational choices in these popular texts also engage viewers' skepticism about information and computer technology.

It is fair to say that cyberpop enculturates subjects to the digital order of things. In magazines like *Wired, Business 2.0,* or (the now defunct Canadian publication) *Shift,* we see representations and interpretations to illustrate how the latest "high tech" can be incorporated into existing cultural processes and individual lifestyles, to "upgrade" the micropractices of everyday life, so that they resonate with the central principles of a networked cybercapitalist economy. To this end, Schwarzenegger films like *Terminator* and *6th Day* offer representations of high-tech culture and subjectivity that introduce innovative ideas about, for example, digitality, identity, and embodiment. Concurrently, cyberpop has the uncanny ability to present characters that actively "rewire" and challenge conventional binary logic and hegemonic knowledge—figures that unsecure cultural ideals about femininity and deconstruct normative definitions of masculinity, for example.

It is widely acknowledged that cyberpop is implicated in the production and maintenance of digital capitalism and oftentimes is apparently complicit with those values. The present book speculates on how cyberpop effectively "cites dominant meanings differently," perhaps to facilitate "an enabling disruption" in the status quo that enables subjects to *think different* about their lives.[12] Within a kind of science-culture feedback loop, cyberpop translates and transmits technoscientific ideas—it is encoded, as Stuart Hall explains, through a kind of interpretive practice that aims for a dynamic synergy between existing norms, values, and discourses and the newly emergent cyberscientific discourses and productions.[13] As Judith Butler reminds us, "A citation will be at once an interpretation of the norm and an occasion to expose the norm itself as a privileged interpretation" (*Bodies* 108). This book considers how layers of encoding in cyberpop reflect its multifunctionality as part popularized science literature, escapist entertainment, "sexy" social criticism, cultural artifact, and infotech marketing—cyberpop (inter)texts are complex and overdetermined.

CYBERPOETICS

Since cyberpop media are in an ambiguous and shifting relationship to the status quo of digital capitalist culture, which they alternately reflect, reify, reproduce, revise, and resist, studying them requires a critical and creative theoretical approach that is imaginative and flexible. Chapter 1 describes a methodology for exploring cyberpop and its relation to digital lifestyles and subjectivities that enables critical consideration *first* at the surface or "screen" level of representational politics. This allows us to appreciate the pleasure, beauty, and innovation of imagined worlds and the spectacles of visual cyber-cultures. And *second*, this methodology enables a deeper reading of the inter-textuality and citationality of cybermedia texts to critically consider how they function ideologically. Through this two-pronged approach, we are then in a position to discern how cyberpop redelivers ideologies and codes that corre-spond to the rules of formation in cyberculture. This methodology, described as a *cyberpoetic* approach, will preserve the playful and irresolvable ambi-guities in, for example, a computer game like *Tomb Raider* that inextricably and paradoxically binds girl power to adolescent male fantasy. Inspired by Donna Haraway's ("Manifesto") work on the cyborg and related figures from the world of technoscience, this methodology can critically comprehend what Katherine Hayles describes as the irresolvable ironies that characterize cyber-pop media.[14]

CYBERCULTURE AS DISCURSIVE FORMATION

After elaborating on methodological concerns and before delving into detailed analysis of the representational politics in selected cyberpop examples, it is important to situate the objects of this book in their cultural context. Chapter 2 is an overview of several key concepts in the network of discourses and prac-tices that constitute cyberculture and, by extension, its popular media produc-tions. Describing cyberculture as a discursive formation (inspired by theories of Michel Foucault (*Archeology*) helpfully clarifies how the key concepts that emerge repeatedly in cyberpop operate as a network or conceptual architec-ture linking technologies to individual subjects, identities, and digital life-styles. In order to provide a framework for the analysis that follows then, we explicate in detail three of the *rules of formation* that operate in cyberculture:

namely, *intangibility, connectivity,* and *speed.* Examining magazine advertisements for digital products and services, and e-commerce management literature advising audiences on how to succeed in "the connected economy," reveals the same collection of key concepts (or rules) used to promote digital capitalist culture, and the development of compatible identities and lifestyles.

TECHNOMASCULINITY

Chapters 3 and 4 continue the discussion of how digital identities and lifestyles are configured and considered in cyberpop, with a specific focus on tropes of technomasculinity. We investigate contemporary popculture representations of maleness designed to be compatible with the imperatives of corporate digital capitalism. These chapters, both of which combine film and media analysis, consider how idealized versions of masculinities are upgraded in such a way that they shift between cultural codes of male and female behavior and various modes of embodiment (and disembodiment). The result, evident in countless examples of cyberpop, is a hybrid form of technomasculinity that sometimes verges on androgyny.

By examining a collection of cyberpop texts (films and print advertisements) that prominently feature a male protagonist in a digitized informatic culture in the not-too-distant future, these ruminations on digital masculinity observe that even across media, the emergent idealized technomasculine icons are remarkably consistent. Each example is a portrait of an *exceptional* young white male and presents a narrative about his quest to escape the drudgery of his life, beat the system, and hack the status quo, aided by computer technologies. The rules of formation in digital capitalist culture (including *connectivity, intangibility,* and *speed*) are reified through this cyberpop, all of which adopts a high-tech (and in some cases a postmodern "tech-noir") digital aesthetic as its *mise-en-scène,* outfitting the hero with arsenals of cybernetic tools for his virtual e-powerment.

At the heart of cyberpop media's versions of technomasculinity is a celebration of the ambiguous figure of the hacker, and an ironic appropriation and popularization of what is known as the "hacker ethic"—a philosophy that emerged from the computer programming and hardware design culture at MIT in the 1960s—by the corporate infotech sectors of the economy. In cyberpop there is a proliferation of representations of the male hacker and his transformation from a stereotypical geeky social outcast to a hero and model of technomasculinity. The elevation of the hacker as male icon depends on his demonstrated ability to manipulate the central commodity of digital capital culture: information. The hacker's technoliteracy is a source of his empowerment, and attaches to his persona an element of wonder, romance, and danger; paradoxically, this proficiency with machines means he is able to participate in the maintenance of the digital status quo and help keep the information economy online. At the same time the hacker is represented as a "console cowboy" outsider, rule-breaker, rebel, anarchist, and at times even a dangerous cyberterrorist.[15]

The discourse of the technomasculine incorporates a classic heroic underdog trope and upgrades it. This hero is represented as an "ordinary guy" (or Everyman) who, through his determination and technological skill, becomes recognized as exceptional. His challenge is to escape from his entrapment in a digitized or data body that inhibits his freedom and interferes with the emergence of his essentially unique persona. Through the trope of the hacker (rewriting computers, identities, embodiment, and the social order), these cyberpop texts illustrate that technological literacy is a highly desirable and transferable skill, and—borrowing from a cybernetic paradigm that suggests "information is information"—that the e-powered digerati can control their destinies and hack anything.

Simultaneously and predictably, however—because cyberpop is characterized by multiple bottom lines, paradox, and polyperspectivity—the films and ads analyzed undercut and complicate both the cybernetic logic and the "newness" of the high-tech rhetorics, set designs, fashions, and special effects by reviving and redelivering "old" content about race, gender, and sexuality. Though it may be true that in a digital paradigm all 1s and 0s are equal across platforms, in cyberpop cultural productions some information is deemed more important, more e-powerful and resilient than other kinds of information. In cyberpop, "the white male heterosexual body [. . .] is nevertheless still privileged and still very much at the center of the action" in much of its popular media.[16] As Lisa Nakamura argues persuasively in her book *Cybertypes*, data about race and gender appear to condition the fate of digital subjects, even in the digital future.[17] Women and racial minorities in cyberpop are more often than not relegated to the realm of the unplugged, the offline, the Luddite, the sex object, or the underdeveloped persona of the sidekick. Female figures become eye candy, and minority figures of both genders are primitivized or orientalized.

CYBERFEMININITY

Chapters 5 and 6 consider the proliferation of representations of virtual femininity in a selection of cyberpop media from the Internet, computer games, and film. These texts implode the discourses around gender, sexuality, and embodiment while at the same time effecting a high-tech upgrade of them—which is not necessarily always progressive politically speaking, but is at least innovative. Because of this multifunctionality, described in earlier chapters as the ambiguity, paradox, or irony that characterizes cyberculture, what is needed to analyze imaginative representations of digital femininity is a cyber-poetic interpretive method. This method must be flexible and imaginative enough to take up various and sometimes seemingly incompatible perspectives on the phenomena of the "pixel vixen"—3-D computer-generated images (CGI) of digital women who are young, slim, fair skinned, wide eyed, and often scantily clad. Through a cyberpoetic lens, rather than reading these representations of fictional, virtual women as simply decorative, it becomes possible to get beneath the surface imagery and consider how these representations play a role in the construction of intelligible modes of digital subjectivity, and the ways they operate as infomediaries in the discursive network that is digital corporatist capitalism. Among other things, the female cyberpop icons analyzed here promote the expansion of technologies of connectivity, interactivity, and personalization, and popularize the discourses of intangibility and cyberfantasy/technoeroticism; pixel vixens accomplish these tasks from the pages of fashion magazines and runways, infomercials and videos, video games and Internet Web sites, and as such they are deeply implicated in and integrated with mainstream cyberculture. Moreover, they accomplish these tasks while oftentimes passing or masquerading as harmless, amusing, pretty, and fully fictional digital mannequins. Pixel vixens are considerably "thicker" than they first seem, and have multiple bottom lines. To *redescribe* the ambiguity inherent in these cyberfigures requires paying close attention to their multifunctionality vis-à-vis digital capitalism and dominant arrangements of power, knowledge, and subjects.

On the surface, pixel vixens appear to be simply eye candy for male users, yet this segment of the present study suggests that they are also technosirens drawing male (and female) subjects to participate in digital capitalism. Under the surface, the CGI girls should be understood as part of the discursive architecture of cyberculture—not merely trivial or entertaining, but also enculturating. A cyberpoetic approach to analyzing virtual femininity as it is configured in the pixel vixens must consider the seduction of the interface between the image and the user, without oversimplifying the human's experience of this "spectacle" or "simulation." Rather than assume Baudrillard's position, in which no critical contemplation is possible before the screen, to redescribe the pixel vixens we must assume that there are "different shades of spectator experience" vis-à-vis these imaginative representations.[18] Assuming a complicated range of possible decodings, the pixel vixen becomes not just 3-D but multidimensional in a semiotic sense, containing numerous and shifting significations.

SHIFT HAPPENS

This book suggests that popular media has the power to shape public consciousness about computer technology and is an important source of the potent metaphors and rich rhetoric that develop into our social imaginary and cultural image repertoire. Cyberpop matters in part because it contributes to the always shifting discursive formation that enframes and configures our ideas about bodies, subjects, and identities. Imaginative ads and films about high-tech lifestyles transmit ideas about which behaviors and identities are compatible with the cybersavvy future, and who is eligible to be the users/consumers/players in the next generation of the information economy. To conclude the present study, we consider in Chapter 7 a selection of cyberpop texts from visual digital culture, artworks that interpret and represent the computerized subject, while challenging the viewer to *think different* about how computers are changing human physiology and psychology. We first examine a selection of contemporary cover art pieces from popular science magazines and immediately identify a rhetorical pattern in the popular press for representing newly emergent cybersciences, the compu-subject of the future, and the kind of high-tech lifestyles that information and genetic technoscientific breakthroughs are enabling. This pattern is significant because it matters exactly how the digital subject is imag(in)ed in cyberpop media, even in its seemingly extreme and far-fetched "Photoshop®ped" versions, since these become sedimented into the existing cybercultural image repertoire. Once sedimented, these icons may serve as models to determine who counts as a digital subject, who will aspire to join the ranks of the digerati—and who will be hailed as a member of generation D—those flexible, connected, and mobile individuals who are technoliterate, online, and fluent in the discourses that represent and reinvent the digital order of things.

Immediately apparent in these artworks and portraits of the digital human is the importance of the technologies and aesthetics of "morphing" and "shape-shifting" to popular conceptions of futural subjects. Thus, next we consider the political and social implications of these digital aesthetics more closely by analyzing an art show entitled *The Unreal Person* and images commissioned for an advertising campaign by Microsoft entitled *Evolution*; we are able to identify ways in which the shape-shifter popularizes ideas about monstrosity and freakery, hybridity, and the abject—and illustrate why this icon is appropriate for (and appropriated by) a networked informatic culture and its cyberpop productions. To further illustrate the point, we look briefly at a contemporary cyberpunk novel by Scott Westerfeld entitled *Polymorph,* which (just as William Gibson's *Neuromancer* incited the public's fascination with cyborgs, virtual reality, and cyberspace) reflects the importance of the morph, the shape-shifter, the hacker, and the concepts of virtuality, speed, connectivity, and shift to the conceptual architecture of digital culture. A cybergothic tale of a hopeful monster whose terrific and terrible flexibility makes "hir" a poster child for the networked economy, *Polymorph* exemplifies the irony and irresolvable ambiguities that characterize cyberpop, insofar as it both cites, refuses, and remixes binary modes of thinking about sexuality, embodiment, gender, and race.

1
Cyberpoetics as Methodology

Irony is about contradictions that do not resolve into larger wholes, even dialectically, about the tension of holding incompatible things together because both or all are necessary and true.

—**Donna Haraway**[1]

The visual, narrative, electronic, and multimedia cyberpop texts analyzed here can be loosely compared to what Donna Haraway calls "technofigurations"—defined as material and semiotic objects composed of complex relations of power and knowledge. Technofigurations are, according to Haraway, "instruments for enforcing meanings" around what gets to count as nature, technology, culture and community, subjectivity and embodiment.[2] Objects of "extraordinary density," technofigurations are established by what Haraway calls "implosions" in the categories that structure Western thought—namely, the oppositional relationships of man to woman, organic to machinic, human to animal, and nature to culture.[3] As composites of imploded binary oppositions, technofigurations combine fiction and fact, the literal and the tropic, the scientific and the artistic, as well as "technical, political, organic, and economic" elements (Haraway 1999: 50). Likewise, cyberpop texts combine fiction and fact, escapist fantasy with cautionary tales, and contain imaginative educational content that increases public technoscientific literacy. Though

Haraway focuses on technofigurations from the cybernetic life sciences (i.e., the gene, the stem cell, and the fetus), her analytic method of *redescription* is particularly valuable for the present study because Haraway insists on appreciating the complex intertextuality and ambiguity of her objects of analysis. Like Haraway's technofigurations, cyberpop media are densely coded texts, compatible with digital capital and implicated in dominant discourses and arrangements of power while simultaneously retaining the trace of a nostalgic cyberpunk feel, a subtle countercultural edginess.

Haraway's method for analyzing technofigurations involves a critical reading of their intertextuality. By "teasing open" the "sticky economic, technical, political, organic, historical, mythic and textual threads" that embody technofigurative objects, Haraway is able to trace or "redescribe" the relations of power between them (1994: 68). Inevitably, Haraway suggests, technofigurations are "thicker than they first seem," and have the uncanny ability to "swing both ways" (1985: 108).[4] Inspired by this work, the current book analyzes and *redescribes* a collection of cyberfigurative popular media (or cyberpop), tracing the intertextual web or "sticky threads" of meaning therein to the rules of formation in cyberculture. We know that films, novels, and other popular cultural production media transmit conceptual frameworks (discourses, values, ideas, and knowledge) to the general public, and in the case of cyberpop, about the place of information and communication technologies in our lives. The discourses embedded in digital culture's artwork and advertisements have material effects, initiating trends, influencing who produces and uses technology, and who recognizes themselves as a computerized subject or member of and participant in technoculture. Cyberpop advertisements and artwork operate to enculturate subjects and play a role in the development of digital literacy, as they introduce and popularize technical terms, compuslang, and marketing buzzwords into the fabric of everyday life (such as "connectivity," "flexibility," and "interface").[5] As a result, cyberpop cultural productions influence how we see and imagine technology, others, the future, and ourselves by transmitting (a limited range of) representations about how these might look in the digital age.

CYBERPOP AND PARADOX

> Unfortunately, what technology gives with one hand, it often takes away with the other.
>
> **—Michael Heim**[6]

Mass media productions including cyberpop can be expected to reflect the digital capitalist culture that produces them, even as they serve up imaginary futural scenarios of digital life. Films like *The Matrix* and *I Robot* and magazines like *Yahoo! Internet Life* and *Fast Company* encourage consumers to participate in digital capitalism and commodity culture. As Manuel Castells suggests, the distinctions between advertising, information, and entertainment are blurred in cybercultural productions, and the difference between *criticism of* and *conformity to* the status quo of digital capitalism is likewise undermined or blurred.[7]

The ambiguity inherent in cyberpop media is due to its paradoxical relationship to dominant configurations of power and knowledge in digital culture. Oftentimes critical of the digitizing of everyday life, the mass media of cyberculture routinely encourage their audience to think carefully about which products and services to consume, and slightly less often they encourage the public to reflect on their implication in the manufacture and maintenance of infotech culture. The target spectators for many of the examples of cyberpop analyzed in this book claim membership in discourse communities that are cutting edge, or countercultural, yet at the same time connected, involved, and implicated in the expansion and operation of the digital status quo. For this reason, cyberpop is sometimes characterized by an ironic or tongue-in-cheek tone, poking fun at social trends while at the same time promoting, romanticizing, upgrading (reinventing), and mythologizing them.

In order to be intelligible to their audience, cybercultural media productions negotiate between "revolutionary" ideas and existing (and established) cultural conventions. For example, as Sherry Turkle explains in *Life on the Screen: Identity in the Age of the Internet* (1997), the most compelling popular cybercultural productions convey theories composed of "ideas that capture the imagination of the culture at large, [which] tend to be those with which people can become actively involved."[8] Thus, in order to be successful, films such as *X-Men* or *Minority Report* must tap into discourses about technology and humanity that appeal to and are familiar to a mass public audience while at the same time delivering messages about the importance of diversity, uniqueness, individuality, and innovation. This negotiation of the "popular" and the "personalized," and the delicate coding of the "new" and the "familiar" is configured in such a way as to encourage the active participation of subjects in the construction of digital lifestyles. Cyberpop cites the regulatory norms of digital culture as they are manifested in its key concepts (for example, speed, intangibility, and connectivity). These citational practices, as Judith Butler explains, are complicit with the dominant cultural order but (perhaps paradoxically) also attempt to innovate, recreate, upgrade, or revise existing relations of power that constitute the status quo (*Bodies* 15).

Katherine Hayles describes this process in *How We Became Posthuman: Virtual Bodies in Cybernetics, Literature, and Informatics* (1999) as part of the "irresolvable ambiguity of cyberculture," wherein "for every solution it offers, it raises a new problem; for every threat that erupts, new potentialities also arise."[9] Hayles concludes that the point is not to resolve ambiguities, but, instead, to take pleasure in the "new moves" and "fields of play" they make possible (Seductions 307). Cyberpop media utilize postmodern strategies and aesthetic techniques such as irony or pastiche, seeking to defamiliarize the spectator, inspire critical reflection and analysis, or invite public debate about the increasing computerization of everyday life. At the same time, cyberpop's key concepts and their underlying discourses encourage the expansion of computer networks, digitization, and global capitalism. This is accomplished by creatively illustrating how the latest technologies can be incorporated into existing cultural processes and individual lifestyles to upgrade them for the digital age. In order to accomplish this, cyberpop references existing social arrangements while concurrently projecting revised and often innovative representations of culture, subjectivity, knowledge, and power—which may or may not be "new and improved."

At the heart of cyberpop, then, is a paradox begging to be *redescribed*, tracing the intertextual mix of the "old" and the "new," the "insider" and "outsider," and the "complicit" and "resistant" discourses therein in order to discern the ideologies and politics of the sticky network of codes transmitted by these digital cultural productions. As Zillah Eisenstein has commented, new media have the ability to "complexly rewire" preexisting racial, sexual, and gendered inequities.[10] Oftentimes, however, these recycled discourses reinscribe conventional binary logics (which privilege the masculine over the feminine, the natural over the artificial, the real over the simulated, and the human over the machine) while, at the same time, they encourage and even facilitate the implosion or shifting of these dualisms into high-tech hybrid forms. Haraway's method of redescription is designed to "make it impossible for the bottom line [of meaning] to be one single statement" (1985: 105). Multiple bottom lines require an analytic of at least "double vision," Haraway suggests, in order to grasp how the networks of power, knowledge, and subjects operate together to maintain, structure, and produce a technoscientific culture (1999: 38).

ANALYZING PARADOX IN CYBERCULTURE

As these technologies emerge in social space the great political question will be what forms of cultural articulation they promote and discourage.

—**Mark Poster**[11]

The importance of cyberpop media lies not only in the representations they transmit and popularize, but also in the "new modes of relation and perception they impose, which change traditional [social] structures" and relationships.[12] As Felix Guattari has suggested, "today's information and communication machines do not merely convey representational contexts, but also contribute to the fabrication of new *assemblages* of enunciation, individual and collective."[13] In order to consider the social and political effects of cyberpop on cultural formations and subjectivities, it is necessary to trace their *encodings* (the ways in which these visual and textual forms reflect and support, criticize and upgrade existing and dominant cultural values, relations of power, and the rules of formation in cyberculture), but also to consider the processes by which they are *decoded* (consumed by their audience). In much of the existing literature on digital capital and its political economy, the active role of the consumer as a user and producer of cyberculture is undertheorized, in part because of the use of "repurposed" analytical models that were not designed with digital and new media in mind. I will consider briefly two of the more popular versions of this repurposed or borrowed analytic before further explaining my own approach to cyberpop cultural productions.

1. Cyberpop As Tools of Mass Deception: Repurposing the Frankfurt Schools' Culture Industry Model

In their work *Times of the Technoculture*, Kevin Robins and Frank Webster view popular SF/sci-fi films and e-commerce management literature as commodities of the culture industry, which (as Adorno and Horkheimer argued in 1944) serve to enforce conformity and encourage passivity rather than promote the development of critical consciousness and active participation.[14] From this perspective, cybercultural productions support a form of mass deception and impede the development of autonomous, independent individuals. According to Adorno and Horkheimer's analysis (repurposed by Robins and Webster), technoscientific and computer technologies and associated popcultural media "parade as progress [. . .] as the incessantly new," but are instead "a disguise for an eternal sameness" (Adorno). The discourses of technoculture, according to Robins and Webster, encourage subjects to be satisfied with the status quo and to consume entertainment that is tantamount to what Adorno called "prescribed fun" and a source of fleeting satisfaction.

Nowhere in Robins and Webster's analysis of the social and political effects of the information and communication technology revolution (they prefer the term "evolution") do the authors consider modes of reception or consumption that allow for criticism or creativity vis-à-vis dominant cultural values, nor is there a distinction made between media (such as television vs. the Internet). Moreover, in their exclusive focus on computer technologies as tools of mass deception, Robins and Webster forgo an inquiry into the complex process whereby the narratives attached to computer technologies are decoded. As a consequence, this work ignores the ambiguous, paradoxical, or contradictory relationship of cyberpop media to digital capital. It also disallows for the possibility of a critical or resistant, media and computer-savvy audience, while at the same time disregarding the role of the consumer in the production of the values and narratives associated with computer and communication technologies. Instead, *Times of the Technoculture* documents the role that information and communication technologies play in the "intensification and reconfiguration" of existing relations of production and consumption.[15] It appears that Robins and Webster see nothing new in "new media."

However, to observe that cyberculture and its communications and information technologies are compatible with the operation of an existing capitalist economy is, according to Hakim Bey, painfully obvious and predictable, even a truism. "Isn't it a cliché," Bey asks rhetorically, "to point out that any communication medium is analogous or mirror like in relation to the dominant social paradigm that coevolves with it? How could there exist a communications medium *outside* the totality it represents?"[16] Moreover, as R. L. Rutsky observes, although it is "pointless to deny that techno-culture and multinational capitalism are deeply imbricated in one another," it is an exercise in reductionist thinking to assume that digital cultural productions are simply reflections or celebrations of "capitalist instrumentality." [17] The current book suggests that what is new and important about cyberpop is the way that it remediates, repurposes, and redelivers "old" ideas in innovative forms, upgraded versions, and new remixes—and close attention is paid throughout to the complicated and media-savvy portrait of the self-consciously implicated and critical, skeptical audience/consumer that is assumed and promoted by these texts.

2. Seduction of the Interface: Repurposing Debord's Spectacles and Baudrillard's Simulacra

Another popular repurposing maneuver effected by theorists and critics of cyberculture involves borrowing the concepts of Guy Debord and Jean Baudrillard concerning spectacles and simulations, in order to suggest that there is nothing new about new media forms. For example, when in an interview Baudrillard is asked, "What potential do the new technologies offer?" he responds:

> I don't know much about this subject. I haven't gone beyond the fax and the automatic answering machine. I have a very hard time getting down to work on the screen because all I see there is a text in the form of an image which I have a hard time entering. With my typewriter, the text is at a distance; it is visible and I can work with it. With the screen, it's different; one has to be inside; it is possible to play with it but only

if one is on the other side, and immerses oneself in it. That scares me a little, and Cyberspace is not of great use to me personally.[18]

Despite the fact that Baudrillard readily admits he is not technoliterate, he is regarded as perhaps the central postmodern theorist of technoculture and new media. His early writing on simulation and the theory of simulacra is regularly repurposed by Baudrillard himself and his followers to analyze the cultural and political effects of computerized telecommunications media. Having not ventured "beyond the fax," Baudrillard remains confident that his media and popculture analyses are applicable to the study of the cultural impact of virtual reality technologies and computer-mediated communication.

In Baudrillard's version, when the user is before the screen, "no contemplation is possible."[19] The user is configured *within* computerized screen culture; in order to "enter" and "play" with the realm of virtuality, the spectator must become immersed in it, engaged in a dynamic of interactivity—but the cost of that experience is their critical vision. Since Baudrillard admittedly has "a hard time entering" into the activities of computer culture—when he looks at the screen, all he sees is "text in the form of an image"—he opts to turn this technological unfamiliarity to his advantage, suggesting that his outsider's perspective affords him a privileged vantage point from which to launch his contemplative commentary. When Baudrillard suggests that the new technologies have a chilling effect on individuals, "freezing" them into passive terminals,[20] one has to wonder if he is expressing his own discomfort surrounding his lack of technological skill.

For Guy Debord (and the Situationists), consumer culture and the commodification of every aspect of life culminates in the production of "an immense accumulation of spectacles."[21] Instead of participating in life experiences, people buy access to images and virtual excursions, becoming trapped in a cycle of endlessly contemplating the spectacles and simulations of life, "the glossy surfaces of the commodity world" of appearances and abstracted images.[22] Debord calls this process the consumption of a "counterfeit life," filled with manufactured and fabricated "pseudo-needs" (68), which eventually converge in "the single pseudo-need of maintaining the reign of the autonomous [capitalist] economy" (51).

In the spirit of Gramsci, Debord suggests that hegemony is created through passive participation in the society of the spectacle—people willingly buy into their own disempowerment by consuming spectacles in the form of entertainment, services, processed news/information, and leisure activities. The spectacle is a tool for the pacification and depoliticization of subjects and culture; it distracts and stupefies people. In agreement with Horkheimer and Adorno, Debord maintains that through the culture industry and its spectacles, private time and leisure is bureaucratized (becomes a paid-for experience, as Jeremy Rifkin would say),[23] and state control (government, dominant powers, corporations) is extended into the microprocesses of everyday life. Yet Debord insists that despite the power of the spectacle and its ability to produce passive, captive audiences for capitalist imperatives, viewers can learn to see behind the curtain. Theorist Steven Best remarks that for Debord, "the late-capitalist world remains accessible to interpretation and vulnerable to active transformation" (60).

In response to Debord, Baudrillard concludes that the theory of the society of the spectacle has lost its explanatory value and relevance and is thus inadequate to analyze the current cyberculture and its popular media (Simulations 56). The distinctions such as subject/object and real/counterfeit have been obliterated through implosion, according to Baudrillard, and with them, the critical theory of the Situationists becomes ineffectual (Best 53). In place of the society of the spectacle, Baudrillard describes computerized virtual digital cultures as "cyberblitz," and part of a current era characterized by the "transpolitical" and the "transaesthetic."[23] In Baudrillard's schema, the "third order" of simulation was defined by the spectacle, the simulation, and the hyperreal, but he suggests that we have now entered into the fourth order of simulation, the order of the fractal or virtual, where there is a radical indetermination and undermining of "all previously secure categories of social knowledge" including the political, economic, aesthetic, cultural, sexual—even the human.[24] In the fourth order there can be no hyperreal or simulations of the real, because the "real" has disappeared or lost its currency. The "trans" categories of the virtual order are unstable, and within them elements are mixed, sampled, recombined, and reinvented, such that the natural order/origin of things is obliterated, and there is a profound indifference as to the proper place, derivation, or history of bodies, representations, activities, or identities. The era of the virtual is the moment of postmodernity, characterized by a celebration of irony, provisionality, and pastiche, hybridity, the remix, upgrade, and sampling. In the age of transaesthetics, spectators are not likely to consider virtual screen culture as "counterfeit," or to see themselves as passive consumers of abstract image-objects, nor are they prone to seek enlightenment behind the curtain or beyond the screen. In the age of virtuality and screen culture, Baudrillard argues, the intangible has become real, or real enough—since the intangible has taken its place and become a standardized element of contemporary cyberculture.

There are limitations inherent in repurposing Debord or Baudrillard's work to explain the effects of new hyper- and multimedia technologies on culture and individuals. To compensate for the differences between electronic mediums—which Baudrillard and Debord sometimes deny exist—these theoretical models routinely make sweeping generalizations that end in a radical skepticism and pessimism about the potential and effects of new technologies.

However, as Andrew Darley suggests, it is integral to consider "the general or shared *and* the specific or distinctive" features between new media and earlier media forms (190). For example, both Debord and (especially) Baudrillard insist that in the presence of the screen or spectacle, the audience is transfixed and unable to formulate a critical response. However, by attending to the peculiarities of visual digital media Darley argues that it is possible to discern "different shades of spectator experience," and "a sense of disparity, diversity, specificity, and nuance," between and within different visual media, including "antagonistic modes of spectatorship" (189-90). The present book will trace the modes of implication, interactivity, and innovation that audiences are encouraged to practice when engaging with cyberpop—therefore a theoretical model of the spectator as *cultural dupe* is inadequate for the present purposes.

Existing theories of simulation and computerized subjectivity need to be upgraded to make them more flexible if they are to be useful for studying cyberpop and new media. Somewhere between the theories of Debord and Baudrillard, neither of whom takes computer technologies as their primary objects of analysis, lie key insights about the complementarity and convergence of visual new media forms and their effects on the spectator who consumes and configures them—and is in turn shaped by this interactivity. This book will reflect on the "ways of *thinking* and *being* that arise in the emerging technoscapes" of cyberculture, and the role that cyberpop plays in developing digital identities and configuring lifestyles that allow for active participation in and critical consumption of computer culture (Escobar 230).

FROM REPURPOSING CRITIQUE TO A DIGITAL ANALYTIC

> I am concerned, however, that we do not cast the same critical light of past approaches on the latest developments. [. . .] [W]e must acknowledge that understanding their operation and character calls for methods that revolve around rather different elements and processes than those we expect to find in immediately prior modes of mass visual culture.
>
> **—Andrew Darley (7)**

> [N]o matter how much digital systems resemble film or television, they are fundamentally different. [. . .] Thus, theorists have to strive to create new modes of commentary that consider more than consumption or spectatorship.
>
> **—Peter Lunenfeld**[25]

Understanding how the popular media of cyberculture operate in relation to its discursive formation requires insights from new media theorists such as Steven Holtzman, whose research on content delivery and multimedia design principles considers the impact of repurposing on digital worlds. Holtzman's observations and insights are relevant when assembling a new theoretical methodology for redescribing cyberpop since, as he writes:

> In the end, no matter how interesting, enjoyable, comfortable, or well accepted they are, these [repurposing] approaches borrow from existing paradigms. They weren't conceived with digital media in mind, and as a result they don't exploit the special qualities that are unique to digital worlds. [. . .] Repurposing is a transitional step that allows us to get a secure footing on unfamiliar terrain. But it isn't where we'll find the entirely new dimensions of digital worlds. We need to transcend the old to discover completely new worlds of expression.[26]

And yet, this emphasis on the "completely new" in Holtzman's description of digital media is contested by Jay David Bolter and Richard Grusin, who suggest that new media is always in a dialectical relationship with earlier forms. They conclude that what is unique and "new" about new media are the particular strategies employed to remediate content originally designed for film, painting, television, and radio so as to redeliver it via the new digital technologies (such as the Internet). "Repurposing as remediation is both what is unique to digital worlds," Bolter and Grusin suggest, "and what denies the possibility of that uniqueness."[27] This is the "enticing and maddening paradox" at the heart of new media and cyberculture according to Eisenstein, who observes that "new" media can just as easily present revolutionary ideas as it can redeliver "old" representations, "rearticulating systems of power and undoing them," both initiating and undermining democratic visions (Eisenstein 7). The best examples of cyberpop employ what Stuart Hall calls "a negotiated code" that cites the dominant cultural values while at the same time offering itself as "an exception to the rule," and the result is explicitly (and intentionally) "shot through with contradictions."[28] To appreciate this kind of ambiguity, a critical approach to cyberpop must not relegate digital culture and its newly emergent media and technoscientific discourses, practices, and knowledges to the "nothing new here" or the "revolutionary" extremes. As Joseph Pelton argues, "To make a successful transition to a cybernetic world we must literally learn new ways of thinking. There must be a new approach. It must be a paradigm that creates a plausible new intellectual and cultural vision of the future. This new cyberspace paradigm means a new renaissance in our thinking."[29] To critically redescribe the patterns and codings of these complex correspondences, unstable synergies, and paradoxical convergences between technoscience, digital capitalism, cyberpop media, and the subjects who inhabit these "technoworlds" requires a digital analytic or what we might call a *cyberpoetics*.

FROM DIGITAL ANALYTIC TO CYBERPOETICS

> One of the pleasures of poetics is to try on a paradigm and see where it leads you.
>
> **—Charles Bernstein**[30]

According to Charles Bernstein and Robert Sheppard, the primary activity of a *poetics* is active questioning about artistic production(s). When a *poetics* ceases to question, it becomes *theory*, Sheppard writes, "retrospective rather than speculative, definitive rather than open to infinitude."[31] Because it is always creative, innovative and tentative, using a poetic model to interpret cultural productions allows the investigator to posit strategic, multiple, morphic, experimental, and provisional readings of artistic productions, according to Sheppard. The concept of a poetics for the study of cyberculture and its popular media seems highly appropriate because the objects of analysis have multiple bottom lines, utilize irony and paradox, and are composed of and operate through irresolvable ambiguities.

The idea of a cyberpoetics is hinted at by Hakim Bey, who suggests that over time in the "big mess" of informational society, ideas, material objects, and practices "begin to coalesce into a poetics or a way-of-knowing or a way-of-acting" (121). Taking this poetics as a starting point, Bey comments that cultural critics can "draw certain pro tem conclusions," about the operations of digital culture, "as long as we don't plaster them all over and set them up on altars" (121). *Theories* of information culture, Bey insists, are too rooted, too firm, "a left-over fetish of dogmatics," and must be replaced with "poetic facts" which are "not assimilable into a doctrine of information" (121). Only through the development of a poetic model for interpretation, Bey suggests, can we arrive at a suitably shifting, mobile, and flexible analysis of the constantly changing high-tech economy and its cultural productions. A cyberpoetics can reflect the speed of change in digital culture by encouraging a practice of critical redescription that, as Bernstein promises, "moves in different directions at the same time," positing and then "disrupting or problematizing a formulation that seems too final or pre-emptively restrictive" (150).

A cyberpoetics needs to reflect the conceptual architecture of digital culture as a discursive formation, resonating with its central tropes, tenets, and organizing principles (including the ones studied in this book, namely, speed/mobility, connectivity, and intangibility/virtuality). Moreover, this poetic approach needs to consider the place of the subject in the loop, as an important component in the creation of cyberculture and its popular media productions. This should lead to an emphasis on interactivity and an assumption of active consumers, and even critical and creative users, rather than passive audiences or spectators. Instead of attempting to furnish final, stable, and comprehensive theories of cyberpop, a poetics can embrace the messiness, multiple bottom lines, and complexity therein. To this end, this methodology resonates with Haraway's notion, in *Simians, Cyborgs, and Women: The Reinvention of Nature*, of "cyborg writing," which "struggles against perfect communication, against the one code that translates all meaning perfectly" and instead "insist[s] on noise and advocate[s] pollution" as a way to underscore the overdetermined, hybrid, and networked concepts of the informatic and informational age (Haraway, 1991: 176). Haraway advocates "embracing something with all of its messiness and dirtiness and imperfection," in order to show that even those cultural productions that are most obviously implicated in dominant power relations can be used as a foundation for seeing differently, redescribing, and perhaps reconfiguring the conceptual architecture and material arrangements of technoscience and digital culture (Haraway 1999: 109).

While considering the political and economic structuring of digital lifestyles and identities, a cyberpoetics must attend to the high-tech aesthetics that are emerging in cyberpop media (Darley 4).[32] This poetics would trace and analyze the particular design choices, formal elements of composition, and techniques employed in new media cultural productions, while also describing the connections or links between these encodings and the sociohistorical and political context from which cyberpop emerges. By considering its formal elements of composition, a cyberpoetic analysis of popcultural representations enables us to ask, as Loss Pequeño Glazier does, "What can you do here in this medium that you could not do before?"[33] Many forms of new media (such as the hypertext poetry that Glazier analyzes) encourage and enable a constant state of change, shift, mobility, manipulability, interactivity, and hyperactivity. Cyberpop is composed of what Glazier calls the "link nodes," which allow for multiple navigational paths and a variety of "bottom lines," as well as numerous interpretations and applications.

Novels, artwork, and films representing digitality and technoscience oftentimes flaunt their "code" in a kind of reflexivity that remind the spectator, player, consumer, or reader that all cultural productions are coded (encoded/decoded) and require interpretation. This encourages the idea that consuming cyberpop can be a critical and even a political activity, and it underscores the active role of the audience as implicated in the production of its meaning and cultural value (Glazier 111). Glazier and other digital media theorists suggest that only by acknowledging the active participation of the public in producing the conceptual networks of cyberculture and its popular forms, does it become possible to understand how "interactivity" is about both complicity with digital capitalism, and also about opportunities for shift, innovation, upgrade, and challenges to the status quo (172). As Johanna Drucker explains in her study of new media typography, it is integral to consider the active role of the audience/spectator in the process of creating the meaning of such forms because often they contain "internal and irresolvable contradictions" requiring the user to creatively and critically negotiate between available interpretations/versions.[34] This interactivity is a key feature of cyberpop productions; a poetic methodology that embraces ambiguity and focuses on the dynamics of interactivity can reflect these complex networks of exchange between digital culture, capital, subjects, and popular media.

A cyberpoetic approach to the films, advertisements, and novels analyzed for this book will trace their loops of encoding and decoding, citation and reinterpretation, consumption and production of meaning, to underscore and insist that there is much more to say about and see in cyberpop media than merely another version of capitalism and a body of participants who are passive and apathetic. Instead, a cyberpoetics can "attend to the local and specific—to the details and differentials of form and reception" and thus "help display the often subtly nuanced character" of cyberculture (Darley 190). As Darley points out, "We must resist the tendency to essentialize: the aesthetic dimension of late modern culture is not homogenous. On the contrary, it is highly sedimented with a multiplicity of image forms and corresponding kinds of spectator experience—even within the mass cultural sphere" (190). The multiplicity of cyberpop forms is part of a growing complexity of digital culture, which Rutsky describes as the emergence of "a dense, 'postmodern' mix of cultural images, sounds, and data, all of which are subject to continual 'unsecuring'—to reproduction, alteration, redesign, editing" (118). One result of this complexity is the proliferation of an aesthetic we could describe as cybernetic pastiche, composed of "assemblages of informational density" (Rutsky 13-14, 117). It follows then, that a poetic approach to cyberpop must appreciate the significance of its remixed, unsecured, and "unfinished quality" (Lunenfeld *Digital Dialectic* 7).

2

Cyber-Commerce and Computerized Subjectivity

Cyberculture is a contested term, so although there are numerous ways to conceptualize it, for the purposes of the present book it is understood as a *discursive formation* inspired in part by Michel Foucault's use of the phrase—a network of linked cultural practices and knowledges (*Archaeology* 38). This network is organized according to particular *rules of formation* or codes, which legitimate a limited range of articulations. Foucault describes the rules of formation as an architecture—the structure or infrastructure of logics, cultural productions, relations of power, actions, behaviors, and ideologies that underpin and support the functioning of a discursive formation. Through decoding this architecture it is possible to identify the processes whereby particular configurations of subjects, knowledges, and power arrangements become hegemonic, normalized, dominant, and authorized—while others are delegitimated or rendered deviant, obsolete, or unintelligible.

The architecture, or conceptual network of cyberculture, and its codes or rules of formation are manifested in a host of discourses including that of intangibility, simulation, virtuality, interactivity, connectivity, hyperrealism, synergism, instantaneity, and velocity. These discourses proliferate in contemporary cyberculture, materializing and materialized by cyberpop productions and practices. In order to speculate about the implications of this discursive formation and its regulatory norms on the establishment of dominant ideas about identity, community, embodiment, culture, technology, nature, and desire, it is necessary to describe the conceptual nodes that operate within the network of cyberculture as its rules of formation. These rules are ideological, semiotic, and material; they organize, construct, and reflect the relations of power and production in the processes of constructing knowledges and subjectivities, and they operate in a synergistic relationship within processes of commerce and consumption. There are other rules we could examine, yet these three are a suitable starting point since they emerge repeatedly, in various guises, within the cyberpop under review.

One way to understand how the discourses of intangibility, connectivity, and speed operate together cohesively within a discursive formation is to consider the concept of digital *convergence*. In technical terms, convergence is the combination of audio, video, and data communications into a single source, received on a single device, and delivered by a single connection in "one big stream of bits."[1] In the informatics sectors of the economy (including computers, communication, and life sciences, for example) this is exactly what is happening, as "the media, telecommunication and computer industries find their activities are becoming increasingly the same" and "traditional functions of telephones, television sets, and personal computers are merging."[2] Digital convergence is a distinct characteristic of the informational age according to Manuel Castells, who describes the process as part of the construction of a complexly integrated economic system and social network, "within which old, separate technological trajectories become literally indistinguishable" (71). One of the results of convergence is that "it can become difficult to distinguish editorial content from advertising messages, or entertainment and news from consumerism" (Herman and McChesney 128).

Similarly, as various media shift and blur together, so too do the ideas they report and reflect. In the same way that digital technologies converge, the rules of cyberculture overlap, connect, and reify each other in a discursive formation or web. Through a process of citation, cut and paste, and what Jay David Bolter and Richard Grusin call "remediation," the codes of cyberculture are repurposed and/or redelivered continuously. Operating in a kind of discursive synergism, the rules produce a set of self-referential norms which are then applied in the design and marketing of computerized machines and digital services, as well as to the operations of corporations, the management of communities and the natural environment, and the construction of subjectivities. Achieving a kind of network cohesion, these blurred conceptual nodes—at once semiotic and material—are the discursive architecture of cyberculture, and they are represented in and amplified by its popular cultural productions. In convergence mode, these rules are manifested in discourses, knowledges, behaviors, and the construction of identities (such as the digerati or knowledge workers). The cybercultural network connects bodies, economies, technologies, subjects, and—importantly—ideologies and value systems. Through cyberpop media the conceptual architecture is maintained, upgraded, popularized, and normalized—in films, Web sites, advertisements, and video games, all of which represent newly emergent technologies, humanizing them, depicting their integration into everyday life at the level of culture and individual lifestyles. In this way cyberpop realizes its role as infomediary and plays a part in both enculturation and hegemony.

To further illustrate how the rules of formation operate in cyberpop, we can utilize a relatively popular (but not bestselling) e-management text by Stanley Davis and Christopher Meyer entitled *BLUR: The Speed of Change in the Connected Economy*.[3] Admittedly this text had no truly significant impact on cultural arrangements—in spite of its inflated claims to offer a "manifesto" for the age of digital capitalism—but, though it did not *effect* cybercultural trends, it concisely and adequately *reflected* them. This text, one of hundreds of similar e-management books that flooded the shelves in the 1990s, is useful as a guide to map the cybercultural discursive formation with its "shifting" or "blurred" rules of digital capital and commerce, management and marketing.

Briefly, *BLUR* traces how the pace of change, invention, and commerce is rapidly increasing in our "hypercapitalist" infotech age. Davis and Meyer chronicle the ways in which information and communication technologies are revolutionizing the concept of time, the future of work, the nature of leisure, and the roles of both the individual and the community in the construction of culture. Connectivity, speed, intangibility, convergence, synergism, and implosion—these are the key concepts or rules organizing cyberculture as a discursive formation, materializing and materialized in the digital economy. They are not simply the buzzwords of corporate infotech; these concepts are, as Donna Haraway (1996) has suggested, the foundations of those powerful imaginative and figurative tropes that bring forth worlds and shape identities.

THE BLUR MANIFESTO: YOUR JOB IS TO MASTER THE BLUR

Has the pace of change accelerated way beyond your comfort zone? [. . .] The fact is, something enormous *is* happening all around you, enough to make you feel as if you're losing your balance and seeing double. So relax. You are experiencing things as they really are, a BLUR. [. . .] A meltdown of all traditional boundaries. [. . .] On every front, opposites are blurring. [. . .] Don't think you'll ever slow down BLUR, let alone bring it to a halt. Its constant acceleration is here to stay, and those who miss that point will miss everything. Your job as a manager, as an entrepreneur, as a consumer and as an individual, is to master the BLUR, to keep the acceleration going, to keep your world changing and off balance.

—Stanley Davis and Christopher Meyer xiii

According to Davis and Meyer, "something enormous is happening all around you" (6-7). Tantamount to a revolution, North America is currently undergoing an enormous cultural transition to what they call the second half of the information age, or the BLUR economy (13). "BLUR" is not an acronym, it describes what they see as the reverberations of this "enormous" change throughout all spheres of society, and accurately depicts the climate of a culture where "on every front, opposites are blurring" (7). Davis and Meyer describe the contemporary North American economy as being in a perpetual state of flux due to massive and continuous implosion of the definitions, distinctions, and categories that have historically ordered societies, communities, businesses, corporations, and individuals. The authors view these changes as positive and progressive, though they acknowledge that BLUR phenomena may at first seem threatening and challenging, as traditional social rules and cultural rituals are not just redesigned but put under the permanent sign of BLUR.

Davis and Meyer build a network model of the connected economy wherein "the individual, the organization, and the economy are all trying to generate value within a consistent set of economic rules"—these rules may be consistent, but they are simultaneously in a perpetual state of change, such that the only real constant is the sense of being permanently "off balance" (118). This set of rules that keeps capital flowing through the global economy should be applied to the operation of successful corporations, and should also form the guidelines for individuals' lives, with synergism and synchronicity between levels as the overall goal. The rules of BLUR economy are comparable to what Foucault might describe as *the conditions for the existence* of the discursive formation of cyberculture. Specifically, the rules of "connectivity, speed, and intangibles" form the "trinity" of BLUR, acting as the "permanent and coherent concepts" that order the contemporary connected economy— what Foucault would call its architecture and themes (Davis and Meyer 84; Foucault, *Archaeology* 34). The trinity of BLUR influences the establishment of social norms and prescriptions that condition individual subjects' lives.

THE BLURRED INDIVIDUAL: COMPUTERIZED SUBJECTIVITY

The second half of the informatic economy requires "flexible" subjects who can adapt to the constant acceleration or shifting of everything, permanent instability, and boundary implosion. Accordingly, Davis and Meyer advise their readers to "Node Thyself," and suggest reconceptualizing the individual subject as a node or site of intersection in a web (or net) of economic connectivity (164). By recalibrating oneself to "enter the world of BLUR [and] move to its cadence," the nodal subject relies less on "prediction, foresight, and planning" to achieve personal and professional success, and instead develops "flexibility, courage, and faster reflexes" for instant and constant adaptation to *speed* (7, 104). This requires, "on a deeply individual level," an extension of the BLURred subject's comfort zone, to enable the acceptance of "some complex paradoxes," the adoption of "some radically new perspectives," and the alteration of "some near reflex-level behaviors" (147).

One of these new paradoxical perspectives is an acceptance of the implosions of work and leisure, public and private, office and home, such that, "now, of course, work goes home with you" (147-49). To the authors, this trend is a positive development that ends the "artificial distinction" between life and work, and results in "a better integrated, better organized world" (237). Their list of "Ten Ways to BLUR Yourself" is designed to help initiate the morphing process whereby "the work you and the home you" meld together into an integrated, BLURred subjectivity and a productive member of infotech culture. This convergence of work and home is indicative of and reflects what Davis and Meyer see as the melding of the individual and the corporation; "good luck finding the point where you stop and the market begins," they write, since "the distinction between a company and the environment it exists in is becoming hazier" (91). Similarly, there is no discernible or important difference between the private self and the public self, since "people simply don't exist separate from their economic selves" (165). As a node in the connected economy of BLUR, it is futile for an individual to attempt to partition their private life from their public work, or to distinguish a sense of intimate and personal identity apart from their patterns of information production and digital commodity consumption.

BLUR culture produces a cyber-citizenry of BLURred subjects, or what Felix Guattari calls "computerized subjectivities" (22). Davis and Meyer inquire rhetorically, "What happens when Connectivity, Speed, and Intangibles converge in you?" (147). Their answer: "It's a BLUR." BLURred or informational subjectivity is, according to Mark Poster, enabled through a "generalized destabilization" in what he calls "the mode of information" (*Mode of Information* 16). The destabilized and computerized subject is, in part, understood to be a collection of informational (or data) assemblages, "multiplied by databases, dispersed by computer messaging and conferencing, decontextualized and re-identified by TV ads, dissolved and materialized continuously in the electronic transmission of symbols" (16). The notion of a concrete and stable identity is BLURred into a new concept of subjectivity as that which is composed of patterns of identifications, modes of interactivity, and network connections/affiliations, which are multiple and oftentimes virtual. The BLURred subject is a subject in process, a "hypermediated self in a network of affiliations, which are constantly shifting [. . .] making and breaking connections" (Bolter and Grusin 232).

At the level of the individual subject then, the convergence of the trinity of BLUR results in the production of the *data body*, "a collection of digital files that validates the social existence of an individual."[4] The data body is a set of identifying informational bits, configured as subjects engage in an informational culture that is increasingly networked by multiplying databases. From Internet "cookies" that record user's preferences and surfing history, to something as mundane as a credit card or ATM transaction, the members of Generation D leave a digitized trail in cyberspace. Being intelligible in digital culture means being "in the system," online, having a virtual set of machine-readable identifiers, or digits.[5] "Intelligibility" should not be confused with freedom or agency, however, since having a data body doesn't equal empowerment, and not all information is equal. The computerized subject's data body enables participation in compu-culture, as Critical Art Ensemble (*Body Count*) observes, "this body explains to others in officialdom who we are. The social being of an individual is determined by these files." The data body is like a virtual double, an avatar, a cyber trace, a placeholder in the matrix, but one over which the subject has limited control. As both Alvin Toffler[6] and Arthur Kroker[7] explain, within an accelerated "blip culture" of information technology like the one *BLUR* describes, individuals exist intangibly as bits and bytes of information in an always accelerating flow of data, with the agency to make choices, albeit from a limited field of possible actions, where there are strong incentives to always make the "choice" to remain connected, and where being a productive and contributing member of infotech culture and Generation D means producing and processing more data.

RULES OF FORMATION: THE TRINITY

Examples of cyberpop texts that illustrate how rules of formation (including the trinity of BLUR: intangibility, connectivity, and speed) are adopted and amplified in popular culture are everywhere. In each example we find evidence of the ways in which the conceptual architecture of cyberculture becomes linked to individualizing powers and processes, configuring behaviors and the range of available lifestyle choices. Redescribing this popular media indicates the multiple bottom lines it contains, which demonstrate how it is simultaneously compatible with and critical of the status quo of digital capital.

THE TRINITY PART 1: INTANGIBILITY—SCREEN
CULTURE, SIMULATION AND TERMINAL IDENTITY

> In the mode of information it becomes increasingly difficult, or even
> pointless, for the subject to distinguish a 'real' existing 'behind' the
> flow of signifiers.

—Mark Poster (*Mode of Information* **16**)

In 1984 Apple Computer Company launched a promotion for its new
Macintosh personal computer that capitalized on the concept of "intangibility"—the first element in the trinity of BLUR and one of the rules of formation
in the discursive network of cyberculture. Both the cyberpop advertisement
and the computer technology it promoted were revolutionary and groundbreaking, insofar as together they introduced a new visual digital aesthetic
of virtuality—and contributed to the emergence of what Baudrillard terms
"screen culture."[8] In the Macintosh, Apple unveiled a graphical interface
technology complete with a virtual desktop and other icons such as files, a
trashcan, and a small animated smiling computer icon. Intended to humanize
the machine—which, incidentally, issued a *hello* greeting when powered up—
these design choices used the rule of intangibility to make personal computers
(PC) more user friendly. By wedding the discourse of virtuality to concepts
of innovation and progress, creativity, personal freedom, nonconformity,
individuality, and democracy, Apple tried to attract a new market of technologically naïve consumers who, although they might not be initially ready to
buy into the PC revolution, would undoubtedly be swayed by these timeless
Western values. Industry insiders and marketers worldwide maintain even
today that the Macintosh promotion was "the best and most influential television commercial ever made."[9] Broadcast only once, Apple's Macintosh ad had
an instant and seismic effect, changing the face of personal computing and
the way that similar products were marketed in the decades that followed. The
Macintosh "1984" cyberpop significantly impacted the cultures of computing
and advertising while also contributing to the cultural climate that Davis and
Meyer describe as the second half of the information age, by ushering in a
BLURred paradigm in which the distinction between the real and the virtual
is losing its relevance.

MAKING THE MACINTOSH

The Macintosh "1984/Big Brother" advertisement was broadcast in a sixty-
second primetime spot during the 1984 Super Bowl.[10] The filming opens
with an off-center establishing shot of a long line of men with shaved heads,
wearing prison garb, some with gas masks, marching single file. Visible to

the left are television monitors affixed to the hallway-tunnel, all broadcasting the same channel. A blue filtered shot shows the men shuffling into a dark auditorium. There they sit in rows before a large screen, transfixed/mesmerized by what appears to be a propaganda film, dominated by the image of a white man's face, wearing glasses, and directly addressing the audience. The speaker's words appear in type on the screen beneath his image:

> For today, we celebrate the first glorious anniversary of the Information Purification Directives. We have created, for the first time in all history, a garden of pure ideology. Where each worker may bloom secure from the pests of contradictory and confusing truths. Our Unification of Thought is more powerful a weapon than any fleet or army on earth. We are one people. With one will. One resolve. One cause. Our enemies shall talk themselves to death. And we will bury them with their own confusion. We shall prevail!

The screen cuts to a long shot of a tanned, muscular white woman wearing red shorts, carrying a large hammer, running, and bursting into the auditorium through gigantic doors. Black-suited guards bearing guns, their faces covered by black helmets, are chasing her. In a slow motion shot she winds up and releases the hammer with a scream, it flies toward the man's image and penetrates the screen, smashing it. As the screen explodes it bathes the men in the audience in wind and blinding light. In a calm, soothing tone—a striking contrast to the monotone of the previous male voice—a male announcer's voiceover reads text that rolls onto the screen:

On January 24th

Apple Computer will introduce Macintosh.

And you will see why 1984

Won't be like '1984.'[11]

The *mise-en-scène* of George Orwell's dystopic science fiction novel *1984* was adopted to suggest the culture at Apple's rival IBM (otherwise known as "Big Blue")—famous for its strict hierarchy and unyielding, inflexible company policies and vision. The "1984" ad portrays IBM as a totalitarian regime, and juxtaposes Apple as the company able to smash the status quo and resist rigid bureaucracy.[12] The tagline for the "1984" advertisement, "Think different" was to become the popularized mission statement for the company, and is still in use for their most recent marketing campaigns. The bottom line, or one of them, was that the Macintosh and its graphical interface technology symbolized something radical and new, through the ideologies of thinking outside the box, innovation, individualism, and youthful vitality.

How exactly did the Macintosh and its cyberpop infomercial resonate with the trinity of BLUR? The discourse of intangibility was of central importance to the Macintosh effect. What truly differentiated the Mac from IBM's personal computers was its technology: Mac was the first PC with a graphical interface and mouse pointer. The graphics-based operating system on the Mac virtual "desktop" shaped a new computing aesthetic (Turkle, *Second Self* 34). No longer did computer "operators" need to have some knowledge of programming in order to execute tasks on the machine by "plow[ing] through dark fields of cathode-green text, remembering obscure commands"; instead, computer "users"[13] could manipulate the mouse to "point and click through a soothing facade of simple, aesthetically pleasing icons: a desktop, menus, folders and files, dialog boxes, a trash can."[14] As Andrew Shapiro explains, "where earlier computer designs had seemed alienating, cold, and confusing, the Macintosh was humanizing, warm, and likeable" (27).

To represent this new virtual workspace as a "likable" and "soothing" aesthetic, in its "1984" promotion Apple substituted an image of a white, blond, athletic, scantily clad female—a sexualized object—for the Macintosh screen itself. Using attractive women as decorations (or "eye candy") to advertise technological gadgets such as cars, watches, or other high-end and status-symbol objects to men is nothing new, and initially it appears as if Regis McKenna's creative team opted for the seemingly "old" strategy of using sex to sell. *On the surface* this rhetorical choice seems to indicate that although Apple explicitly states that psychographic rather than demographic factors defined its target audience of knowledge workers, the advertisement was in fact intended for spectators whose gaze would be captured by the female as sexual object—a Super Bowl television audience that in many respects presumably resembled the one featured in the auditorium (almost exclusively male).

Similarly, although McKenna states that Apple intended for the target Mac consumer to immediately identify with the product and understand him or herself to belong to a new community of users, the "1984" advertisement featured a cast comprised exclusively of white people. This rhetorical choice seems problematic and at odds with the aims of Apple to appeal to a diverse market, since as Sherry Turkle argues in *Life on the Screen,* "We come to see ourselves differently as we catch sight of our images in the mirror of the machine. [. . .] It is on computer screens where we project ourselves into our own dramas, dramas in which we are producer, director, and star" (26).

TBWA/Apple's choice of gendered and racial coding in the "1984" advertising feature almost ensures that minority subjects in the viewing audience would need to take up what bell hooks calls an "oppositional gaze" to put themselves in the picture, and to imagine they could participate in the Mac "concept" and community, because their images were not reflected in the mirror of the machine.[15] These "old" exclusionary representational choices, which present the default subject as white and male, while making racial others invisible and positioning white women as exotic other/outsider, seem unlikely to succeed in attracting the identification of a diverse audience, and yet statistics show that they inspired consumers nonetheless: only 74 days after the "1984" broadcast, over 50,000 Macintosh units had been sold.

It is clear that the representational politics of the "1984" ad did not reflect the demographics of either the knowledge workers that Apple envisioned, nor the real-life employees behind the development of the North American computer technology industry in the US and/or in its outsourced locations around the globe (but mainly in Asia). At the level of the "screen," it appears as if the success of the Macintosh concept/event marketing depended on and reified the stereotype aligning technology with the most historically privi-leged subjects. The Apple slogan "think different" then seems inappropriate, since as Zillah Eisenstein observes, in popular representations of technocul-ture such as the "1984" Super Bowl feature, the computerized subject is pre-dominantly or exclusively "young, educated, affluent, white, male,"—a trend that prompts Eisenstein to conclude, "there is something less than new here" (31). The omissions and reliance on stereotype in the "1984" advertisement are troubling when we consider that Apple was selling not just machines, but also ideologies, tropes, and what they called "Macmessages" that helped con-figure the first decades of cyberculture, and continue to circulate (and some would argue, dominate) today. The popularization and normalization of the Macmessages and their logics of exclusion—which elevated some knowledge workers as models or icons of cybersubjectivity, rendered some invisible, and turned others into exotic objects—calls for critical analysis. However, because the "1984" advertisement is a classic piece of cyberpop, we might assume at the outset that it employs postmodern strategies such as parody, irony, or paradox, any of which should result in the encoding of multiple bottom lines.

BEHIND THE SCREEN: AMBIGUITY AND CYBERPOP

There are several clues that Apple's "1984" Mac ad is, to cite Haraway ("Manifesto"), *thicker than it first seems*, containing paradoxical or seemingly contradictory ideas, some of which will be compatible with the status quo and others that will challenge, question, or creatively upgrade it. Put differently, at the heart of the "1984" advertisement is ambiguity, what Haraway would describe in *Simians* as a productive and seductive messiness that can *swing both ways* (Haraway 1991). To consider the ambiguity of the "1984" cyber-pop, and how it operates to simultaneously resonate with and resist digital capitalism and corporatist culture, it is necessary to *redescribe* the complex network of associations inherent in it—beyond or behind the level of its spectacle, screen, or surface (and representational politics)—to (re)consider how it functions within the discursive formation of BLURred cyberculture.

On the one hand, part of the Mac concept was a celebration of nonconformity. Ironically however, the marketing strategy was designed to sell millions of identical machines. Moreover, Apple capitalized on the cliché "think outside the box" because of its association with innovation and exploration, while at the same time selling machines with a hardware design and operating system that made it impossible for users to change the standard setup, or even to open the computer case without a special tool available only to authorized dealers.[16] Although the "1984" ad appears to be advocating action rather than docile passivity, in fact the graphical interface technology it advertised encouraged knowledge workers to focus on manipulating icons and symbols on the virtual desktop, and actively discouraged them from looking under the hood, or considering what lay behind the graphics, in the mechanics of the machine and its conditions of production.

The creative team responsible for Apple's "1984" promotion presented a popularized version of Debord's theory of the "society of the spectacle." As men sit in rows, mesmerized by the screen into passivity, a radical force explodes into the hegemony of bureaucracy and smashes the status quo. The spectator is invited to look beyond or behind the screen of the totalitarian regime of Big Brother, and given the opportunity to "think different." However, departing from Debord's radical vision of what constitutes social change, the "1984" advertisement advocates trading one spectacle for another, albeit an upgraded and more entertaining and captivating one—perhaps even more mesmerizing by virtue of being interactive. The seduction of the interface (to use Claudia Springer's phrase[17]) between the user and the Macintosh intensifies and reproduces what Debord might call a "pseudo need" of being *connected*—another rule in the trinity of BLUR—to a community of users or the digerati. Just as Debord suggested, the activity of purchasing commodified spectacles, and immersion in the intangibility of screen culture, culminates in the need to buy additional and upgraded digital products and services, expanding the reach of computer technology into the fabric of everyday life, and keeping digital capitalism online.

The "1984" feature presents a dystopian portrait of a totalitarian technoculture, and then switches directions to chronicle a revolutionary moment, looking ahead to predict (and promise) that the Mac (and Apple Computer Company) will effect radical change in the spectators'/user's lives. And yet, ironically, in directing the viewer's attention to the imploding screen and blinding light, TBWA/Apple encouraged the Super Bowl television audience—just like the men shown staring at the propagandistic image in the auditorium—to develop an intimate relationship to yet *another* screen. The "1984" promotion aimed to create a virtual community of users who communicated not with each other, but (interactively) with screens—not unlike the image of the workers in the "1984" auditorium.

Apple used irony to offer *a critical discourse on the present* (to cite Jameson[18]), inspiring the audience to evaluate and reflect on the place of computer technology in everyday life, and the effects of the increasing digitalization of work and leisure. If the information revolution is upon us as the "1984" text suggests, then we should actively shape it to meet our needs, and rebel against big corporations that threaten to erase what is unique and creative about digital technology innovations in the rush to standardize and monopolize (into "A Unification of Thought. One people. One will. One resolve").

Baudrillard suggests that in a screen culture the relations of power involved in the manufacture of technological commodities are relegated to the area off screen, or placed behind the opacity of the screen—thus obscuring the mechanisms of production. Baudrillard calls this the disappearance of the "work-real" (*Simulations* 47). The process is exemplified by the democratic rhetoric of Apple's Macmessages, which promised to "bring computing to the masses," while at the same time obscuring real existing power imbalances between knowledge workers—some of whom were corporate executives and entrepreneurs but many of whom were women doing pink-collar data entry and processing clerical jobs for menial wages—subsuming them all in one homogenizing category.

From an "outsider's" perspective, reading this fragment of cyberpop is a familiar exercise in documenting inequitable representational rhetorics and politics in the mass media. However, the "1984" promotion utilized an industry insider's vision of the corporate climate at IBM. The startling juxtaposition of the monochrome workers—symbolic of IBM's culture—and the hyperreal spectacle of the running female in full color—symbolic of Apple's vision—immediately suggests the arrival of a new digital order, or at least an end to the hegemony of Big Brother/Big Blue, brought about by the underdog, or "rest of us." In the digital culture dominated by IBM, there is little room for innovation, the ad suggests, things are black or white, on or off (1 or 0). In the Macintosh-powered lifestyle (represented by the hammer-wielding runner), computers enable an enhanced, liberated, resistant, mobile culture where everything is different. In the "1984" ad Apple aimed to inspire critical reflection and analysis, or even public debate about the direction of digital culture and the quality of life for computerized subjects, *while at the same time* selling computers that would implicate consumers in the expansion and maintenance of digital capitalism.

Clearly, Apple Computer Company's Macintosh resonates with the discourse of intangibility in BLUR culture. In order to analyze the impact of the "1984" advertisement and the Mac graphical interface on modes of cybersubjectivity, existing theories about media and spectators, screens and viewers, need to be upgraded. The virtual desktop, with its icons of folders and blank white pages and garbage cans where scraps and clutter disappeared instantly from view, presented "a scintillating surface on which to float, skim, and play," while introducing "a way of thinking that put a premium on surface manipulation and working in ignorance of the underlying mechanism" (Turkle, *Second Self* 35). To Debord and Baudrillard, the Mac technology is exactly the kind of spectacle or simulation that depoliticizes, pacifies, and disables the spectator from active engagement or critical contemplation. And yet it is evident that neither Apple nor the millions of Mac users perceived or experienced the virtual interface in these terms. Importantly, the Macintosh "1984" cyberpop encourages what Darley calls "antagonistic modes of spectatorship" and resistance, smashing the status quo, emphasizing the importance of diversity within community, unique individualism and nonconformity, and appealing to its audience with an invitation to experiment, be creative and innovative, rather than following the rules (189).

THE TRINITY PART 2: CONNECTIVITY—VIRTUAL FREEDOM, E-POWERMENT, AND THE PALM PHENOMENON

> We complain about our oversupply of information. We treasure it nonetheless. We aren't shutting down our E-mail addresses. On the contrary, we're buying pocket computers and cellular modems and mobile phones with tiny message screens to make sure that we can log in from the beaches and mountaintops. These devices are fed by our ever-growing militia of information carriers.
>
> **—James Gleick**[19]

The personal connection that Mac users developed to their computers was partly based on the machine's ease of operation and novelty, but also because as Sherry Turkle suggests, computer and communication technologies are "objects-to-think-with" (Turkle, *Second Self* 18). "Computers would not be the culturally powerful objects they are turning out to be," Turkle argues, "if people were not falling in love with their machines and the ideas that the machines carry" (Turkle 1995: 49). Not only did Apple cite Western values such as freedom and democracy for its concept marketing event, the Mac was also promoted as enabling the values associated with a postmodern BLURred economy: speed, flexibility, progress, intangible value and virtuality, compatibility, and connectivity.

Cyberpop ads featuring cell phones, personal digital assistants (PDAs), and Internet service providers (ISPs) stress the virtue of connectivity while preserving a discourse of innovation, creativity, e-powerment, and individuality. In advertising for PDAs, the quality of *connectivity* is a defining feature of the BLURred (computerized) subject. To be connected to the flow of information—the central commodity exchanged in digital capitalism—is synonymous with being informed. As a result, in *The Information Subject* Mark Poster observes that

> Information is presented as the key to contemporary living and society is divided between the information rich and the information poor. The 'informed' individual is a new social ideal (8).

In order to stay informed, the computerized subject must purchase the requisite digital gear and subscribe to communication services, since the flow of information never stops. Being off-line is tantamount to being "out of touch"[20] with the world of work, but paradoxically, cyberpop advertising also promotes the idea that leisure is enabled by (and even dependent on) connectivity, as the distinction between "home" and "office" is BLURred. Within the discursive formation of cyberculture, connectivity means both being in the loop and being virtually "free."

"I'VE LOST MY PALM PILOT AND I CAN'T GET UP"

> I've lost my Palm Pilot. It's just a Palm III, housed in a cheap case bought off the fire-sale table at Staples, lacking a modem or much memory, and really nothing to show off at a dinner party. [. . .] I've gone over the evening in question dozens of times. I've moved my desk at least twice. I've turned my apartment upside down. I've suspiciously questioned friends and colleagues. Weeks later, I still catch myself shaking out my backpack (maybe it's lodged in the corner?), and I'm considering canvassing local coffee shops and laundromats to put up "Have You Seen This Palm?" posters next to the lost kitty pleas. Deep down, however, I believe I've given up. Step 1: Acceptance. Sure, I've got all my data backed up on my desktop; I had even expensed the PDA in the first place. And of course, there's really very little sentimental value attached to this bland-looking digital organizer. It's been gone for weeks, so, like, get over it, man. But still, I can't help but wallow in a pool of denial and stupidity. I can't help but wonder how it is that this small, inanimate object, like so many small inanimate objects, has slowly but surely taken over

my life—and what harm it was wreaking on my overly processed psyche.

—Larry Smith[21]

After misplacing his Palm Pilot™ PDA, Larry Smith spends weeks searching for answers about how and why this separation occurred. Repeatedly turning his belongings, work and living spaces inside out and upside down, Smith obsesses about the Palm's location. Struggling with emotional confusion over his relationship to small inanimate technological objects, Smith tries to accept that he is no longer Palm Powered™, and speculates about his growing dependency on digital tools and toys. In a self-reflexive and heart-broken tone, Smith confesses that he is trying to "accept" that his Palm Pilot is forever gone, and is unsure exactly why he's having such trouble "getting over it." Indeed, insofar as the Palm is a tool for making data portable, losing it could cause a security breach if the memory contained personal information, and replacing it is a costly and time-consuming inconvenience, but Smith's confession suggests that (a) his machine was a relatively inexpensive model, and (b) that no data were permanently lost, and finally (c) there was no special sentimental investment attached to this PDA. So why, then, is Larry Smith feeling so lost himself, "wallow[ing] in a pool of denial and stupidity" and somewhat incapacitated as a result of losing this piece of digital gear? Would it be reasonable to expect that he would have a similar reaction to losing his nondigital address or appointment book? There are at least two reasons that the loss of a Palm Pilot could result in these confusing emotions Smith experiences, which are made clearer by juxtaposing his comments to a recent advertisement for Palm.com (Figure 2.1).

"THE NET GOES WITH YOU"

We live in an increasingly digitized culture within an informational economy, where to be connected to the flow of data is deemed preferable to being unplugged. The modem-equipped PDA featured in the advertising screenshot is a tool that facilitates a portable/mobile connection to the Web or net of digital capital and culture (as is a cell phone and/or wireless laptop computer). These capabilities can make the user feel they are part of the current of exchange in our informational economy: armed with a PDA capable of "beaming" data to another PDA, instantly receiving and transmitting messages via a wireless communications network, and storing all essential personal data in portable form. The user can rest assured they have all their digits properly processed and pocketed, and that they are informed and connected. The owner of a PDA

Figure 2.1   Palm.com's Palm Pilot PDA organizer; the Net goes with you.

can experience e-powerment, a sense of participation in digital culture, and membership in Generation D.

But paradoxically, Larry Smith's Palm III didn't even have a modem. Smith's lost PDA functioned essentially as a digitized DayTimer®, capable of holding small text memos, a calculator, a daily planner/scheduler, phone numbers, and perhaps calorie counting software or digital solitaire, or a small language translating program. Smith's anxiety about losing the Palm Pilot and his sense of feeling disoriented is less about the loss of data (since he misplaced a copy, not the original, which resides safely backed-up on his PC) than it is about the loss of virtual connectivity, and of virtual possession of control over his data body (his digits). Without the small inanimate digital object as a symbol of his connectivity, Smith feels that he is somehow off-line, immobilized, out of the game. As a result, is likely that Smith feels unable to work or be productive, and unable to rest and enjoy leisure time, since as the Palm advertisement proposes, only the subject who is Palm Powered can enjoy a "simply amazing" and balanced lifestyle. If he had his Palm, life would be simplified, the ad suggests, and it could be Larry strolling off into the sunset and surf with his board and his bathing suit, reassured that his handheld "can do practically everything" so Larry could "do nothing" but relax and enjoy the good life, the freedom of the *connected* life.

But the Palm is gone, so Larry Smith joins the PDA-less audience for Palm.com's cyberpop ad, which encourages the off-line subject to feel as if he is tethered to a desk and PC, while the class of successful digital netizens is off playing in the surf. This rhetorical strategy plays on our fears of personal and professional failure in the current climate of Mcommerce (mobile commerce): we are encouraged to believe that physical mobility is an important step to economic (class) ascension, and that mobility and freedom go hand in hand with status and increased personal gain, and are inalienable civil liberties. Thus, instead of experiencing liberation, when Smith finds himself without his Palm Pilot he experiences sensations of entrapment and confusion. The Palm.com advertisement foresees and offers to remedy this condition, by allowing Larry the freedom to go anywhere, facilitated by the PDA's ability to have the "Net" follow him (both the sense of being a *symbol* of his connection to the digital life, and *literally*, in the sense that it provides real connectivity via the Internet, intranets, and mail servers). The Palm Pilot is promoted as a gateway device mediating between work and leisure, managing a BLURred culture and digital lifestyles in which these kinds of distinctions are unclear.

"LIFE: FULL"

Promotional materials for portable digital gear such as Palm Pilots and cell phones attempt to persuade consumers that being digital is not just productive, but that is it pleasurable, part of a digital lifestyle (and even symptomatic of an identity). Since "handhelds can do anything," such as mundane tasks like getting the mail, the advertisement suggests that the user will be liberated from routine duties, and even freed from stifling environments (e.g., isolating cubicles) to pursue leisure activities while experiencing privacy and connectivity simultaneously. Transcending tedious work, "You can do nothing" while the PDA handles "everything"; put differently, however, this explains why Larry Smith feels like, without his Palm, he is unable to do anything: his uncomputerized condition means he has "Life: Empty."

Eventually, having accepted the finality of the situation, Larry Smith upgrades to a deluxe Handspring Visor™—a PDA machine with more memory, features, and aesthetic appeal than the Palm III. Obviously Smith is not alone in his experience of misplacing and then replacing a portable electronic device: in a bit of strange-but-true technology news, it was reported that Prince William of the UK attracted media attention when he mistakenly left his Palm Pilot behind in a taxicab in the spring of 2001. This royal blunder inspired a private company to complete a survey that revealed over 1,300 PDAs, 62,000 mobile phones, and 2,900 laptops had been reported left in London taxis in the first six months of 2001.[22] It is impossible to know how many of the portable electronic devices sold in the US are lost or stolen, but what is perhaps more interesting is that despite the disturbance and distress that losing a cell phone or PDA can cause, consumers will, if their income allows it, replace those devices, perhaps with upgraded versions. Though the sad situation was an occasion for some soul searching and critical reflection about the potential downside of his wired life, the harm to his "overly processed psyche," and costly reliance on small and easy-to-lose digital devices, Smith decides that he needs another PDA.

In what he calls "The Final Analysis," Smith describes his ongoing attempts to achieve a balance in his technologically driven lifestyle, to retrain himself to experience leisure time unmediated by digital devices, occasionally unplugging, disconnecting, and leaving his cell phone, Visor, and two-way pager at the office. And yet, promotional literature for Palm and Handspring PDAs, cell phones, and wireless services are already one step (or likely several) ahead of Smith, offering their products as facilitators of leisure time, of flexibility and personal empowerment, of privacy, or as hybrid tool-toys that can make being "in the Web" or having "the Net follow you" seem like an attractive option for productive workdays and time "off." These messages resonate with the discourse of BLUR, in which being out of the office doesn't mean being "off-line" courtesy of the implosion of the home vs. work binaries.

For example, OmniSky.com (Figure 2.2) reassures those of us who work "insane hours"—and have forgotten what "weekend" means—that we can relax and spend time with family and friends away from the office, without missing a beat of professional productivity by subscribing to their wireless communication service. This will enable users to trade stocks, check e-mail, engage in e-commerce, and search the Web via a PDA device whenever and "wherever you are," seamlessly integrating the worlds of work and leisure.

In a similar vein, Sony Electronics promotes its new handheld CLIE™ with a tongue-in-cheek advertisement depicting a middle-aged couple at a spa, soaking in a mud bath (Figure 2.3a and Figure 2.3b). Their leisure time is enabled by the connectivity afforded by their PDAs. The text rehearses the gender stereotype that women are consumed with the body and emotions (in this case, Web sites featuring "a romantic getaway" for "personal pampering") while men exist in the world of the mind, rationality, science, business, and

Figure 2.2   OmniSky.com digital services; now you can have a weekend.

facts (for example, online information about the chemical composition of mud baths). The ad builds on the use of a heterosexual couple to exaggerate the concept of difference by featuring the female model reclining with a happy expression, compared to the male's uncomfortable pose and outward show of anxiety. This difference, the ad suggests, is due to their dissimilar positions vis-à-vis an informational economy. Perhaps this is intended to suggest that women can be happy and content with *some* information, whereas men need *more* and are never satisfied that they have enough, needing to be continuously in touch with it ("if only he could reach his CLIE handheld right now") —because men are the true producers and processors of information, while women passively consume it, with "no worries."

What is more important, however, is the way the ad underscores the fundamental common ground between these two unlike subjects: they are both

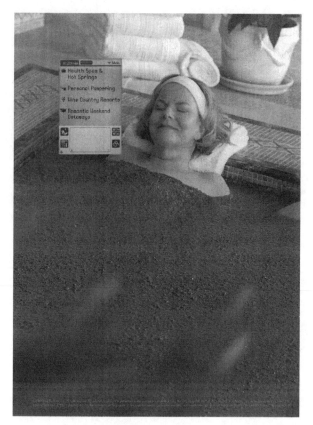

Figure 2.3a Sony Clie PDA, mud bath.

consumed by the acquisition of digital information, and can only experience calm and contentment after connecting with their digital devices. The message communicated is that leisure time is maximized through digital connectivity and data processing (e-)power, and that the compu-subject should never be further than arm's length away from their machines, the tools that organize their lives and even regulate their emotions.

DIGITAL DEMOGRAPHICS AND DIFFERENCE

Clearly the consumer group targeted by this type of cyberpop advertising is not homogenous, and in spite of the fact that Sony marketers know this, still the CLIE advertising campaigns try to make it appear so by exaggerating the discourse of virtual community mediated by common ownership of digital gadgetry. The messages sent about the digital lifestyle are markedly different

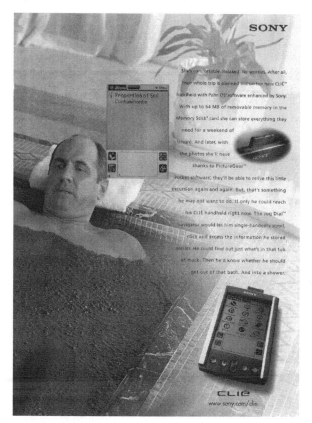

Figure 2.3b Sony Clie PDA, mud bath.

when they are targeted to consumers categorized demographically. Although the mud bath advertisement underscores that at some fundamental level, both men and women need PDAs, albeit for different reasons, another advertisement in the same series illustrates that being digital means very disparate things when considered from the vantage point of racial difference. When we look to advertising for portable digital information devices, some patterns emerge as to which subjects should purchase various kinds of "gear"—and undeniably, visible minority subjects will be directly featured in ads for Mp3 players (Figure 2.4) and digital photography equipment (Figure 2.5). Often these ads for high-tech leisure gadgetry are the only times that black or Asian subjects will appear in digital culture's mass marketing. In what at first appears to be an exception to this pattern, the "Roots Vibrations" advertisement for the CLIE handheld PDA is dominated by a photograph of an African American, but a second glance shows that he is (predictably) a reggae musician (Figure 2.6a and Figure 2.6b). A spotlight picks out a Caucasian couple

I'M LISTENING.

Rio
riohome.com

Figure 2.4   Rio Mp3 player, I'm listening.

in the audience, and a screenshot of their PDA appears below them, featuring stored files on reggae entertainment and cooking. Another CLIE screenshot appears, this one belonging to the black musician on stage, but this PDA is downloaded with information on financial planning and stock management, and a "4 Star Dining Guide."

What is particularly insidious about this advertisement is that in order to be amusing, it exaggerates the unlikelihood of the black musician having a need for this particular financial data. Conventional wisdom and cultural stereotype dictate that these two handhelds have been somehow switched: it is more probable that the white male in the crowd, not the black man, would be closely tracking the stock market and the locations of fine dining establishments—not only due to the fact that (noncelebrity) musicians are generally not wealthy or frequent patrons of "4 Star" restaurants, but also due to the overrepresentation of white men in the world of finance and the most affluent socioeconomic classes. The repetition (and near exclusivity) of images that feature minority women and men with technotoys (music, photographs, Web sites about television, and other low-art popculture data) underscores the logic of the digital divide in cyberpop media. Thus Sony's decision to prominently feature a black man in a promotion for the PDA is somewhat

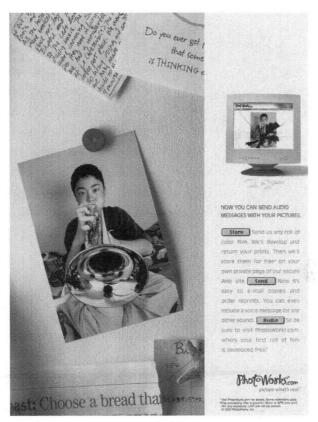

Figure 2.5 Photoworks.com; picture what's next.

of a gimmick; it is likely that in most of the information and computer technology trades, business and digital culture magazines in which this "Roots Vibrations" advertisement ran, it was the only image of a black man featured between the glossy covers—and thus this unconventional representational choice is virtually guaranteed to draw attention to Sony's product. A careful (though unscientific) search through hundreds of high-tech magazine issues will turn up only a very few extremely rare images of black men and women and they are more likely than not to be pictured using technology for fun rather than producing information for work purposes (Figure 2.7). At the level of its representational politics, what makes this Sony advertising campaign for new PDA technologies "amusing" is its reliance on the tired gags of gender and racial stereotyping.

However, getting beyond an analysis of these advertising texts at the level of their surface representations, and considering how they qualify as cyber-

Figure 2.6a Sony Clie PDA, Roots vibrations.

pop media, means considering their ambiguities, and the ways they negotiate their own and their consumer's implication in the formation of cyberculture. To redescribe how the Sony OmniSky ads are both critical of and compatible with the status quo of digital capitalism requires that we underscore their use of irony and paradox, and/or postmodern aesthetic mechanisms (such as pastiche), signaling the implosion or BLURring of metanarratives with historical permanence. How might these cyberpop texts, which seem invested in reifying racial and gendered stereotypes, actually encourage their readers to "think different[ly]" about what being a connected subject in a digital economy means? Likewise, how do these pieces of digital cultural production serve to cite and upgrade the strategies and rhetorics introduced by Apple and the "1984" Mac promotion? It seems clear that these advertisements reify the rule of connectivity in the trinity of BLUR that underpins digital capital; yet in what ways do they communicate a critical or creative perspective on the digi-

Figure 2.6b SonyClié PDA, Roots vibrations.

talization of everyday life? How do the central discourses of contemporary digital culture marketing (following Apple's groundbreaking example) utilize the rhetoric of a privileged insider's perspective to encourage forms of resistant or antagonistic modes of participation in digital culture? By redescribing these texts, they become inevitably thicker than they first seem, as they promote connectivity while negotiating their implication in and relationship to technoculture by employing creative, critical, and complementary rhetorics vis-à-vis digital capitalism and its hegemonic relations of power and dominant discourses.

For example, in the case of Sony's CLIE marketing campaign, what is underscored is the fundamental common ground between seemingly unlike (different) subjects: whether separated by the color line or the gender binary, compu-subjects are at base, connected, intelligible through recourse to the same 1s and 0s. This rhetoric of "net utopia" and its trope that online race, gender, looks, and the particularities of embodiment are irrelevant, is bor-

Figure 2.7   Intertainer Inc.; broadbandfun.

rowed from hacker discourse communities, and was popularized in the early stages of the expansion of the Internet, when users were celebrating the concept of passing as "other" online and identity experimentation. It is a romantic trope that historically has appealed to both computer geeks (insiders) and new online users (the computer naïve). The Sony ad also borrows from the reductive cybernetic concept that "information is information"; following this logic, once online one digital subject's collection of data is in many ways equal to the next one's. And yet, it is clear that although a list of ingredients in a recipe and a list of stock values in the NASDAQ may appear in similar graphics and share the same amount of screen space, and may require the same amount of computational processing power to transmit them, the cultural values attributed to these different kinds of data make them vastly different kinds of "information," besides the fact that their users are differently encoded with racial and gendered connotations as well.

Increasingly, there are no moments where being unplugged makes sense, since as Davis and Meyer suggest, "on every front, opposites are blurring," including the distinctions between "home" and "office," "work" and "life." In the technoculture of BLUR, neither time nor space prevents the flow of information. With the increase in bandwidth and the velocity of infotransmission, our lives are being speeded up in accordance with messages such as "work all the time" and "stay connected." This might be why Larry Smith finds himself caught up and repeating patterns of behavior in a kind of automatic feedback loop, checking and rechecking his knapsack for the missing PDA, moving, replacing, then moving his desk again to look underneath. Without the aid of the tiny machine (technoprosthetic device) to synchronize his life, Smith becomes lost and confused. And lacking the virtual connectivity his PDA symbolized, Larry Smith feels immobilized and "can't get up"—a sentiment that points to another rule in the trinity of BLUR: stay connected, but be sure it is a fast connection, because cyberculture is also about *speed*.

THE TRINITY PART 3: SPEED—TECHNOLOGY THAT FOLLOWS YOU

> Reality is in continual motion, a BLURstorm. [. . .] Miss a day and your world moves on without you. [. . .] In an economy marked by unprecedented Speed, what's valuable is not what's standing still, but what's in motion.

> **—Stanley Davis and Christopher Meyer 8-11**

Part of the trinity of BLUR, the rule of speed describes a cultural climate in which information technologies enable digital capitalism to flourish at an ever-accelerating rate, forcing individuals and corporations into a race to keep informed and effective. Machines and services that enable mobility, connectivity, and instantaneous data transmission are promoted as the essential tools for life on the information superhighway. In order to counteract the technostress and information overload that a BLURstorm inevitably causes, the rule of speed is oftentimes linked to tropes of freedom, recreation, individualism, adventurism, colonialism, living in the fast lane, youth, health, prosperity, flexibility, and risk taking—narratives that are part of the American dream, character, and experience.[23]

In *Hyperculture: The Human Cost of Speed,* Stephen Bertman confirms that "America is increasingly a society on the move, and what was once drive-*in*, is increasingly becoming drive-*thru*."[24] Bertman continues: "As the speedometer of social activity continues to climb, it becomes more and more certain that only those businesses geared to high speed and change will succeed" (110). In the

Figure 2.8   Cingular mobile communication services, technology that follows you.

networked economy of BLUR, thriving businesses, corporations, and individuals must be "fast acting and transient."[25] Knowledge workers need to become mobile labor, recognizing themselves as "free agents," or "bright, creative, high-tech nomads" who are empowered to "make moves" in a climate of downsizing, rightsizing, and outsourcing (Davis and Meyer 151). Speed and mobility are enabled by the consumption of digital gadgets and e-services, which simultaneously manage and intensify the velocity of everyday life in cyberculture.

Mass media reassures its public that if they are online in our networked society, they will not be left behind the pace of change, nor will they be lost in the racing current of information flow. With the correct navigational tools, instantaneous access to the correct data is always one click or call away. Never being off-line means never missing opportunities to be productive, so consumer electronics and communication service plans such as those promoted by Cingular Interactive (Figure 2.8) and Motient's eLink with Yahoo! (Figure 2.9) enable users to have their work "follow" them, even into the restroom.

Figure 2.9 Motient's e-link mobile communication services; Yahoo! in the bathroom.

This cyberpop encourages consumers to "go" (away from the office, or into a bathroom stall), to remain in perpetual motion, with the prerequisite that they stay connected to the world of e-commerce via wireless technologies.

In BLUR culture, "We are in a rush. We are making haste. A compression of time characterizes the life of the century now closing," writes James Gleick in his work *Faster* (9). "Unoccupied time is vanishing," because "We live in the buzz. We wish to live intensely," and "our ability to work fast and play fast gives us power. It thrills us" (10-12). As a result, "all activity becomes crisis oriented,"[26] because as Tim Jordan explains: "The informational space of flows never sleeps. Whether the sun is setting or rising has no effect on the servers and wires that shift information around the globe, and someone or something, somewhere, is always awake in a global system producing more information. [. . .] The space of flows disrupts routine with the certain knowledge that a new piece of information is out there."[27]

The discourses of speed and technomobility refer both to real and virtual phenomena. Portable gadgets allow knowledge workers and compu-subjects the freedom to physically relocate, to listen to music, talk on the phone, or use the computer without being tethered by cords to heavy equipment and offices. And yet, as Donna Haraway has observed, at the end of the twentieth century, "our machines are disturbingly lively, and we ourselves are frighteningly inert" (*How Like a Leaf* 80). Haraway is referring to, among other things, the many jobs in which employees stand at factory assembly lines overseeing the operation of automated machines, behind counters or at windows punching cash registers and processing credit card transactions, or sit at desks, typing on keyboards and answering phones. The emphasis in an informational economy is on increasing the speed of global data transmission, while the human data processor merely pushes the *SEND* key. Acting as a vector through which data processing passes, the knowledge worker can manufacture and transmit information all day long, and not be any more enlightened in the process, since *data* is not synonymous with *information* or *knowledge*. "This is the Information Age, which does not always mean information in our brains," writes Gleick, "we sometimes feel that it means information whistling by our ears at light speed, too fast to be absorbed" (87). The result can be stressful and alienating, leaving knowledge workers with the feeling that they are just cogs (or switches) in the information-computer-technology (ICT) machine.

Oftentimes e-powered mobility is really about virtual travel: sitting in front of the screen of a PDA, cell phone, or laptop, the user is completely inert, a witness to the flow of the datastream as information moves through them and throughout the global communication networks. When Davis and Meyer encourage the reader of *BLUR* to "Node Thyself," they are not referring to this atomized, automaton scenario of digital subject as vector; instead the cyber-economists connect the rule of speed to a discourse of (upward or forward) economic mobility and the agency to control one's professional destiny. In order to associate the concepts of speed and freedom with the acquisition of digital products and services, cyberpop media must address the pervasive sense of technostress that is a side-effect of the e-lifestyle.

> I'm gone for a couple of hours, and I have twenty electronic messages on my computer when I get back. People are working weekends; you can see by the dates. They send things Friday at 10 p.m., Saturday mornings at 9 a.m., Sundays at 9 p.m. Of the twenty messages on my machine, I have to do something about twelve of them. My head spins (Arlie Russell Hochschild, *The Time Bind: When Work Becomes Home and Home Becomes Work*).[28]

The machine also had an unspoken appeal: *keep up*. No one else was around to obey, so it fell to me. The machine expected me to be its equal. It could print two pages a minute—why couldn't I read two pages a minute? Why couldn't I *write* two pages a minute? (David Schenk, *Data Smog: Surviving the Information Glut*).[29]

Echoing Haraway, Gleick admits that despite the fact that "computerization, miniaturization, and the technologies of electronics and artificial materials have all leapt forward," at the end of the twenty-first century Americans find ourselves "more solidly earthbound than most scientists would have predicted" (80). Rather than being able to actually teleport our physical bodies instantly around the globe or journey to distant planets, the main effect of rapid technological change is that "We get dizzy. We feel the instability of our own place in society" (80). The public is becoming increasingly stressed about technology, due to the impossibility of staying on top of information and high-tech innovation. In response, self-help literature is flourishing in a market where people fear falling behind the pace of change, failing to "master the BLUR," and becoming outdated or obsolete as a result.

In response to technostress, information overload, and data smog, a host of products and services are manufactured and marketed to manage the acceleration of everything and the potential loss of perspective and even identity that can result. These products commodify the desire for personalized, individualized information delivery, packaged with a discourse about the virtual adventure, increased mobility, and upgraded quality of life that having digital gear and services can deliver—all designed to offset the knowledge worker's stress about the anonymity of being a "blip" in the circuitry of digital capitalism. At this moment, the discourses of speed and connectivity converge to construct a network of associations for digital technologies that simultaneously humanize and extend the reach of digital capitalism.

PUSHED BY TECHNOLOGY THAT FOLLOWS YOU

Networked communications need interfaces that hop across nodes, exploiting the unique character of distributed communications. Technology that, say, follows you into the next taxi you ride. [. . .] Push media arrive automatically—on your desktop, in your e-mail, via your pager. You won't choose whether to turn them on, only whether to turn them off. And there will be many incentives not to. [. . .] Push media are 'always on.'

—**Editorial,** *WIRED Magazine* [30]

Before the invention of fax machines, personal computers, e-mail, or the Internet, in the 1960s Marshall McLuhan warned that "the speed-up of the electronic age is disrupting"[31] to individuals, since "when things come at you very fast, naturally you lose touch with yourself [. . .] you lose identity."[32] He reasoned that when society functions "at the speed of light," individuals become confused and miserable, due to the inability "to find goals in a world that is moving so fast that no possible goal could remain in focus for ten seconds."[33] More than thirty years later, McLuhan's view is echoed by Paul Virilio who, in his essay "Speed and Information: Cyberspace Alarm!" observes that "with the build-up of information superhighways we are facing a new phenomenon: loss of orientation. [. . .] A total loss of the bearings of the individual looms large."[34] With information overload, it can be daunting and difficult to find the data you need, therefore ICT "personalization" products and services are developed to enable information to follow or find you. Rather than trying to track down data, push media technologies offer to track the user, databasing their preferences and habits, using microtargeted advertising to identify (and in the process, construct) the user's data body, and *push* appropriate product announcements their way.

In *Times of the Technoculture* Robins and Webster observe that computer technologies intensify, reconfigure, and facilitate the processes of "individualization" that are the basic mechanisms for the efficient operation of capitalist/power. Personalization technologies and push media act to reindividualize the cybersubject in blip culture. This process constructs the user's data body by recording their content choices, establishing a set of perimeters around the subject, which act as information filters and nodes to which other digital content providers can link, to further push personalized media. The result is marketing campaigns and products that utilize the prefix "my," such as My AOL, My Yahoo!, My Netscape—and on Microsoft's Windows desktop—My Computer, My Documents, My Files (Shapiro 44). Personalization technologies and push media converge to feed the consumer's manufactured desires and recorded preferences to be connected and informed, in control of their data body and linked (in)to the web of cyberculture, while also being recognized as unique individuals.

MLIFE: NONSTOP

For AT&T this strategy led to a controversial campaign that resulted in a collection of six cyberpop advertising spots aired during the televised 2002 Super Bowl (with a $2 million price tag each). The "mLife" campaign was essentially designed to convince consumers that with a subscription to an AT&T wireless communications service bundle, they could "stay connected and be free." One of the ads featured the metaphoric image of the severing of a newborn's umbilical cord to communicate the (voiceover) message that "we are meant to lead a wireless life"—naturalizing the intensification of cybersciences in everyday life. The mLife (or mobile life) ads were part of what was essentially a rebranding campaign designed to create a buzz about already existing services like e-mail, instant messaging, and cell phone plans with personalized downloadable ring tones. Consumers were invited to "enjoy customization" while using AT&T service plans to become increasingly mobile.

To upgrade the tropes attached to wireless technologies, AT&T borrowed several concepts from Apple Computer Company including event marketing, the use of spectacle, intentionally ambiguous teaser marketing (which did not show the product being sold but substituted other images for it, in this case, montages of happy people), and an attempt to humanize computer technologies. But unlike Apple's "1984" promotion, which aimed to control the conversations around the Macintosh—while paradoxically criticizing IBM for their "unification of thought" propagandistic corporate culture—AT&T Wireless opted to remain intentionally vague about defining exactly what constituted the mLife. Billboards and print ads that appeared prior to the Super Bowl commercial ran taglines asking, "What is mLife?" "Is mLife fattening?" "Is it a new religion?" AT&T Wireless CEO John Zeglis explained that the idea behind this "teaser" strategy was to incite the public's curiosity and to invite consumers to create their own meanings, suggesting that there is an unlimited number of ways to integrate wireless technologies into digital lifestyles.[35]

Mark Siegel, spokesperson for AT&T Wireless, explained that rather than employ "a traditional approach," the company wanted to introduce mLife in "a whimsical, irreverent, unconventional way [. . .] that got people talking."[36] No longer should people think of their phone "as a phone," Siegel advises, but as a device to facilitate connectivity and interpersonal relationships—in other words, like Apple, AT&T Wireless had a goal of getting their consumers to *think different[ly]* about computer and communication technology, and about themselves as users, or better yet, as participants in building digital culture. To do this the branding agency Ogilvy & Mather, contracted by AT&T Wireless, referred to customers as lovers, sisters, and grandmothers, and emphasized that "real" people (visually communicated by minimizing the number of white males that appear onscreen and substituting a collection of gray-haired, adolescent, female, and multicultural subjects instead) can use these telecommunications services as lifestyle products to "manage your life [. . .] and the things you care about." No longer is it enough to advertise the technologies themselves, insists Jeremy Pemble (another media spokesperson for AT&T Wireless), "consumers don't want that" but rather are seeking "simplicity" and ideas about how to use information technology to add value to their lives.[37] Through personalization technology services, consumers are led to believe that the gadgets and services will be configured according to their unique needs, rather than the opposite scenario, in which users must morph into high-speed mobile compu-subjects or Generation D in order to remain in the game. The mLife campaign made an explicit connection between having portable digital technology and connectivity, and living a fast-paced and mobile lifestyle. After its initial launch, AT&T Wireless advertisements explained that the mLife involved taking taxis, going shopping, taking flights, sailing, moving from bar to restaurant to club, and staying in perpetual motion.

Unlike Apple, which did not have the benefit of the Internet as an advertising venue in 1984, Ogilvy & Mather created a Web site for the mLife campaign that maintained the secrecy around exactly what constituted the mLife, and which company was behind it, until Super Bowl Sunday when the connections were unveiled. The Web site had registered 34,000 unique visitors prior to the television spot, and its traffic rose to 681,000 unique visitors on game day (Holland). Industry analysts concluded that although for many viewers, the secrecy and ambiguity surrounding the mLife campaign was irritating, there was enough buzz and curiosity to drive viewers and listeners to the Web site to learn more about the concept, and thus from an advertising perspective the series of cyberpop cultural productions was a success. The remediation of the television and print ads for the Internet site is a clue to how AT&T Wireless envisioned their target consumer group: the ideal audience for mLife is already online, already connected, and perhaps experiencing technostress as a result of an overwhelming amount of digitized interventions into their life. AT&T Wireless offers their audience the opportunity to achieve digital convergence, by subscribing to a bundled mLife package of information and communication technology services, to streamline and simplify the seemingly unavoidable (but manageable) presence of digital technology in everyday life. The compu-subject who is eligible for an mLife is already implicated in the network of cybercultural production, consumption, and exchange—as the heavy Web site traffic confirmed.

The question that Larry Smith poses, about what harm an overreliance on digital devices may have caused to his "overly processed psyche" gets drowned out in an avalanche of cyberpop advertising messages that encourage us to stay in the game, promising freedom, success, productivity, relaxation, happiness and "Life: Full" through digital connectivity and the consumption of evermore sophisticated portable digital products and services. The ads encourage us to integrate computer and communication technologies into every aspect of our lives, delegating to them the responsibility of managing the smallest details of our day, so that they operate in a manner that is eerily similar to what Foucault described as a "capillary mechanism of power," one that "reaches into the very grain of individuals, touches their bodies and inserts itself into their actions and attitudes, their discourses, learning processes, and everyday lives" (Foucault, *Archaeology* 39). Cyberpop advertisements, composed of citations and interpretations of the conceptual architecture of (or rules of formation in) digital culture, operate to configure knowledge, behaviors, relationships, and subjectivities.

Cyberpop media sell products, promote ideologies, and serve as info-mediaries to translate and popularize the cutting edge of emerging digital technologies—but they are inherently ambiguous texts, which, not unlike Haraway's cyborg technofiguration, are mutable, polluted, contradictory, and unpredictable. Constructing a space of accommodation to the economies and hegemonies of cyberculture, advertisements such as the ones reviewed in this chapter might be best understood as examples of Scott Bukatman's *terminal identity fictions*, instructing their audiences on how to "node thyself" and develop a lifestyle that is compatible with and intelligible within an increasingly informatic and virtual digital culture.[38] On the other hand, and at the same time, through adopting a cyberpoetic approach and *redescribing* the multiple bottom lines in these marketing projects, what emerges is a theme of critical resistance to, and creative interpretation of, the dominant modes of information production, consumption, and exchange. Cyberpop advertising borrows from the bedrock of Western values (such as freedom, democracy, and equality), synchronizes these with capitalist imperatives, and upgrades them with postmodern concepts such as implosion, shift, and blur. The result is usually a paradoxical and always an ambiguous representation of subjectivity and culture in the digital age.

3
Technomasculinity and GenderBLUR in *The Matrix*

The dude with no life spends most of his time in a faintly lit office, chugging cheap coffee from Styrofoam cups and training his glazed eyes on indecipherable diagrams. His hair is mussed, he couldn't tell the *Ocean's 11* cast from the Jackson Five, and he hasn't been out on a date with his wife in months. [. . .] You see this figure, staring at his screen, looking pretty much like a zombie—and just grinding away.[1]

—Michael Silver, Business 2.0 (2002)

These excerpts from a feature article in *Business 2.0 Magazine* chronicle the trend of the digitalization of professional sports culture. The essay is a celebratory profile of the achievements, dedication, and technological know-how of John Gruden, lead coach of the Oakland Raiders football team, and "reluctant geek." The accompanying—and only—photograph shows Gruden hunched at a desk in semidarkness, his face illuminated by the glare of a computer monitor, his well-developed forearm stretched out to grasp—not a bulbous firm leathery football but—a tiny smooth electronic mouse. He is described as "ruggedly handsome," has made *People Magazine's* "50 Most Beautiful People List," and admits that his large flat-panel color display monitor is his "best friend." The seeming contradictions inherent in this description are the hook to catch readers' attention. A successful, professional, famous man "with no life," an attractive, heterosexual man whose best friend is his computer rather than his (neglected) wife (or even dog), whose healthy, glowing appearance and hypermuscular physique give no hint of long days and nights at the keyboard in a dimly lit office, who is described paradoxically as both "rugged" and "beautiful." Of all the blurring opposites in this introduction, it is the rugged/beautiful one that points to the upgraded discourse of (techno)masculinity constructed by and reflected in this article.

Unlike *People*, *Business 2.0* is not a lifestyle magazine; its target audiences are IT and e-commerce professionals, and entrepreneurs. Between the covers are articles penned by industry insiders advising how to become (and remain) financially successful in the age of digital capitalism. There is technical advice on purchasing, maintaining, upgrading, and networking computers for corporate environments, and hints on increasing productivity and management skills required for the BLURred world of cybercommerce. Judging by the demographics of the contributing writers, editors, and individuals profiled (such as John Gruden), and the images in its advertisements, it is unmistakably professional white male readers who are expected to subscribe to *Business 2.0*—what hackers call "the suits."

Though John Gruden is not a suit, he is part of the target audience of *Business 2.0*, which now includes professional athletes alongside e-commerce professionals who are embracing the digital age. Initially, Gruden was reluctant to become a computer geek because, as he explains, "the stereotype was, you don't want to be a computer guy; you want to be a football coach" (M. Silver 17). But considering the digitalization of everyday life, today Gruden needs to be *both* in order to remain on the cutting edge and ahead of the competition. The article suggests that everyone, including those who many would consider the epitome of hypermasculinity—such as football players—must become a bit geekier, since in every realm of contemporary digital culture everyone needs tech support. The message in this feature article is that if Gruden, a model of machismo and maleness, can embrace the techie nerd within as part of his celebrity identity, then many lesser men can and should follow "suit"; between the lines, *Business 2.0* selects Gruden as an example to illustrate the trinity of BLURred, networked culture, wherein connectivity is power and technocompetence is fast becoming a required, standard qualification to achieve success in North American culture.

In another issue of the same publication, professional baseball player Curt Schilling is profiled as a self-identified "computer geek" who pitches "fearsome" 96-mph fastballs for the Arizona Diamondbacks and who was named co-MVP[2] of the 2001 World Series.[3] A celebration of the alignment of professional athlete and computer guy is made even more explicit in this feature, as *Business 2.0* encourages the implosion of the historical binary of "jock" vs. "geek" versions of maleness. Armed with a digital camera and laptop computer, Schilling records, rewinds, and replays each of his last 20,000 pitches on "the Dell in the living room of his spring training condo," to study his form and technique in freeze frames. With all of the "noise" and "junk" of the real-time baseball game edited out (such as "home run trots [. . .] tiresome throws over to first base [. . .] dugout shots of the manager picking his nose"), Schilling stores his video clips in a database, enabling him to "play with the data all he wants." Armed with digital image processing software and hardware, Schilling the hybrid geek-jock stands apart from "a lot of the guys [who] are afraid to make the leap" into the age of high-tech sports, admitting, "I couldn't do the job as well as I do without this." The "this" Schilling depends on is not just the Dell laptop prominently featured in the magazine photo spread, but also his professional relationship with an IT consulting team from California, a geek squad responsible for digitalizing (filming, editing, and storing) and shipping the video of 20,000 pitches. This partnership is symbolic of a unique convergence of two versions of masculinity historically opposed: the skinny techie and the muscular athlete made into a model of technomasculinity that is compatible with the digital age and computerized e-commerce corporate (and men's sport) culture in North America.

The popularized discourses of the technomasculine depend on and resonate with the conceptual network or discursive architecture of digital capital for their intelligibility and legitimacy. Ideally then, in an economy that is more about the production, commodification, and management of information than mechanized reproduction, dominant representations of the technomasculine will be compatible with data processing and largely passive days spent in cubicleville. The representations must be "thick" enough to overwrite the emasculating connotations associated with, for example, working at home (vs. in the public realm) and data processing (vs. dictating to a secretary or typist); these activities have long been engendered as properly feminine, and they must be remasculinized or upgraded to be compatible with the future of e-work. To trace the romanticization and celebration or elevation of the hacker as part of the construction of male cybersubjectivities, it is necessary to consider the phenomenon of "geek chic" and the appropriation of the hacker ethic by (techno-)corporate culture.

THE HACKER ETHIC

The historical emergence of hacker subculture and its professionalization has been chronicled extensively in existing literature, including Bruce Sterling's *The Hacker Crackdown*, Jon Katz's *Geeks*, Steven Levy's *Hackers: Heroes of the Computer Revolution,* and Douglas Thomas' *Hacker Culture*.[4] What emerges from this history is a portrait of adolescent computer aficionado that lends itself to stereotype. The figure of the hacker, a computer geek, is typically represented as a young white male who is as painfully awkward about the agonies of his embodiment as he is proficient at computer programming, translating machine language, and navigating electronic networks. Obsessively drawn to the intricacies of computer hardware, the geek develops a passionate attachment to the activities of building, programming, exploring, and testing—or "hacking"—information technology systems.

As Levy explains in great detail in his history of the MIT computer science subculture in the 1960s and 70s, there emerged a "hacker ethic," which represented the aims, goals, and philosophy of this community of software and hardware explorers and inventors. The central tenets of this hacker ethic include an insistence that information and technology should be free and accessible, so as to enable greater creativity, experimentation, and innovation. As well, the hacker ethic promoted a mistrust of suits, authority, the establishment, and an intense aversion to red tape, hierarchies, and boundaries. To the hacker, bureaucracies, Levy explained, "whether corporate, government or university, are flawed systems, dangerous in that they cannot accommodate the exploratory impulse of true hackers" (41). The hacker ethic included the view that computer technology was the key to improved quality of life and happiness; from this perspective, high tech could enrich and change people's lives. In addition, part of the ethic involved an appreciation of a digital "aesthetic" of minimalism, functionality, transparency, and simplicity, coupled with a belief that beauty and art could be created on a computer.

Finally, the hacker ethic promoted the rule that "hackers should be judged by their hacking, not bogus criteria such as degrees, age, race, or position"; this segment of the hacker ethic came to be known as the discourse of "net utopia" (Levy 43). Interestingly, the criteria of sexual difference or gender is not mentioned in Levy's documentation of the hacker ethic and its list of "bogus criteria"—testimony to the exclusively male community of hackers at MIT. This omission, perhaps accidental but clearly important, points to the naturalized alignment of hacker or IT professional with male subject—a connection that was normalized from the earliest moments of digital technology and computerized hardware and software development. We will return to this question of net utopia and the gendering of the hacker later.

The hacker ethic was intended to be a philosophy that was countercultural and resistant, especially vis-à-vis the corporate culture at IBM. By the 1980s the hacker ethic was being popularized in the pages of publications such as *Mondo 2000* and *WIRED*, two magazines that considered themselves lifestyle guides for the emerging digerati. As larger audiences became exposed to the hacker ethic and the computerized machines and programs produced by the hackers, predictably, the ethic was appropriated by corporate culture in order to attract computer professionals to the workforce and to sell digital commodities to the public. Since the ethic was authored by and popularized by an almost exclusively male community of computer professionals, it is useful to consider how its network of discourses and values reflect masculinity. More interesting for the book at hand, however, is to consider how this ethic or philosophy, which came from a group of outsiders, geeks, and underdogs, was networked with traditional representations and tropes of heroic idealized masculinity so as to create an upgraded version of cybersubjectivity compatible with the digital age. A redescription of the hacker figure, and close attention to the modification and borrowing of the hacker ethic by high-tech companies and the entertainment industry, reveals the relationship between digital capital and cyberpop, and illustrates how many popular cultural representations of cybersubjectivity (and the technomasculine versions in particular) are both compatible with and critical of the status quo. Before reading particular examples of this cyberpop, it is useful to consider in greater detail the transformation of the hacker figure in contemporary digital cultural discourses.

GEEK CHIC

"It's a great time to be a geek," argues Jon Katz in his study of hacker culture, because "geeks are literally building the new global economy" and its backbone, the Internet (Katz xxvi). Thus it comes as no surprise that the computer geek/hacker figure is an important element of the discourse of the technomasculine, mobilized by high-tech corporations to encourage participation in the infoeconomy. Cyberpop media feature the hacker, transformed into the knowledge worker or IT professional, as a model of (techno)masculine subjectivity in the digital age. Though twenty years ago they might have been considered social misfits or freaks, today the hacker-turned-ICT professional is recognized as the lynchpin of the information economy.

In the mid-1980s, when Stephen Levy wrote *Hackers*, the term was still relatively obscure to the wider public, but when it gained media attention and was popularized, it had a negative connotation. Levy explains that this was due to the high-profile arrest of several teenagers who had electronically ventured into "forbidden digital grounds," like government computer systems. The media, the law enforcement authorities, and the teenagers themselves identified these activities as "hacking" and "the word quickly became synonymous with 'digital trespasser' [or lawbreaker, or vandal]" (Levy 432). The stereotype of the hacker thus emerged, containing some fiction and some fact: "the hacker, an antisocial geek whose identifying attribute is the ability to sit in front of a keyboard and conjure up a criminal kind of magic" (432). Levy explains that the criminalized hacker-as-outlaw mystique was amplified in both mainstream mass media and subcultural cyberpunk literature, but there was at least one positive outcome: the publicity introduced a wider audience of nonprogrammers to the principles of the hacker ethic. The result was para-doxical: a newfound fear of and respect for computer hackers and recognition by companies that "if they were to lead in their fields, the energy, vision, and problem-solving perseverance of hackers were required," not to mention the security expertise (434). Hackers were either "white hats" or "black hats"—and in a disappointing but thoroughly predictable citation of American "color line" logic, the latter term described the criminal and dangerous public enemies who stole information and sold it, released viruses, broke into company data-spaces, and so on. In fact, the white and black hat categories were misleading, since popular wisdom and history suggests that there are not two varieties of hacker, and in fact technoliteracy can be used for "good" or "bad" ends, which are relative terms and historically variable. Instead of getting mired in the media construction of a black or white binary, we will bypass this example of the conflict model of news reportage and continue investigating the conver-gence of the hacker trope and discourses of the technomasculine by tracing the phenomenon of "geek chic."

The transformation of the computer nerd into the hacker hero was accom-plished by way of a carefully orchestrated cyberpop culture romance with "geek chic," popularized by the media and information technology industry public relations firms, and by the geeks themselves. Nerds were news because in the information age, high-tech skilled computer workers were in demand, and thus the high school outcasts—those who couldn't get a date, joined the math club, failed miserably at sports, but were practiced at and fascinated by electronics and computer programming—became the new models of high-tech success in the 1990s. "The hacker is no longer necessarily or only a nerd," Sherry Turkle observes; "he or she can be a cultural icon. The hacker can be Bill Gates" (*Second Self* 61). It's no accident that Turkle gestures to Gates, the hacker turned Microsoft CEO. Although "it's pretty obvious that over the last decade, computer professionals are much more in the limelight," comments Allan Freedman, a writer for the Computer Language Co. "I think the wealth aspect has a lot to do with it."[5] During the dot-com revolution, Freedman observes, "all the geeks got rich"—at least temporarily (Seeper 2001). Hackers made global headlines during the infotech startup and technostock boom that began in the late 1990s and ended dramatically in the spring of 2000 with the NASDAQ implosion.[6] These "digital hustlers" were "livin' large and falling hard" in the fast lane of the information superhighway, as cyberpop and cor-poratist culture began to notice, encourage, and amplify the geek ascension from outsider to celebrity icon (Kait).

MANUFACTURING GEEK PRIDE

Years ago the geeks would never have been tolerated in the corporation. You played by the rules of the bureaucracy or you didn't play at all. Several things have conspired, though, to make them more palatable. [...] The pace of technology has made it almost impossible to keep up unless you are at least a little geeky. If you want to compete today you had better have a few geeks on your staff.

—Excerpt from an e-mail by "Mark" sent to Jon Katz for his study of hacker culture, *Geeks* (15).

The first annual Geek Pride Festival was held in Boston in April 2000, and the highlight of the event was The Sexiest Geek Alive contest. First prize went not to the most buff physique but to the brainiest contestant. In this geek culture, "sexy" is equated with intelligence, and "coolness" is measured by intellectual and technical achievement. In the words of one female contestant, "A sexy geek is someone who is passionate about what he or she does and is really excited about learning and sharing things."[7]

But it was neither the festival nor the contest that captured world news headlines in April 2000; instead, it was the tech stock market crash that many argue brought an abrupt end to the gold rush in Silicon Valley.[8] Over the next eight months, the NASDAQ dropped to 2300, having lost half of its value by December. Yet industry insiders such as Steven Phenix (who started The Sexiest Geek Alive contest) comment that the NASDAQ implosion didn't hurt true geeks, nor has the "dot-com recession stopped the nerd ascension"—or the celebration of geek chic.[9] This is because the informatics sector, particularly in the condensed area of San Francisco and Silicon Valley, is still experiencing a shortage of high-tech skilled labor despite massive layoffs, which by some estimates translates into a $6 billion annual loss of sales.[10] IT geeks are an increasingly cherished group: in 2000 the winner of The Sexiest Geek Alive contest didn't get any prizes beyond the illustrious title itself. A year later, the contest attracted 18,000 contestants and had no trouble acquiring corporate sponsors (including Gateway Computers and Levi's), who donated merchandise to be awarded to the victorious sexy geek. But, despite the lure of nerdy celebrity, geeks may be an endangered species as research suggests that the majority of the current generation of computer-savvy technokids aspire to be lawyers, doctors, and police officers—the professional idols featured on television sitcoms.

Many IT consultants agree that what is needed, if there is any hope of drawing young people to high-tech jobs, is a techie nerd idol to amplify the trend of geek chic in cyberpop media and rejuvenate or upgrade the image of those who work in the computer technology industries. "Give us, they say, a geek hero, a nerd we can love," observes journalist Lisa Baertlein.[11] And as if in response, "Slowly but surely, high tech is becoming a familiar backdrop as Hollywood increasingly explores the industry's impact on everyday life—the kinds of people and jobs it once stereotyped as nerd bait. Suddenly, nerds are getting a new popculture image."[12]

It is no accident that at the first Geek Pride Festival the three thousand attendees found time between gaming, ogling new computer gear and sexy contestants, and techtalk networking to watch midnight showings of *The Matrix*. In this film, the geek hero/savior that techies were waiting for emerged in blockbuster style and did not disappoint. The analysis of *The Matrix* that follows suggests that there is a connection between the popularity of romantic fantasy visions of the heroic male hacker and the personal empowerment that can come from managing data in an increasingly informatic culture where the reality of computerized corporate life is consoles and cubicles, discipline according to corporate ideology, computerized surveillance, and compulsory connectivity. The film was successful at the box office and well received by geeks and hackers because it adequately portrayed the unease with which techies—and indeed, all cybersubjects—participate in oppressive techno-cratic systems, their position as insider-outsiders, their distrust of author-ity and suits, and other key mantras of the hacker subculture ethic. It was also successful with a more diverse (non-geek) audience because of the way it encouraged the spectator to take up a critical but also paradoxically cel-ebratory stance vis-à-vis information and computer technology. The film adopted a fast-paced, tech-noir aesthetic that appealed to the current of tech-noeroticism that characterizes cyberculture, and it pushed the special effects envelope, which was sure to delight action/adventure audiences. Moreover, the film invited theatergoers to flex their analytic muscles with its complex network of intertextuality.[13] Finally, and most importantly for this analysis, *The Matrix* was successful because it explored the activity of hacking, and it expanded the associations of computer geek to include what *Mondo 2000* calls the "creative reality hacker." This move was what we might call an upgrade of conventional ideas of hacking or hackers, resulting in a portrait of the com-puter user as a critical, creative, and active consumer of digital technology, a subject empowered via technoliteracy to make change.

IN VIRTUAL REALITY "THERE IS NO SPOON": DIGITAL EMBODIMENT AND THE MYTHOS OF TECHNOMASCULINITY IN *THE MATRIX*

The main characters in cyberpunk narratives are the hackers, trans-formed into street-wise rock'n'roll heroes who wear mirrorshades and do 'biz' in the urban sprawl, dealing in designer drugs, information technology and stolen data, jacking into the matrix of cyber-space by means of implanted cranial sockets.

—Jenny Wolmark[14]

The Matrix is a contemporary cyberpunk film about virtual reality environments. In the simulated world of *The Matrix* people lead active lives, have what they believe to be authentic experiences, sensory perceptions, and meaningful interpersonal relationships. However, unbeknownst to them, they are living these lives only in their minds. In the real material world, humans exist as passive docile bodies, oblivious to their physical entrapment in pod-like structures, penetrated by wires and electrodes, plugged into a technostructure that is powered by their organic energy. In the real world of *The Matrix*, humans are not born, they are bred with artificial reproductive technology, a process maintained by the artificial intelligence that has achieved sentience and waged a largely successful war against humanity. In the film, the computers that we increasingly rely on to organize, operate, and maintain our digital culture have become hostile to humans and taken over. People live out their everyday lives, sometimes passionately, oftentimes mundanely, blissfully ignorant of their imprisonment and the horrific conditions of the real world. Their minds are interfaced with a simulation program that projects a virtual reality environment, and that simulated program is called the matrix.

At the center of the narrative is a savior figure, The One who will rescue humanity from the prison of the pods and the false consciousness of the matrix. The One has the power to beat the system and outsmart the machines. This savior can expertly navigate cyberspace, become virtually empowered in a simulated environment, learning the system in order to subvert or crack it. By figuring out the rules and infrastructure of the machine logic, The One can identify its loopholes, backdoors, and weak spots. Once the vulnerabilities, flexibilities or inflexibilities of the system are known, The One can reconfigure the matrix and thus the real world. And who better to do this than a hacker? A computer nerd, a geek, an outsider, an underdog, the person we rely on for tech support, to debug, recover, and rescue us from the helplessness of system failure, hardware incompatibility, data loss, and entrapment in infinite feedback loops. *The Matrix* is a story about the hacker as hero, and more specifically about the young, white, male computer programmer as a model of technomasculinity, a mode of cybersubjectivity comfortable and compatible with infotech culture.

The Matrix tells the story of an ordinary guy who leads a double life: from nine to five, computer programmer Thomas Anderson (Keanu Reeves) exists in the sterility of cubicleville, working for a large corporate software company; by night, alone in his cluttered apartment, he trades the suit for black clothing, switches keyboards, and operates as an outlawed data pirate whose online handle is Neo. In both lives he is a hacker in the original sense of the word, someone who hacks or programs code, an expert in machine language and computer operations. But in neither role is he fully satisfied, since he is plagued by questions about the nature of reality, the meaning of life, and a growing dissatisfaction with his lonely, anonymous existence—Neo experiences a gnawing sense of *this can't be all there is.*

Unbeknownst to Neo, his dissatisfaction is being monitored by a renegade group of freedom-fighting hackers led by Morpheus (Laurence Fishburne), allegedly the most dangerous man alive. This outlaw and his crew have escaped the pods and fled to a secret underground city, where they now live, desperate, impoverished, and hunted, on the run in the labyrinthine sewers of what were once great American cities in the real world—now unpopulated urban wastelands. Morpheus is Public Enemy Number One because his goal is to unplug the matrix simulation program, free the remaining human biobatteries, and wage a war against the machines.[15] Victory depends on Morpheus locating The One: a messianic figure whose existence has been prophesied by an oracle whose hacking skills are unmatched and for whom the matrix will appear transparent, its central logic structures vulnerable. Morpheus believes that Thomas Anderson, Neo, is The One.

As the story unfolds we learn that it is indeed Neo's fate to cause a revolution, but before he can save the world, the first step on the path to enlightenment is freeing Neo's physical body from the pod, effectively waking him up from a deep sleep to what Morpheus—citing Baudrillard—calls *the desert of the real* (Baudrillard, *Simulations*). When he is physically freed, Neo must wake up from the dream that is the matrix, free his mind from the live feed of virtual reality, and learn to think outside the pod, outside the box—like Apple Computer's advertising slogan, Neo needs to *think different*. Neo must accept that everything he knows, all he thought to be real, is actually a fantasy, a simulation. None of his remembered life experiences actually happened, all his memories are false, implanted, virtual. His perception of his own flesh-and-blood embodiment is really only a construction in his mind's eye, a *residual self-image*. In reality he has not grown up in the body he is accustomed to, but rather he has inhabited a body implanted with sockets to facilitate its function as a biobattery. A humiliating turn of events, and a potentially emasculating one, for Neo must accept that he has been penetrated by technology in a profound way, and against his will. With the loss of the integrity of his memory and the sanctified boundaries of his embodiment, Neo experiences profound disorientation, considerable grief, and confusion. He experiences a lingering nostalgia for the pleasures of his virtual life. Until the moment of his rebirth in Morpheus's craft, Neo lived a simulated existence—but his immersion in the matrix is not over, because he must reinhabit the program to study and eventually crack it.

Thus begins a series of dangerous adventures into the virtual territory of the artificial intelligence (AI) machines, or sentinels—dangerous because, as Morpheus explains, "the mind cannot exist without the body," and a simulated fatal bodily injury in the matrix will be perceived by the mind as so real that all psychological operations will cease and the victim will die from an attack both imagined and authentic. Accordingly, the matrix is a war zone for the hacker outlaws, and Special Agents (AI) are heavily armed and in pursuit of Morpheus and his crew. "So I have to learn to dodge bullets?" Neo asks in shock and disbelief. "When you're ready, you won't have to," is Morpheus's cryptic reply. Translated this means—as Neo learns at the close of this first installment of a filmic trilogy—that once Neo has accepted his fate as The One and harnessed his ability to subvert the dominant order, he will be able to rewrite the matrix as he sees fit, deleting rather than dodging bullets. In other words, Neo has to live out a hacker's dream: to inhabit and expertly manipulate the infonet, wherein the hierarchy of power and influence has less to do with looks and personality than with logic and technoprowess, wherein the particularities and agonies of embodiment can be escaped, and to emerge a hero, virtually empowered, a cybercelebrity. The outsider, an anonymous data cruncher, a technogeek, needs to use his skills at navigating cyberspace and inhabiting virtual simulated gaming environments to escape the impoverishment of his everyday life and become liberated from the strict limitations and rules of corporate ideology. His lack of social skills and proficiency at programming will become assets when saving the world from AI Special Agents requires full concentration—indeed, the fate of all of humanity is at stake.

UNTHINKABLE COMPLEXITY

This cyberpunk cautionary fairy tale received mixed reviews when it previewed and debuted on the big screen in 1999, but for the majority of film critics writing in mainstream newspapers and magazines, *The Matrix* was pronounced visually spectacular but philosophically impenetrable and ultimately a failure in terms of its elaborate plot, script, and the director's vision and message. "I wager," one reviewer wrote, echoing many others, "there will be many viewers who still won't have the faintest idea what the matrix is after they've had the royal tour."[16] Those who dismissed the film as "a muddily pretentious mixture of postmodern literary theory, slam-bang special effects, and Superman heroics,"[17] were apt to complain of its "lack of a story"[18] and overabundance of "cybergeek metaphysics and pop-philosophical baggage."[19] Almost without exception however, authors who criticized the film as overly theoretical and postmodern neglected to identify specific examples of either of these elements.

As a result, from reading the majority of reviews published during the month that the film was released in theatres worldwide, one is left with the impression that the film failed on account of being overly intellectual, and having a convoluted and complex script full of a mixed bag of esoteric and obscure references. Reviewers almost uniformly agreed that as visual spectacle, *The Matrix* was groundbreaking in its use of special effects and innovative filming and editing technologies. As eye candy, the film was worth seeing, but it might hurt your brain to try to sort out the storyline.

Though the bottom line for most reviewers was that the film was disappointing, audiences globally disagreed with that reading. *The Matrix* (which cost $65 million to produce) grossed $171 million at the box office. Sony Pictures almost immediately began production on the second and third segments of the Wachowski brothers' script, opting to film the Part II: *The Matrix Reloaded* and Part III: *The Matrix Revolutions*, simultaneously, releasing both in 2003. The cyberpop trilogy delivers enough philosophical and theoretical ambiguity to virtually guarantee that spectators would be seduced into speculating about the various levels of meaning in the script.[20] Long after the visual effects had worn off and were being replicated in other sci-fi and action films, fans of *The Matrix* continued to find pleasure in positing alternative readings.

At the level of plot, audiences were drawn to the plight of the cybersubjects in the unfolding drama-thriller, entrapped in pods and existing in the oblivion of a virtual reality dreamworld, or struggling as revolutionaries seeking to overthrow the technocultural order and the evil AIs. But perhaps more importantly, viewers identified with the underdog hero, a geeky knowledge worker trapped in cubicleville who only very reluctantly accepts that he might be The One who can save the world, but who is immediately ready to embrace the idea that contemporary corporate IT culture is about a program of discipline, bureaucracy, rules, suits, and lack of imagination or opportunities for creativity.

But the complexity and innovation of the film had less to do with its borrowing of a classic underdog hero plot; instead, it was largely due to the filmmakers' use of special effects and a postmodern aesthetic of *pastiche* which relied on a carefully woven and explicit network of citations, a complex intertextuality. The film is composed of a mosaic of fragmented references from popular culture, incorporating elements from numerous filmic genres, religions, and myths. Filmmakers Andy and Larry Wachowski shamelessly borrowed from a smorgasbord of cultural narratives without regard for their integrity or complementarity—morphing elements together to create a composite (inter)text—which drew together Grimm's fairy tales and Zen Buddhism, quantum physics and postmodern literary theory—reflecting the nearly "unthinkable complexity" (to quote William Gibson) of transglobal cyberspace in 2199 (*Neuromancer*). Almost no film critic or spectator could resist tracing the labyrinthine references to other films that the filmmakers looted, for example:

> It's one part techno-Brahmanism, one part holodeck from the Starship Enterprise, a little *Alice in Wonderland*, a bit of *Twenty Thousand Leagues Under the Sea*, and a whole lot of spaghetti western.[21]

> It's Charlie Chaplin's *Modern Times* and Fritz Lang's *Metropolis* for the 21st Century [. . .] Batman meets Bruce Lee [. . .] William Gibson's *Neuromancer* meets *The Last Temptation of Christ* on the set of *Brazil* with Playstation fight sequences to the *Mission Impossible* soundtrack. An information junkie's rush of intravenous *Alice in Wonderland*. Marshall McLuhan on FeedForward. Two hours and fifteen minutes of synapse-popping, cerebrum-stretching parable, allegory, myth, and cultural commentary—all predicated on the religious foundations of communication theory. That's *The Matrix*, the movie (Schuchardt).

As a result, *The Matrix* has been compared to literally dozens of Hollywood productions, from the predictable (*Blade Runner, Terminator,* and *Metropolis*), to the unexpected (*Twenty Thousand Leagues Under the Sea, Naked Lunch,* and *The Last Temptation of Christ*). Although it is true that after this exercise in tracing the intertext, many journalists felt confident dismissing the script as a clever assemblage, and ultimately a random collection of "mindless mayhem"; audiences, on the other hand, enjoyed the pastiche immensely (Rosen 1999). As film theorist Chad Barnett notes in a recent scholarly analysis of *The Matrix*, popular media reviews such as the one penned by Roger Ebert, underestimated "postmodernism's grip on contemporary American culture."[22] As a result, almost without exception, reviewers were unable to predict not only the six Academy Awards the industry awarded it,[23] but also the huge fan base that *The Matrix* was about to draw, or its appeal, not just to PhDs, but to anyone working in a stifling office culture, those routinely immersed in the virtual culture of the Internet, viewers who enjoyed flexing their analytical skills with a sophisticated script about culture, spirituality, and technology, film buffs of a dozen genres, the MTV generation who is accustomed to "remix" and "sampling" artworks, and, of course, hackers and geeks who finally had their nerd hero courtesy of Hollywood.

Of the numerous lines of inquiry to pursue in this film, two stand out as reflecting the key concerns of the current book. In what follows we consider how the complexity of the film reflects what Zillah Eisenstein called the essential *paradox* of cyberculture, and underscore how this cyberpop is both critical of and compatible with the status quo of digital capital corporatist culture. The second line of inquiry focuses on the modes of engendered and raced identity popularized in the film, specifically the representation of technomasculinity therein, which relies on a trope of the nerd-hero and effectively blurs maleness into androgyny, which we might even describe as queered masculinity.

PARADOX: TECH NOIR AND THE DYSTOPIA
OF TECHNOCULTURE

The Matrix represents our current technocultural predicament, in terms that reflect, challenge, criticize, and reimagine the impact of computers on everyday life for millions of people in American culture. *The Matrix* shows the underside of the American dream; in this case, the fallout from the vision of a utopic global network of connectivity and "friction free" cybercapitalism (to quote Bill Gates).[24] It juxtaposes the glamour of high-tech lifestyles with the banality of cubicleville and the desolate conditions for the disenfranchised who exist off-line. *The Matrix* performs as both escapist entertainment and sexy social criticism. It was designed to challenge some conventions and uphold others, but above all, to make audiences think critically about the place of technology in our lives. For example, the new world order that Neo must bring into being is without borders or boundaries; it is the world of BLUR, a utopic product of the hacker ethic. In the real world, people have lots of high tech including weapons and computer terminals, but contra the hacker ethic, this does not improve their quality of life; instead we see them dressed in rags, impoverished, hunted, imprisoned in darkness underground. The blissful ignorance there-is-no-steak-but-it-sure-tastes-delicious-anyway world of the matrix is a garden of Eden in which humans are ignorant and enslaved but generally at peace, and by contrast, the real world is postapocalyptic destruction.

In showing the underside of the technocultural status quo, *The Matrix* is an example of tech noir, a genre of film that relies on irony, pastiche, spectacle, and postmodern politics to represent imploded technocultures in the not-too-distant future. Set in a postapocalyptic urban landscape, and featuring characters whose lives are synchronized with the computerized machines that dominate many scenes, tech-noir films such as *Blade Runner, Terminator I & II, GATTACA*, and *The Matrix* emerge at a cultural moment when revolutions in informatic sciences are challenging many naturalized social conventions and epistemologies.

GENDERBLUR: TECH NOIR AND ANDROGYNY

As in classic noir of the 1940s and 1950s that reflected cultural anxieties about postwar American values and sex roles, traditional gendered conventions are made particularly unstable in *The Matrix* through amplifying what theorists have called a crisis in masculinity. Neo the hacker hero often appears to be a passive observer rather than being in control of the action; confused, anxious, and trapped by his conflicting desires. He battles with the agonies of his embodiment, suffering due to his *lack* of courage, strength, or self-containment, and is often wounded and vulnerable or temporarily disabled, symbolically castrated or penetrated. The classic and neo-noir male hero is always represented as insufficiently heterosexual; feminized, androgynous, and/or sexually ambiguous, and Neo is no exception. Masculinity in crisis within classic and contemporary noir depends upon a dangerously blurred positionality vis-à-vis the feminine. Correspondingly, tech noir offers a highly scripted, exaggerated, and often threatening version of cyberfemininity which borrows elements from the femme fatale persona, though often fails to take full advantage of this complex and potentially transgressive filmic trope. As a result, the technomasculine hero in this tech-noir film appears feminized, and the femme fatale is masculinized, or a better way to put it is that in *The Matrix*, both genders become androgynous, as their personas shift, blur, and morph.

The androgyny or queered technomasculinity scripted into *The Matrix* did not go unnoticed by reviewers. The actor Keanu Reeves, cast as Neo, was described in feminine terms or as androgynous by numerous authors—comments about his character's masculinity being insufficiently macho are likely linked to Reeves' racial heritage, a point we will return to. Both the sex-gender binary and colonialist racial logic (including the color line) are incredibly resilient systems, so much so that even in a film that celebrates the breakdown (or hacking) of boundaries, racial and gendered difference becomes more flexible, even blurred, but it does not implode.

TECHNOMASCULINITY AND ITS OTHERS

Like most cyberpop, *The Matrix* is a mixture of "new" and "old" discourses about technology, gender, bodies, power, and so forth. For example, it has become commonplace to see white male subjects "jacked in" to computer technologies, while minority male subjects (and all women) are likely to be represented as hostile to and suspicious of technology, as "modern primitives,"[25] or in a naturally closer symbiotic relationship to "Mother Earth." *The Matrix* does not break with this tradition, and on the surface we see mixed-race and African American men with names like "Tank" and "Dozer," which imply blue-collar technology, such as heavy-duty earth-moving machinery. In stark contrast to Neo's pale, skinny hacker's body, both men of color have hypermuscular physiques, neither of which is outfitted with a socket to permit them to enter virtual reality. Neither Tank (Marcus Chong) nor Dozer (Anthony Ray Parker) have access to the matrix, which may initially seem to be a good thing, but which also means that they never experience what Cypher calls blissful ignorance, and are instead confined to live out their lives in the wasteland of the earth, underground or holed up in Morpheus's ship, navigating the labyrinth of sewer systems. As Amanda Fernback suggests, in cyberpunk fiction "the technoman is complete and the unwired man lacks," or put otherwise, "those bodies not 'jacked in' or in some other way wired are incomplete."[26]

Mass-marketed versions of technomasculinity oftentimes rely on their opposition to the unplugged subject, who is represented as overly rigid, primitive, Luddite, or trapped in the "meat." Predictably, the (male) subjects who fail to qualify as technomasculine heroes are often racial minorities, but (and this is a new strategy) whereas in previous eras the underdog male character would be represented as insufficiently heterosexual, overly feminine, or physically disabled, in cyberpunk media technomasculinity incorporates genderBLUR, and thus these stereotypical qualities, which would disqualify a character from hero status, no longer carry that kind of abject power. Race, on the other hand, still operates as a complicated and overdetermined layer of difference in films such as *The Matrix*. Perhaps because of its appropriation of the hacker ethic and its discourse of net utopia, which insists that race should be irrelevant, it could be expected that the Wachowski brothers would make enlightened choices about representational politics in their screenplay. And the fact that they really do not, and instead use old stereotypes about race and gender, indicates the bankruptcy of the discourse of net utopia; in other words, in the real world of film production and box office draw, the particularities of bodies matter.

What sets Neo apart from the "others" is not his whiteness, because as the role was cast, Reeves—whose hapa identity is well publicized—appears Caucasian but is actually mixed race, thus his ethnicity is more complicated than may be readily apparent on the surface.[27] Neo is exceptional because of his technoprowess and his insider/outsider status. Neo is truly a "mixed" character: a lynchpin of the infotech economy and a data pirate simultaneously, a hacker who loves machine language and computers, but who is determined to destroy the computer systems that order the world of 2199. We realize that in *The Matrix*, in order to achieve authentic technomasculine hero status, The One must be a member of the digerati. It is only possible to achieve success, to challenge and recode (or hack) the digital order of things, this cyberpop suggests, by being a player in the game, implicated, online and connected, rather than a critical outsider.

In *The Matrix,* connectivity is not only a prerequisite, it is a mode of physical embodiment. Within the course of the film, we watch as Neo is transformed from a wimpy, bored, anonymous nerd, hacker/programmer trapped in cubicleville, the land of suits and bureaucracy, to a martial arts master, an expert at handling heavy artillery, a swaggering, black-leather-trench-coat-wearing, Uzi-toting, badass. With an uncanny freedom to self-define, within the virtual reality of the matrix, Neo can theoretically appear in any guise he can imagine, he can inhabit different configurations of embodiment, and in none of them does he have a visible socket in his skull. And yet the importance of this socket to Neo's sense of self cannot be underestimated. It is the socket in his head that allows for a direct mind-computer interface, it is his connection to the matrix that facilitates his escape from the postapocalyptic real world. In cyberpunk fiction, even the most intrusive and intimate connections with computer technologies are usually represented as pleasurable. This, of course, is part of the technoeroticism that characterizes cyberpunk, and it is what makes the genre a valuable source of rhetoric, images, and tropes for the computer industries.

COMMODIFYING GEEK CHIC, APPROPRIATING THE HACKER ETHIC, TECHNOMASCULINITY IN INFOTECH ADVERTISING

> Call it a hyperhip wet dream, but the information and communications technology industry requires a new active consumer or it's going to stall [. . .] This is one reason why we are amplifying the mythos of the sophisticated, high-complexity, fast lane/real-time, intelligent, active and creative reality hacker [. . .] A nation of TV couch potatoes (not to mention embittered self-righteous radicals) is not going to demand access to the next generation of the extensions of man.
>
> —**Editorial,** *Mondo 2000* [28]

> It's particularly sad and poignant for me to witness how comfortably the subcultural contempt for the normal, the hunger for novelty and change, and the basic anarchistic temperament that was at the core of *Mondo 2000* fits the hip, smug, boundary-breaking, fast-moving, no-time-for-social-niceties world of your wired mega-corporate info/comm./media players. You can find our dirty fingerprints, our rhetoric, all over their advertising style. The joke's on me.
>
> —**R. U. Sirius, founding editor,** *Mondo 2000*[29]

The geek ascension that is represented by *The Matrix* blockbuster film is evident in contemporary advertisements as well. In terms of engendered cybersubjectivity, the blurred technomasculinity personified by Neo is becoming a mainstay of marketing schemes by high-tech companies. The complex and paradoxical negotiation of tropes of the masculine in cyberpop representations includes imagery and narratives about the exceptional male who is e-powered through possession of digital gadgetry to rise above all "others." Similarly, a discourse of technofetishism and "gear lust" is routinely addressed to male consumers and audiences, as an anecdote to their possible "lack" of (e-)power. Finally, the trope of "geek muscle" is popularized, as nerds become mighty males through their position in the network. I have selected three advertisements as examples to explain how cyberpop represents versions of the technomasculine ideal that resonate with the trinity of BLUR and reflect the phenomenon of geek chic.

Cyberpop advertisements bridge the gap between fiction and real life, intertwining mythical stories about empowerment, individuality, and success with commodity consumption and the construction of concrete lifestyles, relations of power and production. In advertisements for high-tech products and services, evidence of the appropriation of the figure of the hacker and of the hacker ethic is overt. This enables the ads to employ an ambiguity vis-à-vis the technological order of things, since hackers distrust authority, bureaucracy, and suits, and yet they are also the digerati. Contemporary computer tech ads often have a tongue-in-cheek approach to the computerization of everyday life, and take up a savvy, clever, creative, and simultaneously critical position about their (and their consumers') implication in digital culture.

Since the primary target audience for high-tech goods and services is assumed to be predominantly male, cybercultural popular media advertisements feature versions of technomasculinity that are compatible with consumption of digital goods and services and that encourage participation in corporate culture (romanticizing cubicleville and promoting connectivity as empowerment). These advertisements exemplify Bukatman's *terminal identity fictions* as they are narratives that model modes of cybersubjectivity that accommodate the digital order of things. As the editors of *WIRED* state explicitly, the expansion of the information and telecommunications revolution depends on the manufacture of a new active consumer group who appreciates the qualities of technological sophistication, creative intelligence, and the fast-paced, innovative, and constantly shifting computer-enhanced, online, and networked lifestyle. In order to construct this discourse community, marketers selectively appropriate and carefully upgrade the principles of the hacker ethic to harness a rhetoric that reflects the "hunger for novelty and change," the "subcultural contempt for the normal," and the "smug, boundary-breaking, fast-moving" pace that *Mondo 2000* editor R. U. Sirius describes as characteristic of nascent hacker community in the 1970s and 1980s. The joke that Sirius refers to, and the reason for his disappointment and dismay at this appropriation, is that cyberpop advertisements and multinational tech-nocorporations borrow the hacker ethic not to encourage the dissolution of boundaries or to free information, but rather to increase the commodification and consumption of information and hardware, and to recruit knowledge workers to cubicleville in cybercapitalist corporate culture.

The Exceptional Male: E-Powerment through Connectivity

According to thingamajob.com (Figure 3.1), "Life 2.0 Begins" by posting your resume with their Web site database service. No longer will you be anonymous and isolated; instead you will be connected in the flow of the datastream. Ironically, in order to escape the enforced passivity of this situation, you have to play by the rules and list your resume on their Internet job board. The advertisement illustration is reminiscent of the haunting pod scene in

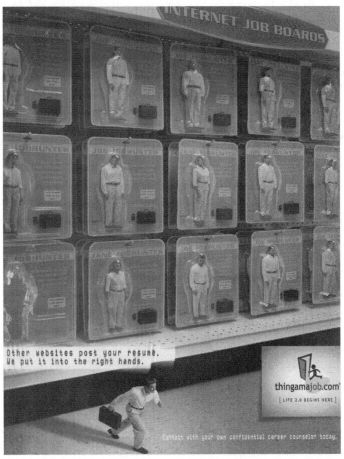

Figure 3.1 Thingamajob.com, Life 2.0 Begins.

The Matrix, picturing people entrapped in sealed plastic containers—resembling toy action figures hanging on display. The other knowledge workers are encouraged to follow the lead of the tiny white male action figure, who has broken out of the mold and is seen scurrying away. This exceptional male has hacked the order of things and taken his toy briefcase of data with him; he has escaped conformity while wearing a uniform reminiscent of Abercrombie and Fitch to begin *Life 2.0*, unique and different, courtesy of another Web site that offers personalized services to an individual in charge of the navigation of his digits rather than entrapped by them.

Interestingly, the packaged people who remain are not all male and white, they are considerably more diverse in terms of race and gender, but the exceptional subject is the white male, a theme that is repeated in most ads that show both white men and ethnic others. Featuring a workforce reminiscent of the multicultural rebel hackers led by the lone white male hacker Neo in *The Matrix,* this advertisement repeats what is quickly becoming a trend in cyberpop media: an overrepresentation of white males as Everyman heroes, as the model for the exceptional digitized subject, whose uniqueness is not only encoded in his data body (i.e., in his genome, or digitized credit or medical history) like all computerized subjects, but also seems to exceed this categorization due to his "natural" leadership abilities.

The thingamajob.com cyberpop ad illustrates that the information technology sectors need to signify, romanticize, amplify, and appropriate the innovation, insatiable curiosity, risk taking, playfulness, and creativity of the hacker culture in order to deliver its upgraded products and services to digital culture—and to protect the security of its investments in the commodification of data. Companies like Apple Computer, Microsoft, AT&T, and Intel are determined to convince computer types that working for mainstream corporate IT culture doesn't mean selling out, becoming a "suit," and being trapped in the anonymity of cubicleville (or the pods!), bowing to the bureaucracy and hemmed in with red tape. And so, even though knowledge workers may find themselves in a suit or uniform, in a cubicle, programming/processing data in a panoptic environment, in popular media we see representations of the digital subject as a member of the digerati, or Generation D, encouraged to "think different" (Apple Computer), "think outside the frame" (NetMedia.com), innovate, create, and become virtually empowered by being wired, intimately connected to computer technologies.

Irony: Technomasculinity and Gear Lack/Lust

The ironic and tongue-in-cheek tone of many technofigurative advertisements are directed to a male audience. They contain potentially emasculating, feminizing elements—for example, the image of the male IT worker may inhabit a body that is relatively small or frail (rather than muscular), that body may be penetrated in various ways or signify a "lack" (rather than signifying the phallus), and sometimes that "lack" may be the seeming absence of a libido, or at least, insufficient heterosexualization, and bad object choices that result in gear lust and technofetishism, rather than interpersonal human relationships. The hacker figure Neo in *The Matrix* was burdened with all of these traits and conditions, and yet he triumphed over them to save the world and emerge a cyberhero because he was able to become virtually empowered in the simulated reality of the matrix, with a little help from a male mentor figure who coached him in matters of self-confidence and martial arts, of course.

At registrars.com (Figure 3.2) the white male sits in a vulnerable position, his ankles and wrists exposed awkwardly, as he confesses his digital envy and professes his electronic (virtual?) impotence. The expertise of the male doctor, who sits to the side, is both amplified and interrupted by Internet technology, as he opts to record possible domain names such as the truncated and thus inadequate "richpsychologist.com" and "DrRichardsonpsycho.com" before settling on the extra long "Dr.RichardsonPsychologist.com." Registrars.com continued this insider rhetoric with another advertisement featuring two men pictured from their thighs down, presumably naked in the shower discussing the length of their domain names. This penis envy is an insider's joke, because hackers don't care about embodiment, supposedly. On the Internet, size doesn't matter, as Jon Katz explains:

> Geeks live in a digital world, one much more compelling than the one that has rejected or marginalized them. Being online has liberated them in stunning ways. Looks don't matter online. Neither does race, the number of degrees one has or doesn't have, or the cadence of speech. Ideas and personalities, presented in their purest sense, have a different dimension (**xxviii**).

This is a familiar version of net utopia: the no-race-or-gender in cyberspace concept, the online-no-one-knows-you're-a-dog idea, the enticing promise of unlimited opportunities for virtual passing and pure individualism untainted by social customs about difference and otherness. A myth, and a powerful one, especially compelling for "those who confront the severe limitations reality imposes in the form of corporate ideology, determining social structures, and the physical body itself," according to Anne Balsamo.[30] As computer programmer Brenda Laurel confirms, "I know from 15 years' experience with computer guys that we have a class of people we call nerds who are radically uncomfortable with their bodies and their sexuality."[31]

The tone of the registrars.com advertisement is thus ironic, acknowledging the absurdity of technofetishism but promoting longer domain names just the same. While it pokes fun at the stereotype of computer nerds and their

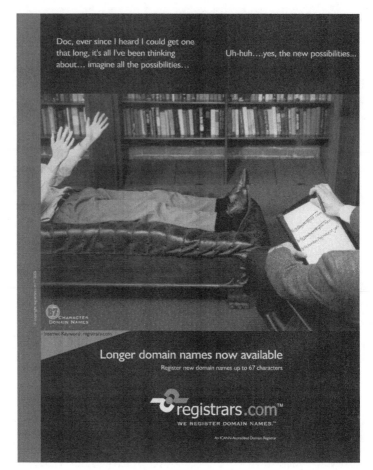

Figure 3.2   Registrars.com, URL envy.

unattractive and insufficiently masculine bodies, it promises the audience that more connectivity leads to greater technoprowess, self-confidence, and productivity. No longer is the penis size what matters, registrars.com tells the spectator, nor is it muscles and physical attributes long associated with desirable male bodies; instead, like the professional athletes (football coaches and baseball players) profiled at the beginning of this chapter, real male heroes need technology if they are going to compete in fields where, not coincidentally, few females are present.

Upgrading the Hacker: Technomasculinity and Geek Muscle

For Corel, the bulging bicep of the male bodybuilder signifies the e-power that can be had by purchasing WordPerfect for the Linux operating system (Figure 3.3). Superimposed on the grimacing straining model's physique is a text document, to inspire the data processor to flex his word-processing skills. It is significant that Corel selects the hypermuscular image to promote its software for Linux, since (unlike Microsoft Windows, for example) that OS was developed collaboratively amongst the global hacker community, and its source code distributed publicly without charge. Linux is widely regarded as a public production in line with the hacker ethic of subverting bureaucracy and keeping information free. Linux is considered a rare example of the uncommodified products of hacking, and is thus celebrated as a victory in the global hacker community. The fact that hackers were able to code and distribute the Linux system, and disrupt (to some extent) Microsoft's software monopoly is viewed as a stunning victory for the underdog, the little guy, and the geek subculture.

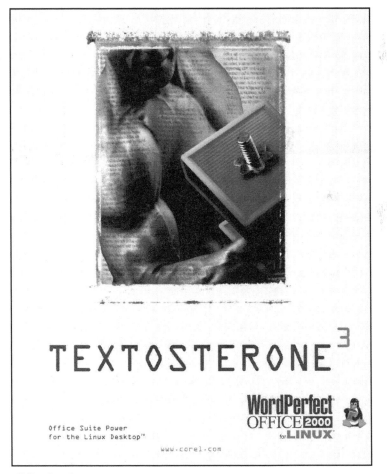

Figure 3.3   Corel, textosterone.

This explains Corel's choice to feature an exaggerated, hypermuscular, Terminator*esque* image of the male body, knowing full well that the male bodies behind the coding of Linux are likely dissimilar to the illustration. Corel opts for "the spectacle of hyperphallic cyborg masculinity, a fetishized masculinity" disavowing male lack (or the nerdiness of the hacker, stereotypically) by constituting itself through "the magic of the technopart" (Fernbach 239). In her analysis of the *Terminator* films, Amanda Fernbach describes the use of technoprops such as guns and motorcycles (or in the Corel ad, a barbell) to signify phallic power while ironically also revealing masculine lack (239). A cursory glance at any selection of mainstream advertising in digital culture magazines reveals immediately that the Terminator version of technomasculinity is rarely used in ads outside of promotions for games and science fiction film. Corel's promotion for Linux software stands out among the hundreds of pages of advertising for Microsoft and Apple OS, as does the unconventional, fantasized (fetishized?) image of technomasculine power. But that might be changing. The distinction that separates the hypermuscular and hypermasculine subject from the nerdy technogeek is blurring, as we saw in the case of *Business 2.0* celebrity athlete profiles, showcasing their computational prowess.

The geek is an important cyberpop icon for the information technology sector to encourage participation in cybercapitalist infoeconomy. Similarly, the appropriation of the hacker ethic results in representations of the technomasculine, which are paradoxically both compatible with and critical of corporate culture. The hacker mythos is a romantic underdog narrative that complements the American Dream—insofar as it suggests that beyond appearances, everyone can make a significant contribution to society, even the unpopular nerd who doesn't reflect the traditional masculine ideal. Beyond that, it is an attractive trope to many audiences, because it encourages those with less power to mistrust authority and the suits, to resist the bonds of bureaucracy, and to pursue creative and innovative projects.

As well, the versions of geeky technomasculinity featured in these films, novels, magazines, and ads are empowering at least for white men, because they suggest that one unlikely hero can change the world as if it were simply a matter of recoding it. Examples abound of cyberpop that demonstrates a new flexibility of maleness, and the convergence of previously dichotomous tropes of masculinity, in the paradoxical hybrid geek hero persona. In these narratives of technomasculinity there is evidence of BLUR and remixing, but they are not so radical as to significantly disrupt the racial codes that overlay and interface with gendered epistemologies.

4

GATTACA, Gender and Genoism

It lays down for each individual his place, his body, his disease and his death, his well-being, by means of an omnipresent and omniscient power that subdivides itself in a regular, uninterrupted way even to the ultimate determination of an individual, of what characterizes him, of what belongs to him, of what happens to him.

—Michel Foucault[1]

It didn't matter how much I had lied on my resume. My real resume was in my cells.

—Vincent Freeman, *GATTACA*[2]

As Manuel Castells and others have argued, the informatic revolution has two components: developments in computer and communication sciences, and breakthroughs in the biological sciences. This chapter departs slightly from a focus on information computechnologies to consider the other side of the informatic age: namely, the impact of the genomic revolution on popular cultural productions and ideas about gender, race, identity, and embodiment. In what follows we examine the dystopic science fiction film *GATTACA*, a story about the digitalization of the human genome and the potential social reverberations of this explosion of knowledge and power. In this film, computer imaging, genomic databases, technological modes of surveillance, and high-tech medical procedures are paired with controversies about what it means to be human in the digital age.

The genetic code is of paramount importance to the narrative of GATTACA, and it is wedded to already existing ideas about the supposed naturalness of chromosomally based sexual difference, and the codes of a binary sex-gender system. Cyberpop media generally repurpose popular or public discourses, metaphors, representations, and ideologies in complicated ways, such that they can be interpreted as simultaneously resisting and reifying the status quo of digital capitalism. Thus, even as this film introduces radical concepts such as the data body and genomic determinism, in many ways it illustrates how these "revolutionary" concepts *complement* rather than *disrupt,* and remediate or redeliver traditional ideas about both the eugenics and white supremacy as well as the binary and hierarchical sex-gender system. Because there are always multiple bottom lines in cyberpop texts, exactly what makes this film dystopic is sufficiently ambiguous that it can be interpreted in various, seemingly opposed and contradictory ways. One of those possible readings would argue that the dystopia of GATTACA is most evident in its representation of the future of developments in genomic science through the rhetoric of a cautionary tale—suggesting that this field of technoscience is a potential threat to the privilege enjoyed by those persons who can fit into a classic liberal humanist conception of subjectivity, namely able-bodied, economically privileged, white, straight, male individuals from first world nations.

Despite the promotional hype for GATTACA, which warned of a future in which designer babies would be purchased or cloned, and eugenic science would prevent anyone with any form of disability from being born, in fact the most frightening element of this film is the way in which it explains how breakthroughs in genomic science can operate in the service of maintaining the present day status quo of racial and gendered inequities. On the surface, this film is dystopic because it tackles controversial developments in technoscience, and illustrates how revolutionary breakthroughs in genetics could challenge all traditions and existing paradigms, changing everything for the worse; however, *redescribing* the film as cyberpop means noting how it cites a network of concepts about bodies, gender, science and technology, power and knowledge. It is possible to see that this film is equally dystopic because it reveals that this "new" science will not effect radical social enlightenment, or bring about a more equitable North American culture at all.

In terms of its aesthetics, GATTACA borrows conventions from the emerging genre of tech noir, to accomplish what B. Ruby Rich describes as "a rewiring of the [noir] genre's circuitry to the currents of the present, flashing across the screen some fascinating messages about the fears and dilemmas of our age."[3] These dilemmas are connected to the genomic revolution and the growing presence of computerized communication and surveillance technologies in the fabric of American life. The tech-noir elements of this film make a significant contribution to its representation of gender and power relations, particularly insofar as it borrows from classic noir conventions, to amplify the underside of the American Dream; that is, the crisis in masculinity that results in times of social upheaval, and the cathected and ultimately unknowable figure of the femme fatale.

FROM DOLLY TO *GATTACA:* GENE ANGST

As Barbara Katz Rothman has observed, "Genetics is the contemporary frontier in science."[4] Among other things, this means that in the world of science fiction, genetic narratives are popular and proliferating. In the summer of 2000, news headlines proclaimed that the Human Genome Project Initiative (hereafter HGP) was completed, such that scientists had successfully mapped the three billion "chemical letters" that compose the human genome.[5] This scientific milestone captured news headlines worldwide, but it was only the latest announcement of accomplishment from a field that had been making startling breakthroughs and news headlines for a generation.[6] What was "new" about the HGP in the public mind was the claim that this project would enable scientists to decode and recode the program of what it takes to be human.[7] But even that wasn't exactly "news" because in order to justify using American taxpayer money to fund the project, such exaggerated claims had been flying around in the media almost since the project's inception. Announcing the completion of the HGP wasn't as earth-shattering to the lay public as it might have been if not for the fact that the public was well prepared for it, partially due to another genomic science breakthrough that occurred three years earlier: in 1997, Dolly the cloned sheep was introduced to the world, the first mammal to be born (and survive) who had been cloned from a mature adult sheep cell. When Dolly was unveiled, op-ed pieces filled pages in newspapers worldwide, representing an outpouring of what has since been called public "gene angst"—a suspicion that genetic science has gone too far, is playing with Mother Nature, and risking unforeseeable (but probably dire) future consequences for the human race and the biosphere. Part of this widespread public "biofear" (to adopt José Van Dijck's phrase) is attached to the spectre of human cloning, to worries over the commodification of human life and the body, and to historical connotations between genetics, eugenics, and Nazi science.[8]

This was the cultural context into which Sony Pictures and Jersey Films released *GATTACA*, set in the not-too-distant future, and representing a culture that functions according to the laws of genetic determinism, selective breeding, and an inescapable genomic class/caste system. The film reflects and engages public bioethical concerns about the connection between genetics and tampering with the natural order of things, "playing God," and tinkering with the human spirit or the uniqueness of the individual. Recognizing that the cultural climate was perfect for a genetic thriller, Jersey Films presented a fictional interpretation of what the other side of that horizon might look like. GATTACA capitalized on, utilized, reflected, and amplified the public's gene angst about a totalitarian sociobiological cultural order that might result from advances in genetic research.

BIOENGINEERING AND THE GENOMIC ORDER OF THINGS

In GATTACA, the HGP has been completed, and geneticists have identi-fied the genes that account for a range of psychological and physiological characteristics and conditions in the human subject. With this information they are able to use recombinant DNA technology to design an individual human's genome. For a price, any "undesirable" genes and genetic sequences (such as, we are told, those that are linked to obesity, alcoholism, and depres-sion) can be deleted from an embryo's DNA, and the chemical codes for more socially advantageous qualities (such as height, strength, and intelligence) can be added. This results in a two-tiered class system: those who are "Valid" (designer babies whose DNA was screened and manipulated before they were born), and the "In-Valids" (those persons who were born without the aid of computer-assisted genetic designers). The latter population of "blackjack births" and "genojunk" cannot compete with the Valids whose GQ (genetic quotient) is the product of laboratory intervention (screening, sampling, and editing), and optimization enabling them to achieve "infinite levels of per-fection." Membership in the class of the genetic elite qualifies a subject for professional employment; conversely, In-Valids—whose genomic fingerprint (we are told) predisposes them to criminality—form an underclass faced with myriad obstacles, including the impossibility of finding a career or obtaining health insurance. The In-Valids populate what Judith Butler calls "the zone of uninhabitability," an excluded site of the abject, against which the Valid genetic elite self-defines, forming a potentially disruptive or threatening force that must be controlled and monitored (Butler, Bodies 3).

Giving new meaning to Freud's dictum "biology is destiny," these genomic class/caste stratifications are inflexible; from the moment of birth, a subject's future is permanently inscribed in the chromosomal text that resides in every cell of their body. Moreover, the translation of the information in this text, the sequence of genes located in the double helix of DNA, is publicly available to whomever might be interested in reading it; again, for a price, a thriving com-mercial genetic screening industry will provide a printout of any individual's genetic blueprint or "data body," requiring only a microscopic fragment (specimen) of urine, blood, hair, or skin cells to scan. As Scott Bukatman comments, through this process "the body is inscribed and defined, paradoxically extended and delimited by these pervasive, invasive technologies" (234). No privacy laws protect GATTACian citizens from exposure, and subsequently, their psychological and physiological genetic portraits are available to possible employers, insurance companies, and even potential mates. In this culture sociobiology is business as usual, as any genetic deviance in the data body is policed; as one inhabitant observes correctly, "we have discrimination down to a science"—and they have a term for it: genoism.

TECHNOLOGIES OF EMBODIMENT:
THE CORPOREAL CONTRACT

Not surprisingly, the only employment available to the In-Valid Vincent Freeman (a man whose genetic script reveals myopia, a learning disorder, and a heart defect that is predicted to kill him before he is 30) is as a janitor at *GATTACA* Aerospace Corporation. Vincent's (Ethan Hawke) goal is to become an astronaut and fly in *GATTACA* Corporation's first mission to Titan (one of the moons of Saturn). He has the intellectual and physical capabilities to do so, but his flawed DNA that serves as his resume means he will never be considered material fit for participation in the colonization of the universe. Vincent's ambitions exceed his genetic capabilities, and here we have the dilemma that provides the central narrative for the film: to escape the limitations of his body and achieve his mission, Vincent must do the impossible—acquire new DNA.

Vincent demands that those around him read between the lines (or helix) and recognize his worthiness. He steadfastly "refuses to accept the hand he's been dealt" and resorts to "extreme measures" to secure his place in the professional ranks at *GATTACA* Corporation. Securing the services of German, a "gene broker" (Tony Shalhoub), Vincent begins an elaborate scheme to "pass" as a Valid using a "borrowed ladder"—the genetic identification/identity of another man, Jerome Eugene Morrow (Jude Law). When German (whose name seems to promote a reference to the historical connection between genetics and Nazi science, perhaps intended to overshadow the American participation in the eugenics movement) assures him, "You could go anywhere with this guy's helix tucked under your arm," Vincent signs on the dotted line. Thus begins a complicated (and homoerotic) exchange of bodily fluids, an intimate corporeal contract between two men. Turning his apartment into a medical lab, complete with microscopes, needles, and catheters, Eugene gathers, packages, and sells (fragments of) his body to Vincent. Together they invent a composite subject named Jerome Morrow, a hybrid persona constructed through the intermingling of their bodies and minds, and one who is, as a result, an In-Valid on the inside and a Valid on the surface. For clarity's sake, I will refer to this invented subject as Jerome$_2$. Cloaked in the identity of a member of the genetic elite, Vincent passes as Jerome$_2$ (while the original Jerome resorts to using his second name, Eugene), having purchased the coveted Valid status, which opens doors for him at *GATTACA* Corporation.

GATTACA is properly classified as science fiction, appropriating from the cutting edge of biotechnological research and imaginatively interpreting the sociocultural impact of the genetic revolution as part of a narrative about the technoscientific construction of culture, subjectivity, and embodiment. The film's tagline: "there is no gene for the human spirit," gives us a hint that *GATTACA* is perhaps best understood as an example of what David Porush terms "cybernetic fiction," which "Insists that humans somehow elude mechanical reduction, that there is some meaningful silence left over—some irreducible, inexpressible, and unmasterable remnant or trace for which cybernetic quantification of information cannot account."[9]

The sleek, silver, streamlined surveillance technologies we see in every scene of *GATTACA* monitor molecular biodata, quantifying psychological and even some psychological processes, manufacturing a subject's genetic qualifications (GQ) in machine-readable computer-compatible language, and policing the border between the Valids and In-Valids. However, these screening-security technologies ignore what Elizabeth Grosz describes as the psychic interiority of the subject: those qualities that distinguish humans from machines and animals, such as the imagination, courage, determination, and the soul or human spirit.[10] The machines are digital tools, and cannot creatively interpret or read between the lines (or chromosomes) to comprehend Vincent's unique, unquantifiable humanness, his "unmasterable" self, his will or "spirit"—that which is supposedly chemically unverifiable and invisible, undigitized. Insofar as it is dystopic cybernetic fiction, *GATTACA* causes the spectator to think about how the body is implicated and the subject is made intelligible (or will be, in "the not-too-distant future") according to genomic epistemologies. Through identifying with Vincent, the audience is (partially) reassured that—just as we saw in *Blade Runner, The Matrix, RoboCop*, and *The Terminator*(s)—although the computer technologies we design and depend on may become increasingly smart, autonomous, and even hostile, we will always outwit them because of our irreducible humanness—the unsequenceable, untranslatable spark of the self that does not appear on any genetic map.

Who is this "we," the cybersubject of the technofuture who will beat the system and outsmart the machines that run it? *GATTACA* screenwriter/director Andrew Niccol describes Vincent as a representative of "us" (the audience), someone with whom "we" can all identify and see as a reflection of ourselves, complete with our own very human limitations. It seems misguided and naive to imagine that this character (or any character) could succeed on screen as a representation of generic genomic citizenship, passing for the spectator as a symbol of the "human" spirit. Two generations of contributions to an enormous corpus of feminist film theories have, we hope, successfully convinced us that there is no such thing as a "generic" (unraced, ungendered, etc.) human character on screen, any more than there could be a generic spectator.

In Niccol's script, it is no accident that the subject who is empowered to negotiate and hack the technoscientific social order is both white and male (not to mention able bodied and a practicing heterosexual). Two references come immediately to mind that support this choice: first, in our information culture, it is well known that adolescent males are overrepresented in the computer hacker culture, and have been since the 1960s. In the film, this explains the choice of a young white male character who hacks the genoistic social system, gains illegal entry, infiltrates and studies the operational logic of the corporation, and successfully evades surveillance programs in order to get an educational experience or to protest a corrupt ideology or politics, for the risk of it, or just for the thrill and fun of it.

Secondly, as stated above, the cultural referent for the film is the Human Genome Project, whose scientific model for "*the* human genome" is also, not surprisingly, male.[11] However, the overdetermined gender scripts on which this film depends do not end there. *GATTACA* also imports the technoromantic cyberpunk discourse of the utopic transcendence of physicality, and all the gendered implications that accompany it. Within this narrative convention, not only is it exclusively male (and overwhelmingly white adolescent) subjects who are able to negotiate their place in the technosphere, but it could hardly be otherwise, since the essential and deterministic links between women and the body, female and nature, femininity, sensuality and the flesh, are taken for granted, left unproblematized—and often denigrated through a subtle or explicit distain for "the meat."

The film depicts a dystopic science fictional view of a future culture in which everything from a subject's employment opportunities to their options for selecting a romantic partner is predicated on their GQ. In *GATTACA* we witness one "exceptional" man's struggle to have his capabilities recognized and rewarded, despite his possession of "inferior" DNA that firmly positions him as a member of the genetic underclass and severely limits his individual freedom. Explicitly then, the film is a story about discrimination in the twenty-first century, and the ways in which genomic science has furnished American culture with new ways to distribute and demarcate difference and disenfranchisement among subjects. On closer examination, however, *GATTACA* illustrates the ways in which the concept of genoism complements existing forms of discrimination and differentiation between subjects: for example, patriarchy and white supremacy.

In order to be intelligible, on a narrative level the film filters this concept of genomic subjectivity through the lens of existing cultural discourses about bodies, biology, and identity. It also borrows from the folklore of a male hero using his imagination and creativity to triumph over the oppressive and corrupt set of power relations that would constrain and limit his personal success. The film accomplishes this through its narrative construction and its casting choices, insofar as, predictably, the hero is white and male as are all characters with speaking parts in positions of institutional power (doctor, police, CEO). The protagonist's love interest is a young attractive white female whose character is underdeveloped, and he is surrounded by nonwhite actors and actresses who have nonspeaking and/or marginal roles, with "bad guy" personas. Genoism, racism, and sexism are shown to be compatible and mutually reinforcing systems for maintaining socioeconomic inequity in the not-too-distant future, just as they were within the eugenics movement and within contemporary American culture.[12]

As part of its narrative construction, *GATTACA* perhaps inadvertently illustrates that even in a future culture where DNA-based information is used as the referent of a subject's identity and sense of entitlement, there will still be an overwhelming significance attached to the "sex chromosomes" (the biodata upon which we construct ideologies of gender) and to the biologically unbounded concept of race, which serve to regulate the social order today and historically. As such, *GATTACA*'s filmic narrative combines groundbreaking models of the future of digitalized subjectivity with age-old scripts about gender, race, and embodiment. The result is a story about the way that discourses of gender essentialism, naturalized white privilege, eugenics, and biological determinism are refigured and reified through genomic technoscience.

It is here that the telltale signs of tech noir can be discerned. Like noir, *GATTACA* is a kind of hybrid text, combining elements from melodrama, detective fiction, mystery, and the social problem film, in this case with the added twist of science fiction. It takes what is becoming a dominant conviction, that the Human Genome Project is evidence of technoscientific progress, and will lead to improved quality of life, the possible eradication of social inequities, and empowerment for all—and problematizes it. Other social conventions are upheld by the film, such as inequitable gendered and race ideologies, the connection between disabled bodies and dysfunction or nonproductivity, and the norm of compulsory heterosexuality. *GATTACA* shows us the dark side of the American Dream, where not just anyone can become the president, civil liberties are unprotected, and there is no such thing as universal opportunity based on merit—with the exception of genetic "merit." As feminist film theorists have suggested, noir film can be read as an accurate portrayal of a patriarchal society, albeit oftentimes a complex and critical one. Similarly, in *GATTACA* the audience is presented with a story that combines scientific fact with fiction, and a startlingly new social order that has an uncanny resemblance to our present one. The signature feature of noir film, the femme fatale, is both present and absent in *GATTACA*, signifying that the film has an ambivalent relationship to the genres it borrows from—and suggesting that tech-noir and cybernetic fiction are examples of postmodern pastiche appropriate for the bioinformatic age, as has been noted by several critics and reviewers.

GENOMIC FEMININITY

> Bodily fluids flow, they seep, they infiltrate; their control is a matter of vigilance, never guaranteed. [. . .] [They] are engulfing, difficult to be rid of; any separation from them is not a matter of certainty.
>
> —**Elizabeth Grosz (24)**

> I expel *myself*, I spit *myself* out, I abject myself within the same motion through which "I" claim to establish *myself* [. . .] It is thus not lack of cleanliness or health that causes abjection, but what disturbs identity, system, order. What does not respect borders, positions, rules. The in-between, the ambiguous, the composite.
>
> —**Julia Kristeva**[13]

When we consider *GATTACA* as a piece of cyberpop media it is predictable that we see the familiar tale of a white male who, due to his strength, bravery, ingenuity, self-confidence, determination, intellect, and selfish pursuit of his own desire, beats the system and is liberated from a stifling social order that is unappreciative of his uniqueness. There is a correspondingly predictable script of genomic femininity. Vincent's corporeal contract with Eugene is the first of two intimate and high-risk couplings that he undertakes as a result of his passionate desire to fulfill his dreams and affirm the validity of his identity. Vincent's passing performance as a Valid is so convincing that he wins the affections of unsuspecting Irene Cassini (Uma Thurman), his fellow employee at GATTACA Corporation. Described as a "fabulous babe" by media reviewers, Irene is a dangerous *femme fatale* who seduces Jerome$_2$ and causes him to risk all that he has achieved at GATTACA Corporation, blinded as he is by his desire for her. In a moment of what is presented as reckless abandon (but appears erotically bankrupt), Jerome$_2$ has sexual intercourse with Irene, leaving telltale traces of sperm, skin, and saliva on/in her body and her bed. Although he becomes intimately involved with Irene, he cannot trust her (or anyone) with his secret (his body), and realizing this dangerous and foolish transgression—into meatspace as the cyberpunks say—he launches into a narrative woven of lies, and flees her embrace. Irene knows she is being deceived, and says as much, but Jerome$_2$ seems unconcerned or oblivious. If Irene demands further explanation, it is offscreen, since we see her, their relationship, and everything else exclusively through Jerome$_2$'s privileged perspective—and that is a narrow bandwidth indeed. Just as he earlier severed the emotional bonds to his mother, Jerome$_2$ abandons Irene in an attempt to preserve his power, autonomy, performance, and professional success. But does he need to leave her?

On one hand, Jerome$_2$ doesn't need to leave the women in his life, he just wants to be free to follow his dreams to outer space, and so he cuts ties to earthly things (symbolized by the feminine) and seemingly effortlessly deletes his sexual desire, lust, and arousal, as part of his triumphant transcendence.[14] We see Jerome$_2$ abandon his female relationships not so much because of who these women are, or due to his overwhelmingly strong feelings for and attachments to them, but mainly because they are simply not crucial to the success of his quest. His dramatic exits are unnecessary, since the women in Vincent's and Jerome$_2$'s life are disposable, whether they are In-Valids (his Mother) or Valid-but-not-quite-Valid-enough (Irene), they are powerless, naive, passive, and frail beings, unlikely to be in a position to aid or derail the progress of the exceptionally Valid Jerome$_2$ even if they wanted to. We watch Jerome's mother use genetic screening technology to guarantee that Vincent's younger sibling is born Valid—but Vincent triumphs over his mother's intentions and his genetically superior brother anyway. Similarly, Irene uses genomic screening technology to spy on Jerome$_2$, sneaking a hair from his desk and rushing off to have it sequenced, but again, Vincent has all bases covered and he beats the test by planting a borrowed Valid's hair as bait. Even when women use technology in the film they cannot compete with the hero, nor interfere with his quest.

Even so, on a symbolic level, Vincent and Jerome$_2$ must sever connections with women because in *GATTACA* female embodiment (especially the womb and the vagina *dentata*) and proximity to it (as a child or a lover) is a dangerous thing that could prove men's undoing.[15] The film adopts uncritically, and thus reproduces, a gendered narrative that designates female bodies and feminine embodiment as *de-gene-rate*, something tinged with contagion and disorder that a hero must avoid and from which he must escape.

Irene represents lack and weakness that is anathema to Vincent, and the horror of entrapment and stasis to the upwardly mobile Jerome$_2$. At the end of the film, as we watch Jerome$_2$ revel in the accomplishment of his victorious liftoff and departure to Titan, we assume that off-screen Irene is exactly where she started: firmly planted with her feet on the ground, watching the sky through the glass ceiling at GATTACA Corporation, literally—the building has a transparent roof affording a view of the stars. Irene is a spectator to the triumph of GATTACA Corporation's technoscientific accomplishments, but never a participant. Although she is qualified for space travel and assured by the Project Director that her "place in line" for a future mission "is secure," at the same time we realize that her chance to transcend earth's gravitational pull will never materialize. Instead of exhibiting the kind of courage and determination that makes Jerome$_2$ "the right sort of person to be taking us to Titan" (quoting the Project Director), Irene acts through a blind and naive faith in the genomic order of things. This allows Irene to contentedly agree to put her life on hold for a year as she patiently and passively waits for his return so that they can continue a relationship started under false pretenses. To the audience though, this doesn't seem like much of a sacrifice, since Irene's persona is undeveloped, marginal, and lacks psychological depth. Irene is already on pause, she doesn't make things happen; things happen to her and she responds. She is a desired object, not an agent like Vincent.

It is then disappointingly predictable when GATTACA Corporation's Project Director Josef Gregor (Gore Vidal) instructs Irene to put aside her astronomic research to serve as "Liaison Officer"—what appears in the film as a stereotypically feminized pink-collar "hostess" position. Would a liaison officer ever be allowed to travel to space? Supposedly, yes. As one reviewer suggested, *GATTACA* is a story about "a futuristic society where it's not *what* you know, or even *who* you know, but who you *are* that counts. The only 'network' you use to get a job at GATTACA Inc. [*sic*] is the double-helix network of your DNA strand."[16]

However, not all viewers would agree with Edmonds. We learn that, not unlike present cultural conditions, discrimination based on gender (and other markers of identity such as race, class, and age) in GATTACian society is both illegal and business as usual. The film presents elements of a feminist utopia, a culture where *officially*, being a woman should not limit one's climb up the corporate ladder; simultaneously however, we note the uncanny coincidences within the film, when the XY genetic ladder leads to upward mobility and expanded career choices, but subjects with two X chromosomes are passed over for promotions and opportunities based on who they are and what they are made of. Clearly there is another discursive network operating in *GATTACA* linking gender and genetics.

Irene was born with a heart defect, a physical condition she shares with Vincent, who also has a weak heart. The similarities between them, however, end there. This is not surprising considering that as Elizabeth Grosz observes, "one and the same message, inscribed on a male or a female body, does not always or even usually mean the same thing or result in the same text" (156). So although Vincent and Irene's genetic scripts may resemble each other insofar as both exhibit hypertrophic cardiomyopathy, in this sociobiological society, perhaps the most crucial piece of biodata determining how a subject is positioned socially—and by extension, how they construct their identity—is the presence or the absence of the Y chromosome. We come to realize, as the story unfolds, that Vincent and Irene could not be more different, in fact, their compositions are antithetical. Luckily, those two weak hearts can still beat as one, and their difference doesn't preclude them from falling in love, which predictably, they do.

The physiological similarities between Vincent and Irene are offset by an exaggerated construction of their psychological and emotional *difference*. The erotic attraction between "opposites," which serves to naturalize the heterosexual dynamic in the film, is reinforced by Irene's utterly passive and icy disposition vis-à-vis Jerome$_2$'s passionate and fanatical pursuit of his personal goals. As actress Uma Thurman explains, "Irene simply accepts her fate," whereas "Vincent refuses to accept his limitations and thwarts them constantly—he has the courage and audacity to do so."[17] Irene's character is envisioned by her creator Andrew Niccol as, "somebody who would lie down and die at the allotted minute because she would feel guilty if she lived a minute longer than her [genetic] profile proscribed. [. . .] Irene is a woman who is very definite about her shortcomings, who is very firm in her belief in her frailties" (Official *GATTACA* Web site). The audience is too, since even if Irene is dressed and coiffed to resemble a femme fatale, and even if she lures our hero into dangerous territory, her persona is thoroughly contained, predictable, and utterly unlike the powerful and ultimately unknowable femme of classic noir. According to Niccol, Vincent's persona also "has frailties" but they do not prevent him from driving himself to extreme levels of exhaustion and desperation, pushing at the boundaries of his capabilities, to overcome them. For Vincent, Niccol insists, "there's no such thing as *you can't do this*" (Official *GATTACA* Web site). Chromosomally constructed sexual difference predisposes him to the qualities of will, courage, and human spirit, whereas for Irene, the XX condition determines her passivity and essentialized frailty. Thus even though Irene has a Valid GQ classification, she cannot compete with the faithbirth Vincent, who is her genetic inferior, in the battle of whose "human spirit" is stronger, because Irene can never escape her biological bonds as female, or the corresponding social imposition of femininity. According to the logic of Niccol's script then, Irene can therefore not "pass" as a generic "human" subject because of her chromosomal classification, the indelible mark of sexual difference. This prevents Irene from contending with Jerome$_2$ for a place on the "manned" Titan voyage, makes her ineligible to be the Everyman that Niccol assumes all theatergoers identify with, and disqualifies her from being the hero(ine) in this film.

Unfortunately, the Vincent/Irene binary is too simplistic to be convincing, and their affair seems passionless. Instead of the charged dynamic between the genders in classic noir, in this film, scenes in which the lovers appear together are picturesque long shots rather than close-ups, filled with awkward stilted dialogue rather than clever *badinage*, or—in a particularly desperate attempt to make their one sexual encounter visually innovative—shot upside down, with a blue filter, reflected in the dark glass of a patio window.[18] By opting for the stereotypical female-lack version of Irene rather than a complex interpretation of genomic femininity, Niccol sacrificed the opportunity to humanize his characters, and the critics complained loudly about the cardboard personas and "wooden flirtations" of Vincent and Irene (Sobchack, *Virginity* 43).

Although GATTACian society functions according to genomic discourses and a genetic caste (class) system, a (familiar) imbalance of power between the genders is clearly part of the maintenance of social hegemony. *GATTACA* presents the story of one male subject's resistance to inequitable social conditions; but what modes of resistance to the technological order of sexed, sexualized, and engendered embodiments are possible or imagined for female subjects? Vincent passes successfully as Jerome$_2$ by rendering his true identity transparent. He transcends his body and its particularities, irregularities, and imperfections, though leaving a trail for others to follow, composed of microscopic fragments from his purchased identity. But what of the women in the film? Can they too become transparent and escape their fate as spectacles for a male gaze in this not-too-distant future? Are female subjects able to resist the genoism that characterizes their culture by recourse to technology? Can women "pass" and transcend their embodiment and the mark of gender?

Some female "subjects" never have a chance to find out. Although the controversial billboard promotion campaign for the film challenged audiences to consider the ethics of designer babies, in fact within the film itself we see that the act of selecting an embryo's *genetic* qualities is inseparable from selecting its *sex*. When Vincent's parents decide to have a second child, they have learned from their "mistake" (i.e., Vincent) and they seek out assistance from a geneticist. It is only *after* they decide about the presence or absence of a Y chromosome that Vincent's parents begin to discuss the finer points of their future son's chemical characteristics. They unabashedly admit that they want a male child, a choice that is not nearly as controversial in the filmic narrative as their anxieties around tinkering with the embryo's genome, to eradicate any other undesirable characteristics. The fate of the remaining three fertilized embryos we see magnified on the geneticist's computer screen (two females and one male) are unknown to us; perhaps they are frozen or discarded? This eugenic moment of selective breeding illustrates the fears that bioethicists and feminists have voiced, as reproductive technologies are used to screen out future female subjects.[19]

Other female subjects do have a chance, theoretically. Irene, as an example of a "made woman"—a female subject whose genome is the result of genetic engineering—achieves the coveted Valid identity, but does it get her very far (compared to Jerome$_2$ the self-made man)? Apparently, Irene conforms to GATTACian cultural norms and expectations without question or protest. Just like Vincent's mother, who supposedly learned her lesson by having her first child without genetic assistance/interference and decides to do it the "right" way next time, Irene uses (bioinformatic screening) computerized technology not to resist genoism but to participate in it. Irene's static one-dimensional persona marks her as a dupe of the sociobiological order; she appears to believe in the concept of genetic merit and the rigid class/caste system that reflects it, even when it is clearly not in her best interest to do so.

GENOMIC MASCULINITY

Whereas Irene has faith in technoscience, Vincent has none. This positions Vincent as an outsider within, and accounts for the instability of his character. Irene is sure of herself and her shortcomings, but Vincent, on the other hand, has faith only in himself in spite of the dominant view of faithbirths as de-gene-rate. His isolation from others, due to the required distance he must maintain to protect his passing performance as Jerome$_2$, causes him to grow increasingly paranoid and neurotic. We watch Vincent explode in frustration and fear in scenes with Eugene and Irene, only to swagger confidently when at the office. Vincent is the hero, a winner who has made it inside GATTACA Corporation, but he is not in control of his life, and is instead caught in a web of conflicting desires, motivations, and relationships. Like the classic noir hero, Vincent's ability to be a role model is compromised throughout the film by his rootlessness, bachelorhood, criminality, emotional turbulence, unsuccessful and tragic encounters with women, and quasi-gay relationships with men. Coupled with his attempts to pass as a Valid subject, Vincent carefully scripts his performance of successful masculinity as masquerade,[20] so as to convince Project Director Josef (who holds Vincent's key to the Titan voyage) and everyone else that he is made of the "right stuff"—and to hide his obsession with his very real physiological lack and the problematic gap between Vincent's self and that mask of hybrid subjectivity, Jerome$_2$.

Irene's persona is the antithesis to Vincent's, but this is only the first of two important character juxtapositions that operate to produce him as hero material. In *GATTACA* we are presented with two very different versions of technomasculinity in the figures of Vincent and Eugene. Despite any physical similarities they might have, we see that their personalities are polar opposites. Eugene Morrow has no backbone, metaphorically speaking, and is represented in the film by his severed spine and inability to walk. It is implied that his disability reflects an inner weakness of character, a flawed sense of self, crippled by internalizing impossible standards of perfection expected from a Valid individual. He is a pathetic drunk, with no drive and no will to live. Born into a life filled with all of the advantages accompanying a Valid GQ, coupled with the old-fashioned bonuses of being both white and male, Eugene is as a result so overwhelmingly privileged that when he places second instead of first in a swimming competition, he attempts suicide (unsuccessfully, leaving him disabled). Drowning his sorrows in liquor, and wallowing in self-pity, Eugene cannot accept a silver medal, cannot conceive of not being number one, or of the compromise of being trapped in a wheelchair, or of having to worry about money. Eugene begrudgingly accepts his fate, to be stuck in his body and resigned to an undoubtedly painful and humiliating regime of gathering his own urine, blood, vomit, fingernail clippings, and other abject substances, to harvest them for their commercial genetic value (in other words, Eugene becomes reduced to "you-gene").

Isolated and abandoned in a wheelchair-inaccessible apartment dominated by a huge swirling (double helix inspired) staircase, obsessively and frantically collecting and cataloging his bodily wastes as he winds his wheelchair around in the makeshift laboratory, Eugene is alone all day while his benefactor Jerome$_2$ is at work at GATTACA Corporation, and then waits alone all night while Jerome$_2$ socializes. In a startling ending to this degrading life condition, the film concludes with a eugenic moment as Eugene commits suicide (successfully this time), communicating to the viewer that this life, entrapped in the confines of the meat/flesh, doesn't matter, is illegitimate, since its use-value has expired at the same moment that Jerome$_2$ succeeds in his mission, or perhaps much earlier, at the moment Eugene became paralyzed.

And yet somehow *GATTACA* represents Eugene's suicide as a dignified ending, even as an appropriate and legitimate choice, as if to insinuate that any form of In-Valid embodiment is a fate from which white male subjects must escape, by any means necessary. In a parallel sequence of match shots, claustrophobic close-ups of Eugene's final moments huddled in the incinerator are coordinated with shots of Jerome$_2$ strapped into the confines of the spacecraft, lifting off to Titan, to underscore the corresponding but painfully different "escapes" that these subjects are entitled to.

That Eugene is as firm in his conviction that he should die as he is that Jerome$_2$ should live, points to the assumption of white male entitlement that predominates in the film. Eugene (and Andrew Niccol, and perhaps the audience) is certain Vincent should not be discriminated against, and he is steadfastly wedded to his own self-pity, because as Hannah Kuhlmann observes, in contemporary American culture neither of these men "would of course ever be limited by his body" and thus it is far-fetched and difficult to accept that in the GATTACian dystopic future, a white straight educated male with disposable income could not have the ability (or the right) to escape the confines of abject embodiment.[21] It is genoism in *general*, and this narrative in *particular*, the terrible story of a male subject who is entitled to but denied success based on unjust cultural (not natural or biological) rules, that qualify this film as dystopic. Put differently, the dramatic quotient of *GATTACA* depends on the terrifying specter of loss of male and white privilege via technoscientific progress that threatens to level the playing field, or at least redraw the lines of advantage, potentially relegating white men to the bottom of the social ladder, paralyzing them while "others" take their places in the professional classes.

A NEW UNDERCLASS

Before he embarks on his passing performance/scheme, Vincent belongs to "a new underclass" of unengineered In-Valid subjects, whom we see represented as janitors or incarcerated as criminals. Notably, all members of Vincent's custodial crew are white and male, an uncanny reversal of present-day economic reality, where racial minorities and women are disproportionately represented in these underpaid and undesirable jobs, making up the "old underclass" to which Vincent's "new" crew is juxtaposed.

Instead of seeing minority subjects represented in predictable roles in the film, we find in *GATTACA* at least two examples of black men in authority positions that may at first seem unconventional. There is the nameless geneticist figure (Blair Underwood) who aids Vincent's parents in making racial and gender-specific choices when they create a designer baby.[22] Perhaps ironically, this white-coated black male scientist explains patiently to the parents that he has "taken the liberty of removing any potentially prejudicial" characteristics from the genetic composition of the embryos they may select to have implanted—emphasizing that as per their request, he has screened to ensure "fair skin." Essentially, this geneticist creates an intolerable situation for Vincent, as his genetically engineered brother Anton (Loren Dean) is born, with whom he battles in a sibling rivalry that is life threatening on several occasions.

Secondly, in a flashback scene we watch as a twenty-something Vincent tries to get employment and is forced to submit to an illegal urine test to screen against admitting an In-Valid GQ. The (again, nameless) personnel officer/interviewer (Clarence Graham) who hands him the cup for the test, and who authoritatively stands behind a desk and between Vincent and a job opportunity, is also a black male. As the scene unfolds, Vincent's voiceover explains how technoscience has caused cultural degeneration, accompanied by a shot of Vincent sitting on a bench beside a black male and a white female outside this employer's office. It is impossible to miss the innuendo, that is, the injustice of a white male having to compete with black men and/or women for a job. The casting choices are significant, as it becomes clear that in a genoistic culture, racial others will use the tools of science to redress the historical precedents set by centuries of white supremacy. Does this scenario contribute to the features that qualify the film as dystopic? Who is the new underclass in this film if not the straight white men who today enjoy much privilege?

In contrast to these black male professionals who seem to stand in the way of Vincent's socioeconomic ascendancy, *GATTACA* Corporation installs a white male doctor as its resident physician, Lamar (Xander Berkeley), and Project Director Josef (Gore Vidal) a white male employer, both of whom prove themselves capable of bending the rules and keeping a secret. These authority figures so completely and unequivocally support Jerome$_2$'s goal of space travel that they each jeopardize their own positions of power, taking dangerous risks to help him achieve success. Why do Lamar and the Project Director Josef help Jerome$_2$ if not because they believe that he deserves and is somehow entitled to escape the fleshly bonds that should not matter, and should not distract from his real qualities and strengths? By the same token, it is significant that we see neither of these gate-keeping figures reading between the lines to accelerate Irene's progress to Titan. Instead, Josef is rooting for his protégé Jerome$_2$ in whom he likely sees a reflection of a younger version of himself, and similarly Lamar gives Jerome$_2$ a leg up because he reminds him of his own son. This leaves the viewer to ponder the extent to which the triumph of Vincent is not the story of Everyman as Niccol suggests, but rather the victory of the old boy's club over technoscientific progress, or perhaps their complementarities. Either way, these white males see an important resemblance between Vincent's achievement and their own self-interests, and in the postphotographic moment of GATTACian culture where appearances are less important than bioinformatic quotients, this can only be described as nostalgia for and reenactment of a previous era's romantic notions of male bonding and a brotherhood that looks after its own.[23]

THE BODIES THAT MATTER

In the final shot of the film, as Jerome$_2$ leaves on his mission to Titan, and the camera pans across his fellow astronauts, we see that the crew is not only multicultural (we see two black subjects and one Asian subject) but also includes a female, who is presumably a Valid. But this brief panning shot representing racial and gendered diversity is so fleeting—ending predictably in a lingering close-up of Jerome$_2$—and just so much background, that it cannot succeed in convincing the viewer that racial and gendered others have equal opportunities vis-à-vis the white male hero, whose authorized story continues to unfold in a voiceover even as the camera gives us a momentary glimpse of these silent supporting "other" characters strapped into the spaceship.

We get the sense that other characters in the film support Vincent's flight from the body, as if it is reasonable, appropriate, and just. Perhaps they instinctively recognize that he possesses a transcendent human spirit, and that it would be unfair and perverse to detain it/him. In a genoistic culture, Jerome$_2$ is naturally entitled to have doors opened for him because he is (passing as) genetically superior, but I would argue that it is also because he is white, male, and heterosexual—older throwback signs of privilege from an era in the not-too-distant past (i.e., today). In the end, Vincent does not triumph because of his human "spirit" or soul, but largely because of his access to and connections within a network of powerful white men.

GATTACA presents one possible configuration of the relationship between the coevolution of genetics and global, capitalist, neocolonialist, and corporate interests—adopting a critical, even a dystopic view of the future of genomic technoscience. But it accomplishes more: GATTACA illustrates the way in which science is part of the culture that develops it, mirroring the biases, values, prejudices, and paradigms that structure the social sphere. Even in this film, which explicitly presents a biologically essentialist future, we see that it is not only DNA which, as Michel Foucault suggests, "lays down for each individual his place, his body, his disease and his death, his well-being" but also the culturally constructed data of gender and sexual difference which "characterize him, what belongs to him, what happens to him," or her (Foucault, 1977).

Tech-noir cyberpop productions like GATTACA and the cult films it is sandwiched between, Blade Runner (1982) and The Matrix (1999), capitalize on the public's technoscientific angst or biofear, emerging at a moment in history when innovations in the genomic and informatics sectors of the economy are heralded by many as causing cultural confusion and upheavals in tradition. Interestingly however, as feminist-minded observers well know, even in an "imploding" and "boundary-shifting" postmodern moment such as the one into which Dolly the sheep and GATTACA were launched, popular culture is filled with representations of gendered and raced embodiment that are remarkably consistent and resilient.

5

Cyberfemininity: Pixel Vixens

When technology intersects with the body in the realm of representation, the question of sexual difference is inevitably involved.

—Mary Anne Doane[1]

Cyberpop media texts materialize a cultural imaginary composed of, among
other things, icons representing modes of subjectivity, which circulate as part
of a popular image repertoire. These icons frame and configure our ideas
about real bodies and subjects, transmitting a sense of which forms are compatible with the technosavvy future, and who is eligible to be the users/con-
sumers/players in the next generation of the informational economy. The
choices made around representing the body and the subject of the future
matter, especially since in our net culture, information is transmitted, downloaded, cut and pasted, cross posted, linked and networked instantaneously.
Cyberpop figures are cited and recited; they inform each other intertextually.
As Judith Butler has explained, this kind of repetition is a crucial part of the
process by which particular images, discourses, and models of gender and
the body become popularized, normalized, and naturalized.[2] As we habitu-
ally consume (and produce) these representations of subjectivity, becoming
accustomed to these figurations, we are in the process of becoming "technoliterate," acclimatized to cyberculture, fluent in its specialized vocabulary—in

other words, enculturated. Thus, Haraway insists that "how we figure techno-science makes an immense difference" to which narratives, stories, and discourses become dominant, because such figurative tropes are "instruments for enforcing meanings" around subjectivity, identity, community, technology, and embodiment in cyberculture (Haraway, Game 60).

SEDUCTION OF THE INTERFACE: PIXEL VIXENS AND THE VIRTUAL HYPER-FEMME

Technology has no sex, but representations of technology often do.

—Claudia Springer (8)

Today *Ananova* received a marriage proposal from a stranger via e-mail. He had seen her at work; admiring her from a distance, he watched for weeks and listened to her voice. It was not an unusual experience for *Ananova*; she has received other e-proposals. *Ananova* even has a fan club or two; she is becoming a virtual celebrity. Her web of acquaintances and friends is global. What is unusual is that *Ananova* is a computer program, not a real female. She "lives" on the Web, working as a newscaster (Figure 5.1). *Ananova* is not an anomaly; cybergirls are proliferating.[3] A graphic interface construct masking software and database, the pixel vixen humanizes infotechnology, but she also aims to seduce the user into a virtual relationship, a personalized infomediation—translating data according to one's preferences, interests, needs, and desires. This proposed relationship between a human male user and a virtual female celebrity was the subject of cyberpunk author William Gibson's novel *Idoru*:

> "What did Blackwell mean, last night, about Rez wanting to marry a Japanese girl who isn't real?"

> "Idoru," Yumazaki said.

> "What?"

> "'Idol-singer.' She is Rei Toei. She is a personality-construct, a congeries of software agents, the creation of information designers. She is akin to what I believe they call a 'synthespian,' in Hollywood."

> Laney closed his eyes, opened them. "Then how can he marry her?"

> "I don't know," Yumazaki said. "But he has very forcefully declared this to be his intention."[4]

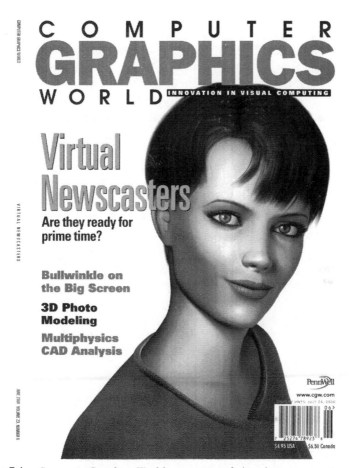

Figure 5.1 *Computer Graphics World* cover story of virtual newscaster *Ananova.*

As the novel progresses, Laney meets the idoru *Rei Toei*, is irresistibly drawn to her, and finds the experience exciting but frightening and even overwhelming. Laney tries to look away and avoid her gaze, reminding himself: "She is not flesh. She is information. She is the tip of an iceberg, no an Antarctica, of information. Looking at her face would trigger it again: she was some unthinkable volume of information" (Gibson, *IDORU* 233).

Rei is artificial intelligence (AI), a computer program simulating a human female; *Rei's* passing performance becomes more convincing by engaging with humans and learning to mimic them. In his marriage to *Rei*, Laney's acquaintance Rez merges with the personality-construct, becoming virtual, leaving his body behind, uploading his conscious mind to the Net, and is assimilated into cyberspace in a kind of *jouissance.* In the course of the novel, Laney grows to understand and appreciate Rez's infatuation with the idoru, and he must repeatedly resist the seduction of the shimmering pixel vixen and her invitation to leave the fleshly world behind.

Cyberpop inspired by the idoru (originally from Japan, roughly translated as "virtual celebrity character") appears in contemporary Western cultural media, not only in science fiction and cyberpunk literature, but in information and computer technology marketing materials. Versions of idoru are used to humanize, personalize, and sexualize information technologies, and in the process encourage the consumption of digital gadgets and electronic communication services. This chapter focuses on five of these virtual "hyperfeminine" figures launched at approximately the same historical moment (1999-2000): the cyberassistant *Mya* from Motorola Corporation, *Webbie Tookay* the virtual supermodel from Illusion2K and Elite Model Management, the virtual newscaster *Ananova*, the (as-yet fictional) search engine *Syndi* from *Artbyte: The Magazine of Digital Culture*, and in the following chapter, the virtual celebrity *Lara Croft* from the *Tomb Raider* Playstation® game. The pixel vixens are cyberpop icons not unlike the cyborg figure Haraway popularized in her classic "Manifesto." The pixel vixen, too, is "enmeshed in an intertextual web of power relations, knowledges, values, ideologies, discourses, histories, temporalities, and geographical spatialities" (Haraway, *Leaf* 108). This figure has been appropriated, mobilized, compromised, and "used in all these inappropriate ways," and yet Haraway insists that this doesn't mean we should "give up the game" of resignifying, rereading, redescribing, and reinventing figures like the cyborg or the idoru (108). In what follows we analyze both the design choices made in composing these graphical interfaces, how they reify and contest the rules of formation in cyberculture, and the ideas about technology, gender, and digital subjectivity these synthespian infomediaries communicate.

The choice to begin by juxtaposing a "real" pixel vixen (*Ananova*) with a fictional one (*Rei Toei*) from a cyberpunk novel reflects the centrality of paradox to the construction of digital culture. The pixel vixen is *both* real *and* fictional: it is real in terms of having material effects on people's lives and playing a role in the formation of digital lifestyles, and it is fictional insofar as it operates in conjunction with an elaborate fantasy narrative. In her book *Virtualities: Television, Media Art, and Cyberculture*, Margaret Morse explains that "an information society will not be experienced by most users at the level of its technological foundation or as algorithms and abstract symbols"; instead they will interface with user-friendly data that has been "reengaged with personality and the imagination" (5). Morse suggests that an informational society "inevitably calls forth a cyberculture" that is personal, humanized, and compatible with current configurations of power, knowledge, subjects, bodies, and identities—even as it offers upgrades or high-tech versions of the next wave of these components for the digital future (5). The idoru exemplifies the process Morse describes. They are promoted as our allies in the battle to stay on top of the tidal waves of data transmission, latest-breaking news, stock market blip, fashion trend, traffic accident report, or new cell phone number; the virtual female is a tool that will facilitate the user's navigation of what Baudrillard called the "cyberblitz" or data smog that characterizes the networked e-society (Shenk 21).

Ananova and other pixel vixens are used as spokes"persons" or talking heads promoting the values of digital capitalism: the irresistible idoru signifies and sells connectivity, e-powerment (through personalization technologies), and intangibility (BLUR). "She" is an object of technoeroticism, encouraging users to establish a very personal attachment to their computer technologies. At the same time, however, the CGI (computer-generated image) girls can be redescribed as examples of cyberpop that have the potential to challenge, resist, or threaten the status quo, especially the associations of technology and masculinity—because these figurations make explicit connections between femininity and cutting-edge emergent technologies. Also, the pixel vixens implode notions of gender essentialism by explicitly foregrounding their feminine encodings; as a result, the constructedness of femininity, the intentionality of performing femininity is made very clear. Within an aesthetic of digital artifice the idoru accomplishes a denaturalization of femininity, foregrounding what we might call its tools or architecture.

The result is that the idoru can be interpreted as further objectifying women, and more interestingly, as parodies of ideal femininity. Although they appear to be representations of virtual women, on closer examination the idorus are better understood as simulacra, with no "real" referent. Perhaps it is overstating the case to claim that pixel vixens can threaten the hegemony of digital capitalism, but as cyberpop, they at least advocate a positionality that is creative, critical, and self-aware in its implication in the construction of digital culture. These figures, like Apple's "1984" advertisement, encourage consumers and users to *think different* about the digitalization of everyday life from an insider's perspective. Moreover, they promote a kind of implosion in the binary of work and play, serving as the faces of an informational economy and mediating the flow of data, all the while entertaining the spectator with tongue-in-cheek touches that are reminiscent of video game culture.

"SHE IS NOT FLESH. SHE IS INFORMATION."

Technology is the fetish of cyberpunk; desire is translocated from the heterosexual norm onto the technology itself and onto the heavily fantasized cyberspace that it generates.

—Amanda Fernbach (244)

Some of the graphical choices in designing virtual females are predictable: on the surface, the pixel vixens reviewed here are similar in appearance to the never-ending stream of images of blond, Caucasian, teenaged, size 1, legs-to-there, heterosexy, wide-eyed, air-brushed or digitally remastered virtual seductresses that dominate advertising in Western culture. In this way the pixel vixens may be fairly unremarkable examples of eye candy. However, under the surface the pixel vixens are supercomputers, wireless technologies, the latest 3-D graphic art and voice-recognition software, database programs, search engines, even artificial intelligences—the cutting edge of high-tech innovation. This makes the idoru a gatekeeper of what Laney rightly described as an "unthinkable volume of information." In a culture where a subject's identity, history, wealth, and health are increasingly dependent on and configured according to the information stored in myriad databases, a gatekeeper or infomediary occupies an important, powerful, and privileged position in the network, as the one responsible for keeping records and managing data, privy to the professional and personal digits, without which the computerized subject would cease to be intelligible within an informational economy and culture.

MYA

In 1999 Motorola Corporation introduced their Web-W/O-Wires™ program, a hardware and software combination they would sell to wireless Internet service providers. Subscribers could use voice-recognition software to access Internet-based data over the phone, which would be read by a computerized voice, synthesized to sound "female." In our image-driven visual cyberculture, the successful marketing of this voice-activated service (called Myosphere™) depends in part on the creation of a graphical icon to attract consumers' attention. Thus Motorola commissioned Digital Domain, the special effects company formed by James Cameron of *The Terminator* and *Titanic* fame, to develop *Mya*, a pixel vixen to appear in Web-W/O-Wires advertisements and be the face of Motorola's Myosphere (Figure 5.2).

Mya made a highly visible public debut as part of the televised production of the 1999 Academy Awards, showcased in a sixty-second primetime infomercial. On Oscar night the television audience was introduced to "Tinsel Town's freshest face, and latest It girl"; a 3-D CGI animated *Mya* character emerged from a limousine and proceeded to strut down a virtual red-carpeted catwalk, drawing gasps from the simulated crowd of onlookers and digitized paparazzi. In full pixelated glory, *Mya* appeared tall and ultra slim, wearing an iridescent floor-length shoulder-baring gown in an indescribable shade of not-quite coral/pink/silver, clinging provocatively to her supermodel phy-

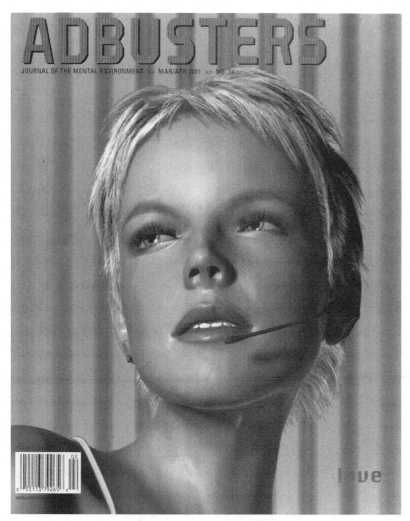

Figure 5.2 *Adbusters* cover story features Motorola's cyberassistant *Mya.*

sique, and complementing her shimmering white skin and chic, short, gleam-
ing platinum-blond hair. Immodestly, *Mya* announced that she would soon
"change your life," and confirmed, "Yes. I read the Web to you." *Mya* will act
as an infomediary—serving up data (from the Internet, stock reports, sports,
weather, traffic reports, local news, and your PDA), and shipping out information (placing phone calls, leaving electronic and voice messages).

After her explosive (and expensive) splash into the public realm, *Mya* virtually disappeared back into the computer labs that are coding and uploading
her. This isn't surprising, since her CGI form was designed as a spectacle to
attract us to her real asset: her voice—after all, she is an information reader.

Figure 5.3 *Artbyte Magazine* cover story features Internet search engine character *Syndi.*

Mya is not simply a fictional character, she is also the mascot for serious biz in the infotech world: mediating a user's most personal digits. The word *My-a,* sounds very much like it could be the root of *my-assistant,* which reflects the direction that infotech companies are moving in, to offer increasingly personalized services, enabling users to filter and configure their information intake according to individualized preferences and needs (as in *My AOL, My Computer, My Yahoo!*).

As part of our informational culture of speed, digitalization, and automation, it is crucially important that the pixel vixen is perceived as "a character that people instantly like," because, as Julie Roth, Motorola's director of marketing explains, "It is important for people to develop a personal connection within the virtual world."[5] Margaret Morse would agree, explaining that

"As impersonal relations with machines and/or physically removed strang-ers characterize ever-larger areas of work and private life, more and more personal and subjective means of virtually engaging with machines and/or distant strangers are elaborated" (Morse 5). With this cyberpop, Motorola is marketing the perfect virtual secretary, always on call, at her post and ready to serve, consistent and reliable, and most importantly perhaps, without the ambition to climb the corporate ladder, not apt to leave on a honeymoon, and guaranteed not to require maternity leave. *Mya* manages the mundane—data within virtual "in" and "out" boxes—but what makes her extraordinary is her sultry voice on the other end of a telephone, on-call 24/7, ready to make appointments and e-mail messages more appealing. *Mya* may be the celebrity "It" girl, the fantasy pixel vixen in a slinky gown, "the darling of the e-world" and "the name on everyone's lips"—as her infomercial states—but part of her appeal is the fantasy that this virtual celebrity female is not too busy being famous to give the user her complete attention, day and night.[6]

Although Geoffrey Frost, vice president of consumer communications at Motorola promises, "We may give you your choice of personalities" for the synthespian construct that fronts the Myosphere technology—by electing to use the figure of a blond, blue-eyed, Caucasian, seductive animated female character to launch their service, Motorola is not only promoting the predict-able sexual sell, but they are also helping to normalize the assumption that the consumer of information and computer technology products and services is both male and straight.[7] In this sense, the *Mya* cyberpop figure can be read as depending on, borrowing from, and retrenching sexist stereotypes.

In spite of Motorola's claims to the contrary, their CGI girl did not "spring out of nowhere;" *Mya* and other pixel vixens are part of a historical trajectory that includes not only the obvious predecessors such as the fembot and cyborg, but also the phenomenon in which female bodies are used as ornaments or accessories in advertisements (and at trade shows) designed to sexualize and humanize technofetish objects from fast cars to fast computers to fast Internet connections for (predominantly) male consumers. But there is a limit to the amount of anthropomorphizing involved in the creation of a successful pixel vixen: Motorola envisioned *Mya* as a spokesperson [*sic*] with "a face, a name, and a personality," and decided to "humanize her," but they were careful not to commission photo realism, and insisted that the graphic designers exagger-ate the pixel vixen's digital "nature" (Roth 2000).

In *Mya's* case her hyperreality was achieved through making both her skin and dress appear to shine and shimmer with a distinctly inhuman (alien?) luminescence. This shiny quality was a requirement, explains Fred Raimondi (visual effects supervisor and animation director at Digital Domain) since "in the first shot we showed them [at Motorola] she looked too real, we had to pull her back" into the realm of artifice, which is considered to be a large part of her appeal (Barboza). This digital artifice needed to be added on, however, since the design of *Mya*, like all of the pixel vixens profiled in this chapter, was based on film footage of a real (human) woman. The process of designing *Mya* began, Raimondi explains, with the casting and filming of a live female model that was then "deleted." The design team then added simulation details, since the goal was "not necessarily a photo-realistic woman, as the client didn't want to go in that direction," according to Raimondi (Blair). In fact, being too lifelike may spell virtual or literal erasure for the pixel vixen, as was the case for the nameless cyberbabe that *W Magazine* commissioned for a cover photo, but then opted to delete/cancel. A composite of four human models, *W*'s pixel vixen was axed because the figure was "too perfect," according to Edward Leida, *W Magazine's* design director, and was "missing the nuance that would make her unique"—or uniquely digital.[8]

As Robert Hamilton suggests, these feminine icons are built according to an exaggerated digitality: "artifice becomes part of the charm and much of the reason that these images are appealing to their audiences."[9] However, Hamilton continues, "the extreme separation from reality hinders (although doesn't necessarily prevent) any normative social function that these images may have." In her analysis of virtual reality environments, Anne Balsamo observes that new computer technologies "do not guarantee that people will use the information in better ways"; instead Balsamo finds that "it is just as likely that these new technologies will be used primarily to tell old stories—stories that reproduce, in high-tech guise, traditional narratives about the gendered, race-marked body" (132). Some of the graphical and narrative choices surrounding the pixel vixen promote and rehearse sexist stereotypes that objectify women and eroticize male dominance. At the same time, on close examination of their encodings and decodings, their design, and their reception by male and female audiences, the idorus become thicker than they might at first seem, slightly ambiguous, and while predictable and stereotypical, they are also innovative and full of playful possibility.

ANANOVA

> *Ananova* is a creature of the Web. She is born of digital DNA—the bits, bytes and data streams of information that course through the veins of the Internet.

—from the official site, Ananova.com

Ananova was conceived in 1999 and made her debut in an Internet launch in June 2000. On the surface, like *Mya*, *Ananova* appears as a young Caucasian female, with a slim shapely figure, short stylized hair, and full makeup including deep crimson lipstick. *Ananova* smiles a lot, and has a habit of cocking her head to the side, and looking upwards with enormous anime-like hyperreal blue eyes. Her profile indicates that *Ananova* is 5 ft 8 in. and 28 years old. She is described as "quietly intelligent," though "in reality she [is] hyperintelligent and capable of carrying out thousands of tasks a second, interacting with many different people at the same time," yet "she's not a show-off."[10] *Ananova* "works" as a virtual newscaster on the same 24/7 shift that *Mya* will have.

Underneath the digitalized surface of her graphical design, and between the lines of the imaginative and elaborate fictions designed to humanize her, *Ananova* is a superintelligent computer program with a search engine that roams the Internet and looks for news-breaking information about current events. A fraction of this data is processed and read by a computer-simulated feminine human voice, while a 3-D computer graphic animation serves as a talking head. In addition to appearing on the Internet, there are plans to make *Ananova's* cybercasts (like *Mya's*) available through wireless service providers to mobile devices (PDAs, cell phones, digital watches, wireless laptop computers), thus somewhat multiplying and diversifying the user base, reaching people with different levels of access to electronic resources. *Ananova* is an infomediary and a vector or conductor hyperlinking users to the flows of information that structure digital culture. One of the goals of the *Ananova* project is to develop a personalized push media service with the ability to track and "know what you are interested in and alert you the moment something happens that's relevant to you."[11]

The enthusiastic reception of *Ananova* and the growth of her fan base cannot be wholly accounted for by the quality of the Ananova.com site's cybercasts. Even with the fastest Internet connection, like many Webcasting news sites, the streaming video feed animations often stall, become distorted, and "pixelated," and the sound and transmission quality is unpredictable due to net congestion and other factors. In order to facilitate users' attachment to this cyberpop celebrity and thus the service, and to encourage the formation of virtual relationships and thus brand loyalty, a significant amount of space on *Ananova's* official Web site (www.Ananova.com) is utilized to concoct elaborate fictions about the pixel vixen's personality. We are encouraged to believe that *Ananova* is an example of ALife (artificial life) or AI (artificial intelligence), and to think of "her" as a human-like smart machine that can correct its/her functioning as a result of experience and human interaction. *Ananova's* goal, the mythical narrative indicates, is to become more human, or perhaps posthuman, since she is also presented as self-reflexively, unabashedly, and proudly digital, virtual, and unnatural.

Like *Mya's* designers, the team constructing *Ananova* had to walk a fine line between humanizing their character and maintaining her cybernetic qualities; thus *Ananova* has unnaturally green hair, and the site includes behind-the-scenes information about her coding and uploading, complete with 3-D models of her "pixelated" skeletal frame. We learn that *Ananova's* visage is a composite of features from the faces of famous and ordinary people, painstakingly selected from over 100 images then morphed together.[12] Yet these digital details do not discourage users from identifying with *Ananova*; the Web site features *Ananova* look-alike contests, where female fans, some of whom have dyed their hair green, submit photographs showing their resemblance to this virtual character.

In this feedback loop, real women attempt to model themselves after a virtual female, who is not modeled on a real woman, but a morphic composite. And if you can't look like *Ananova*, you can have her look like you instead; in the future, fans can order up a personal configuration of the cybercaster that suits their individual tastes. Her owners confirm that the green-haired-white-skinned-youthful-female version of *Ananova* is simply a prototype, and in the future, "we fully intend to allow every individual to customize *Ananova*, right down to age, race and gender" (Ananova.com). What is more likely, in the age of nakednews.com, the Web site that features fully nude female (and male) newscasters, is that users will become accustomed to white, young, sexualized, and feminized icons resembling *Ananova* or *Mya*, as they proliferate and become normalized in digital culture.

The *Ananova* project is a remediation of traditional newscasts, promoted not as an alternative venue for receiving information about world events, but rather as an improved form of news transmission. *Ananova* is allegedly "capable of sourcing a million different stories and delivering them instantaneously to a million different people, depending on their interests" (Ananova.com). Her designers brag, "Try getting Dan Rather to do that."[13] But is the virtual newscaster as pixel vixen a threat to the news establishment, personified by veteran anchorman Dan Rather? Instead, the design choices that *Ananova's* designers dismiss as arbitrary accurately reflect and reify the inequities of the media industry when it comes to selecting female news anchors. For a female to become a success in broadcast media, she needs to closely resemble the *Ananova* character, with the exception of her green hair; in fact, she likely has to be white and blond, and certainly young looking and slim figured.

As Robert Hamilton suggested, the virtuality and digital artifice incorporated into the design of the pixel vixens, even their exaggerated artificiality and tongue-in-cheek elements, do not guarantee that they will not have negative side effects in terms of the messages they transmit about gender. Between look-alike contests, fan clubs celebrating virtual celebrity, and animations livening up PC desktops, the *Ananova* phenomena may seem to be silly and harmless fun; however, the repercussions of this modeling of an unattainable, virtual ideal femininity as the face of the digital future, and the idea that femininity can be customized to order, seem more controversial when we consider the case of another pixel vixen, *Webbie Tookay*, who is a virtual supermodel taking the fashion industry by storm.

WEBBIE TOOKAY

She is never too tired to work and she is available all the time. [. . .] Also, she does not have a personal life that interferes with her work and she doesn't age and she doesn't gain weight.

—Luciana Abreu, Director, Illusion2K Virtual Models and Actresses Management[14]

Webbie can eat nothing and keep her curves. . . She can be on time, or in two places at one time, and you know she will never get a pimple or ask for a raise. Sometimes I wish all models were virtual.

—John Casablancas, Founder, Elite Model Management (La Ferla)

In 1999, the same year that *Ananova* was conceived and *Mya* was produced, Elite Model Management entered into partnership with a Brazilian company called Illusion2K and Atlanta-based Giant Studios to design a $1 million project: virtual supermodels billed as "a new concept of beauty for the next millennium."[15] For a licensing fee, these animated mannequins are "available for any kind of work in any media" including Internet, films, video, advertising, and fashion shoots (Illusion2K.com). According to Illusion2K director Luciana Abreu, the virtual supermodel is part of the trend toward personalization technologies, insofar as "the client comes to us and tells us what they need, and we will produce [a virtual model] to perform exactly what they want" (Silverman).

The first of these virtual models to be publicly launched is a light-skinned, blond-haired, blue-eyed, young and slim-figured digital mannequin. As the prototype, *Webbie Tookay* is, like *Ananova* and *Mya* before her, a digital hybrid: she is a composite of fragmented body parts and facial features, drawn from Elite's top models, combined to reflect "the perfect measurements" according to the company (see <www.elite3k.com>). Reportedly, "parts" such as the legs, the chin, or the breasts, of "a voluptuous blond, a stunning Latina, and a beautiful Asian woman" were morphed together to create her (inexplicably Caucasian and even Aryan) look (Illusion2K.com). However, the database of model "types" provided by Elite's roster (which historically has included megastars Kate Moss, Linda Evangelista, Claudia Schiffer, Tyra Banks, Amber Valletta, Isabella Rossellini, Giselle Bundchen, Naomi Campbell, and Cindy Crawford) proved insufficient for Steven Stahlberg, the Swedish animator who designed *Webbie*. Stahlberg admitted he needed to edit and improve or upgrade the composite graphic image to "slim her down, make her chin a little smaller, make her legs a little longer," though at the same time Luciana Abreu claims that "she is not that skinny," and her figure reflects "the major tendencies of today's models."[16]

It is probably a good thing that Illusion2K is more concerned with creating a perfect simulation rather than with the pursuit of "realism," if the example of fellow pixel vixen *Kyoko Date* is relevant. According to Robert Hamilton, Japan's *Kyoko Date* was created as a pop music star, but it soon became apparent that she could not compete with other fully simulated digital females such as *Shirori*—star of a best-selling computer game. The difference between these two idorus, according to Hamilton, was that *Kyoko* was constructed (like *Webbie*) through morphing together images of "fragmented" body parts from photographs of top models, in this case from Japan's Horipro Agency. As a result, she appeared excessively "real" and could not satisfy the market of predominantly male audiences for idorus in Japan—who were more comfortable with the fully fictional and fantastic *Shirori* than with all-too-human looking *Kyoko*. Hamilton concludes that "there seems to have been a fatal flaw in logic when creating" *Kyoko Date*, insofar as her designers underestimated the appeal of the virtual, the draw of the digital, and the fantasy of the simulated synthetic female, and got carried away with trying to make a pixel vixen that could pass as real.

Reportedly, Illusion2K plans to launch a Web site featuring newscasting and other features, perhaps giving *Ananova* and *Mya* a run for their money. The target audience for the *Webbie Planet* Web site is the 14-25 age group, according to Elite, a market they hope will form a virtual community of fashion-conscious e-commerce around the *Webbie* character. "We want to develop a relationship [with] visitors to the Web," Abreu said, so that users will "become *Webbie's* friends and they will give her information" (Silverman). Ideally, *Webbie's* visitors/friends will be a source of data for marketers about their fashion preferences, budgets, average sizes, and so forth. The connection between the rhetoric of "personal relationship" and "friendship" and the business goal of collecting market(ing) research helps to explain why Motorola promotes *Mya* as "everyone's best friend," because she constructs and manages a database of users' personal digital histories, information that presumably will be a commodity that Motorola can sell.[17]

In order to facilitate this virtual community and friendship, *Webbie* is humanized to the extent that she (like *Ananova*) is marketed with a simulated personality profile, programmed to be "concerned about what's going on in the world"; she is especially interested in environmental politics and reproductive freedom (Illusion2K.com). *Webbie* is described as a very happy young woman who uses beauty products, adores chocolate—which does not pose a problem since she cannot gain weight—loves disco and animals—especially dogs.[18] And despite her flexibility, *Webbie* does draw the line at wearing fur, according to Abreu. This shouldn't compromise *Webbie's* career, however, because her other qualities clearly outweigh any troublesome personal politics: namely, *Webbie* has perfect skin, hair, stable weight, and perhaps most importantly, she has no complaints about working long hours, and no demanding "boyfriends, lawyers, or personal managers" to advocate for her rights, fees, or freedoms. Designer Steven Stahlberg aimed to create a "woman who would be physical perfection without the mental and verbal grief" of a real human female.[19]

When asked whether the use of virtual supermodels will have any trickle-down negative effects on real women working in the fashion industry as models, spokespersons for Elite foresee no problems, since "there are things only a human can do." Matt Madden, Director of Research and Development for Giant Studios (an animation studio) is more specific about the ways in which the technology could liberate and benefit human models, suggesting that real-life Elite models could be digitized, so that "different versions" of them can be stored in a computer and reused or "restructured" in order to "produce an appealing marketing piece for less cost."[20] The real-life model "would own a piece of that" repurposed product, Madden reassures. Furthermore, "obviously you wouldn't capture or portray a supermodel without their permission," Madden concludes, most especially because in order to achieve the highest level of simulated realism, "you would always use their voice and probably their motion as well" (Schiff). Whether or not he intended to, Madden's insights make it clear that the virtual supermodel project is a form of remediation, an upgrade, marketed as a superior form of female model, without the interference of emotions or the physical limitations of an organic human subject.

SYNDI

Look into my eyes, click on an icon, and we're off. There's a metropolis of possibilities inside. After a time, I become more discerning. I learn your tastes. I look for you on my own. I don't just search for you. I search for the ideal you.

—Syndi, Artbyte Magazine 1999 (Figure 5.3)

But then again, we're all just a set of codes. It's what you do with them that counts. [. . .] In a world blanketed by media, we need a portal for our emotions, an image to love. Images are so real.

—Syndi

Mya and *Webbie* are still in development and at this time there is scarcely any information about them circulating on the Net apart from official press releases. In comparison, *Ananova* is now cybercasting, and her site includes "the A-Files," with official background information about her, more of which can be found on her (seemingly officially sanctioned) fan sites, such as "Club Ananova." But the most complete dataset of background information on the design, programming goals, and vision of a pixel vixen belongs to *Syndi* the "creative agent," "celebrity portal," and "search engine with subjectivity," designed by artist Jim Anderson for *Artbyte* magazine.[21] This is ironic because *Syndi* may be the most virtual pixel vixen of all, since she is print bound.

To date, *Syndi's* existence is confined to a collection of articles and images in *Artbyte*, an avant-garde digital art and culture publication. Unlike *Mya*, *Ananova*, or *Webbie*, who are 3-D CGI animations operating "for real" on the Internet or television, *Syndi* is a pure cyberfiction trapped and frozen in the glossy, distinctly static paper pages of a magazine. There we find what we could call her "blueprints"—detailed descriptions about *Syndi's* potential as "an intelligent agent who can mirror your needs creatively" (Anderson, 1999). Theoretically then, *Syndi* incorporates the user's preferences, needs, and desires, searching the Internet for information you might not even know you want—she is a vector for personalized push media technology.

In terms of her relationship to the other pixel vixens, *Syndi* is closest to *Rei Toei*, the AI idoru from the pages of William Gibson's novel, since *Syndi* is a purely conceptual and artistic project. However, her "physical" resemblance to *Mya* and the other digital females is uncanny, as is her intended "use" as a tool for the information age, an infomediary role. Unlike *Mya*, *Ananova* or *Webbie Tookay*, *Syndi* doesn't appear to be in development, for sale, seeking corporate sponsorship, or trying to attract and please a Real Life (RL) user base (outside of *Artbyte* subscribers). Perhaps as a result, the creators behind the fictional *Syndi Project* are extremely candid about the fact that if *Syndi* were to malfunction, become incompatible with the network, or outdated, or "fail at exchange with other points in the system, then she's erased" (Anderson, 1999). Information is not just *Syndi's* job, it is her lifeline. Not unlike the replicants in *Blade Runner*, *Syndi* can be "retired." This might give us cause to wonder about the cyberethics of erasing/deleting a digital female who has been carefully humanized, and with whom users have been encouraged to develop a personal (if virtual) and intimate relationship.

Like *Ananova*, *Webbie*, and *Mya*, *Syndi* is actually designed to be in many (virtual) places at once, meeting the needs of innumerable users simultaneously. And yet like magic, it appears that each user has her full attention. This is heady stuff, an exercise in virtual empowerment, as *Syndi's* creators acknowledge: "People who interact with *Syndi* feel fulfilled, inspired, important, and enlightened" (Anderson, 1999). Margaret Morse concurs, arguing that "the responsiveness of images to our commands and the ability to act at a distance in the world by simply saying or pointing or gesturing can create a feeling of omnipotence that [. . .] can be terrifying or delightful, depending on the context and cultural frames constructed for virtual realms" (Morse, *Virtualities* 15).

UNSECURING GENDER

What exactly is the radical potential of the pixel vixen? If we consider Haraway's claim that the cyborg figure is notoriously unfaithful to its origins, together with the professed intentions of the CGI designers to offer flexible "skins" for their services, some interesting possibilities arise. For example, if part of the idoru's function is to be a placeholder in cyberspace for the user and their data body, what could be described as the idoru-avatar, and if, as Sherry Turkle (*Second Self*) suggests, users have a desire to see themselves reflected on the screen, then it is quite probable that, if the technology is flexible enough, we will see a radically diverse population of synthespian newsreaders, search engines, and virtual assistants, which continue to diversify as the user base of the Web expands. There is evidence to support this possibility, if we look to the developments in female online gaming communities as documented by several researchers including Allyson Polsky. As women and girls began playing computer games, Polsky observes, "they began producing experimental skins that challenge real world gender ideals and aesthetics of both their male peers and the male-dominated gaming companies."[22] Specifically, these gaming avatars were oftentimes hybridized and monstrous or alien female figures, pointing to the trend toward a posthuman paradigm for future digital identities.

Furthermore, if the option to customize the pixel vixens is truly made available, then the original versions, which were predominantly female, light-skinned, and blond, would be revealed as simply the preferences of the original design team—and this would decenter the pixel vixens as "models" and make them appear only as "versions" that can be upgraded through customizing. (As Sandy Stone notes, "many of the engineers currently debating the form and nature of cyberspace are young men in their late teens and twenties, and they are at times preoccupied with the postpubescent. This group will generate the codes and descriptors by which bodies in cyberspace are represented.")[23] This would be an important development, since the idea of an upgrade is associated with "improvement." R. L. Rutsky, in his analysis of digital and cyberpunk aesthetics, describes the capacity that new media and cyberpop has for constant remixings, especially in terms of its capacity for "continual unsecuring"—for "reproduction, alteration, redesign, editing" (118). If the promises of Motorola (*Mya*) and Associated Press (*Ananova*) are made real, the customizable "skin" options for idorus may allow for de- and reconstruction of representations of digital humans in ways that unsecure modernist (and even postmodernist) discourses about humans, technology, bodies, gender, and race.

Webbie Tookay and other CGI girls both reference and resist the codes of femininity, in the process revealing that the information of gender is part of the social programming of cyberculture, it is intentionally encoded rather than naturally occurring, and thus while gender codes may be essential to the functioning of subjects and culture, they are also hackable. On the one hand, the pixel vixens *mark up* the information that is femininity in such a way as to draw attention to its unnaturalness, artificiality, and playful possibility. Their unreality is exaggerated in an aesthetic of digital artifice. At the same time, in their recitation of certain stereotypical codes and behaviors associated with patriarchal paradigms of femininity and heterosexuality, *Mya, Ananova, Webbie,* and *Syndi* replay and perhaps upgrade the technologies or mechanisms of feminization and gender performance in disappointingly predictable ways, showcasing superslim, white, heterosexy femininity as the epitomization of what is desirable for female cybersubjectivity.

The pixel vixens play a powerful role as infomediaries, facilitating, transmitting, and popularizing—not just the infotech they are created with and for, but also—a high-tech cultural imaginary. They are the poster girls for Generation D, encouraging users to consume and covet technogear and infoservices. Models for the well-connected, mobile, flexible, fast-paced digital lifestyle, CGI girls seduce us with promises of e-powerment through immersion in the mode of information, mediated by, of course, the pixel vixens and their sponsors. In the process, they become a component in the creation of cyberculture, part of its iconography.[24]

6

Technoeroticism and Interactivity:
The *Lara Croft* Phenomenon

At the intersection of technology and eroticism lies technoeroticism,
the passionate celebration of technological objects of desire.

—**Claudia Springer (1)**

From what Sandy Stone calls *cyborg envy* to gear lust to intense almost "interpersonal" relationships that develop between humans and our machines—
technoeroticism involves an experimental unsecuring of the binary separating
the organic from the "machinic," or the real from the simulated (Stone, *War
of Desire*). Technoeroticism can take many forms. For Haraway, it's the pleasure of the cyborg myth. The seduction of symbiosis and potent fusions. In
his essay on "The Erotic Ontology of Cyberspace," Michael Heim connects
technoeroticism to a fascination with digital aesthetics; for Heim, virtual
worlds replace the messy complexity and ambiguity of everyday life with the
beauty of "precise structures" and a world "clothed in beaming colors" (82).
For Sherry Turkle, technoeroticism is the "holding power" of the machine
and its screen, the seductive interface between humans and their computers,
based on virtual interdependence, trust, and even love (*Life on the Screen* 6).
We become passionately attached to our machines. To achieve this connec-

tion, Claudia Springer explains, cybertechnologies are often feminized—and in a culture that aligns the feminine with an ethic of care, this encourages empathetic bonding, so that our machines can seemingly reflect, extend, and absorb the user's ego. Likewise, in cyberpop, as Judith Halberstam observes, "technology is given a female identity when it must seduce the user into thinking of it as desirable."[1]

This was the idea behind Apple's groundbreaking "1984" Super Bowl advertisement for the Macintosh, which featured a scantily clad blond female icon standing in for the machine and selling us screen culture. It's a resilient logic, such that a generation of computers, consumers, and Super Bowl fans later, another sexy, blond, white cyberfemale (*Mya* the virtual assistant) is used to sell us *personalized* computer technologies in a half-time TV spot courtesy of Motorola. From Maria in *Metropolis* to *Mya* by Motorola, to the robotic beauties of two remakes of *Stepford Wives*, the manufactured cultural fascination with artificial females evidences a technoerotic impulse and an alignment between femininity and artificiality. The question becomes then, what kind of cybercultural values are encoded in the visual rhetoric of technoeroticized cyberpop, how do they enculturate? And, knowing that cyberpop is both celebratory and critical of the status quo, how does technofetishism reify the rules of formation in cyberculture, and unsecure them? With these issues in mind, we are now in a position to consider the productive ambiguity of *Lara Croft*, a cyberpop figure that reflects and resists the discourse of technoeroticism.

Of all the pixel vixens in the world of cyberculture, one in particular has been remediated from computer games to comic books, to feature films, and even to human look-alike contests. The pixel vixen *Lara Croft* is the name of the central character in *Tomb Raider*, an action-adventure-strategy game designed by Sony for Playstation® and for use on home computers. *Lara* is no longer limited to the virtual reality environment of the *Tomb Raider* computer game, as it is reconfigured and repurposed for numerous applications, morphing from a fictional character to a "real" phenomenon in her own right, with an adoring audience of digerati. As such, *Lara*'s programmers and fans join with journalists, and cultural critics writing for magazines, journals, newspapers, and online, to excitedly compare the merits of this pixel vixen to "real women," and speculate about the virtual lust of two generations of ("real") men (and women) seduced by *Lara*.

This cyberpop icon achieves notoriety as a cultural phenomenon, functioning as part of the trinity of BLUR in network society by reifying the values of connectivity, speed, and intangibility. As part of the flow of information that characterizes (and creates) the current cyberculture, the *Lara* persona and brand is especially interesting because it is an interactive fiction, encouraging users to develop virtual relationships and be seduced by the screen. By examining the codes of this cyberpop figure, analyzing her official and unofficial representations and popular interpretations, in this chapter we trace the ideologies about gender, technology, power, sexuality, and digital capital that are (explicitly and inexplicitly) embedded in her programming and responsible for the widespread appeal of this pixel vixen. The heroine of *Tomb Raider* has as many bottom lines as she does remediated versions and upgrades; some of those spinoffs are more successful than others, some are compatible with feminist analytics, while others are paradoxically and predictably stereotypically sexist.

BACKGROUND: TOMB RAIDER

The object of the *Tomb Raider* game is to locate and liberate ancient treasures and artifacts from centuries-old tombs, caves, and other remote locations around the globe, while defending oneself, or rather, enabling *Lara* to defend herself, against a host of enemies. The neogothic aesthetic of tombs, caves, mansions, and other labyrinthine settings are unstable environments, flooded, crumbling, booby-trapped, and inhabited by hostile others. To negotiate these terrains requires enormous athletic skill, strength, and endurance (for jumping, climbing, kicking, running, diving, and swimming), courage (for dodging swinging blades, lightning bolts, attacking bears, tarantulas, raptors, and assorted bad guys), not to mention an aptitude for handing various weapons (shotguns, handguns, Uzis) and fast-moving vehicles (motorcycles, speedboats, and snowmobiles).

Luckily, *Lara Croft* was designed for just such a life: each version of the game comes with a dossier of fictional background information (a cyberbio) about the central character; we learn that *Lara* is an archaeologist by trade, a tireless and fearless extreme-sports-loving type of adventuress, highly trained in handing arms. *Lara* is a loner by nature, single and orphaned (no dependents or family) with a fairly flexible schedule (independently wealthy). In *Tomb Raider,* the challenge is to make it across a cavern or through a cave, and to do so means putting *Lara*'s virtual life on the line. This, it seems, is a scenario already complex enough without adding in worries about the ethics of shooting opponents (human and animal) on sight and with intention to kill, or the destruction of ancient natural environments including ritual burial sites, or the theft of cultural artifacts. But then again, this is a first-person shooter video game, not exactly a genre well known for its narratives of cultural sensitivity, respect for others, enlightened gender attitudes, or nonviolent conflict resolution.

Tomb Raider is selling a fantasy, a type of virtual reality environment the player can become immersed and lost in, an escape from the mundane routines of the everyday into a fictional world of intrigue and adventure. The central character is an important element of this fantasy, operating as a component designed to seduce players into the realm of interactivity that will keep them at the screen through their identification with and (virtual) participation in her travels, trials, and quests—through numerous editions of the Playstation game. But *Tomb Raider* is also selling more than interactive fiction, technoeroticism, and fantasy; it is also promoting the central tenets of digital capitalism, the key conceptual tropes and ideologies that structure the discursive formation of cyberculture. The success of *Tomb Raider* and its protagonist *Lara Croft* is explained by tracing the links between this cultural production and the network of discourses and rules of formation that form the conceptual architecture of digital culture (such as intangibility and virtuality, speed and mobility, connectivity and interactivity).

CYBERCELEBRITY, DIGITAL SIREN

Between its release in 1996 and April 2000, *Tomb Raider* sold more than 21 million games, earning $500 million, including merchandise sales. The game and its pixel vixen protagonist *Lara* are the subject of more than 56,000 (official and unofficial) Internet fan sites.[2] Moreover, *Lara* has been extensively remediated: there exist *Lara Croft/Tomb Raider* comic books, candy bars, action doll figures, and clothing lines. *Tomb Raider* is an international phenomenon, promoted worldwide and produced in several languages. *Lara* is the subject of numerous art exhibitions in the US and Europe, and appears on television in the US and Europe selling products including cars and soft drinks. "She" has appeared on over 200 international magazine covers including *Time, Rolling Stone, Newsweek,* and *The Face.* In the US media there are many examples of anthropomorphized *Lara: Details* magazine selected her as one of the sexiest women of the year. *Forbes* magazine included *Lara* in its list of the wealthiest celebrities. *Entertainment Weekly*'s "It" issue included her as one of the "100 most creative people," and *Time Digital* voted her one of the 50 cyberelite (along with Bill Gates and George Lucas). Gucci reportedly paid $30,000 to use the character to model their fashions, and Irish rock band U2 contracted Core to provide images of the figure onscreen as part of one of their world tours. Paramount pictures invested $100 million to make a *Tomb Raider* feature film starring Angelina Jolie. As a result of this extraordinary publicity, aggressive marketing, and extensive remediation, the popularity of *Lara* extends beyond the community of computer gamers; she is recognized as a global virtual celebrity (or idoru) and cyberpop icon for the digital age.

Exactly what is so seductive about *Lara Croft*? On the surface or screen level, it is impossible to overlook her hyperreal-curvaceous figure, the product of the same adolescent male fantasies responsible for at least three generations of female amazon and fembot comic book graphics. Described as "Beyond-Barbie" *Lara Croft* cuts a voluptuous figure in her 88-24-36 dimensions;

Figure 6.1   Rendition of Eidos Interactive's *Lara Croft* pixel vixen.

dressed in Lycra® microtops, Neoprene wetsuits, string bikinis, and the like (Figure 6.1).[3] The *Lara* idoru is eternally young and beautiful, always available to "play," and is 100% under the control of the user. Part of the pleasure of engaging with *Lara* is that, like a toy (and unlike "real" women), she doesn't talk back (*Forbes* magazine observes: "When *Lara's* got a problem, she doesn't talk it through, she blasts it to smithereens."[4] Similarly, a Core Design spokesperson compared *Lara* to "Barbie with guns.") *Lara* doesn't make demands, and she can be switched off if the user gets bored or the *Lara*-user predicament gets too complicated. With a deep English accent that her creators suggest American audiences love, *Lara* makes sighing, groaning, and grunting noises as she runs, jumps, kicks, shoots, swims, and (unfortunately) whenever she gets attacked and dies—sounds which some male users admit they find erotic.[5]

With all of this going for her, it is understandable that *Details* and *Entertainment Weekly* pronounced *Lara* one of the sexiest "It" girls around. Sex does sell, but *Lara's* polygons are not the only reason she's such a blockbuster hit. At least as important if not more crucial for her success is the fact that *Lara* is a very specific type of fantasy girl: she's made of not just curves and courage, but pixels and programming. And in a culture that is obsessed with being wired the success of the *Lara Croft* video game figure is *virtually* guaranteed because of her capacity to network with the user in a feedback loop of interactivity. Likewise, by extending this observation, we could have foreshadowed that the filmic version of *Tomb Raider* would not be as successful as the game versions, because of the lack of interactivity between the (rather passive) spectator and the pixel vixen's action-adventures on the silver screen—a point we will return to.

Lara Croft encourages technoeroticism; it is very likely true that, as game designer Stuart Campbell suggested, "*Lara*'s popularity comes down to two words. And the second one is jugs."[6] Yet it is more accurately the figure's virtuality and intangibility that is the key to fans' fascination and attachment. As in the case of *Mya, Webbie, Ananova, Syndi, Kyoko Date* and other pixel vixens, it is *Lara Croft*'s digital nature, cybernetic artifice, and interactivity that account for her success in many complex and contradictory roles: dreamgirl and cyberbabe, avatar and body double, feminist caricature and postfeminist role model, eye candy, mechanism for enculturating terminal subjects, escapist entertainment, and advertisement encouraging the consumption of digital commodities. Here we consider each of these roles, with special attention to how they exaggerate or depend on a discourse of virtuality, one of the key conceptual nodes in the discursive formation of cyberculture. In order to redescribe the *Lara Croft* figure through a cyberpoetic lens, it is integral to keep in focus the ambiguity of pixel vixens. By doing so it is possible to show how they are more than cartoon figures or digital titillations, but rather figurative nodes in a network of discourses about gender, technology, power, information, subjects, bodies, and desire, which resonate with, resist, redeliver, and repurpose the status quo of the digital capitalist culture that produces them.

ELUSIVE DREAMGIRL

> It is a fantastic game. [. . .] The woman looks great, and has such unbelievable breasts, and despite all of this, I still have her totally under control. When does that ever happen in real life?
>
> **—Mark, gamer, cited in official marketing publication of Eidos Interactive[7]**

Rebecca Schneider argues that the seductiveness of fantasy girls or dreamgirls like *Lara*, lies in their unattainability. Schneider writes, "Their inaccessibility simply enflames the desire for access, compelling the purchase of the commodity pitched. Though the product is infinitely acquirable, one can never deplete the product's elusive double, the dreamgirl on its surface [. . .] Dreamgirls sing the inexhaustible value of what you can't possess though it is in your own hands."[8] In a considerably more politically troubling analysis, Toby Guard, the graphic designer responsible for *Lara Croft*, also underscores inaccessibility as the chief seductive aspect of his figure, admitting that *Lara* represents "an empowered woman [. . .] not a smutty sex object, but an inaccessible gun-toting bitch."[9] *Lara* is an elusive virtual dreamgirl in several ways: in the game itself, *Lara* remains virtually one step ahead of the player at all times. *Tomb Raider* is *Lara*-focused, and the player sees the action through her perspective, or from a vantage point just behind or beside her. This makes *Lara* appear intimately close but strangely just out of reach, as if she is on the other side of a transparent looking glass that acts as an impenetrable barrier. *Lara* spends almost all of her time in the game focused on her quest, paying little attention to the player. This can make the game seems somehow voyeuristic, almost as if we are watching *Lara*'s movements secretly, through the screen, instead of controlling her every flickering pixel. Cultural critic Miranda Sawyer compares *Lara* to "the perfect girl who passes you in the street, whose face you just miss, who never sees you, who you never see again" (Sawyer). The combination of physical perfection, unattainability, and uncontrollability (what Guard misogynistically refers to as the appeal of the "bitch") are the codes designed to seduce the spectator into an interactive (virtual) relationship.

In order to see *Lara* again, and to catch her gaze, we must look to how this pixel vixen is featured by Core Design in promotional materials. This is a second aspect of *Lara*'s virtual dreamgirl effect: in contrast to how she appears in the actual game products, the *Lara* CGI is represented in advertisements and media promotions for *Tomb Raider* in ways that suggest she is centrally focused on seducing the viewer rather than on her archeological career, or even on defending herself from hostile enemies. *Lara* directs a level gaze at the consumer, beckoning them to buy the game(s), take them (and her?) home and directly, and privately, engage with her. However, once home, in the game itself, the *Lara* character appears extremely "pixelated," often at an extreme distance, looking the other way. We can get virtually closer to her only outside the game, for example in advertisements where she is smoothed out into 3-D graphics, increasingly animated CGI ones.

There are at least two versions of *Lara Croft*: one exists in the game, and the other exists as a fantasy in the minds of her players and fans, even her programmers.[10] This second, imaginary *Lara* has a considerably larger audience of spectators and fans who are not necessarily gamers at all. And thus it seems fair to say that she is perhaps more powerful and influential in this virtual representation. Smiling and winking and busting out, popular representations of this pixel vixen might seduce us into thinking that the dynamics of technodesire and the seduction of the virtual are achingly simple. But when she is in her graphic element, the computerized environment, this cyberpop icon is actually extremely demanding, putting players through their paces, challenging them to join her in risky life-or-virtual-death adventures. This is serious gaming business, and while the player may sweat, curse, and cringe, *Lara* epitomizes grace under pressure; a virtual professional, charging forward, she hardly looks back (at us).

This illusive doubling raises several questions. What is going on when a virtual female successfully seduces two generations of (mostly) men to spend $500 million on 21 million versions of her—only to, immediately upon getting home and unwrapping, turn her back on these players and focus on her own selfish quests, leaving them (or us?) behind? Do we need more complicated theories of technodesire, cyberpop media, the pixel vixen, and virtual celebrity, to explain the fandom (and slash fiction) that surrounds *Lara* (and similarly, *Ananova*), amplifying her exposure as an icon in cyberculture? How to account for the proliferation of Web pages, the Hollywood films, and the other cultural productions that are part of the *Lara* brand, if not for the fact that the concept of the virtual or the intangible is incredibly compelling, more seductive even than the challenge of succeeding through levels of a complex computer game? It seems misguided to suggest, as some critics have, that at the root of technodesire for the pixel vixen is men's attraction to virtual dreamgirls because they are easier to control, less trouble, less demanding, and quieter than real women. This may be true. Or it may be the case that the pixel vixen has nothing to do with real women at all, and the real seduction is the interface, the intrigue of engaging with the intangible. Or, because cyberpop representations have irresolvable contradictions and multiple bottom lines, it could be and is likely *both*—a possibility we will return to consider later.

AVATAR AND BODY DOUBLE

> If you've been amazed at how Lara Croft can pack all of that[. . .] er[. . .] *energy* into shorts and a tank top, wait until you see what she can do in your pocket.
>
> **—advertisement for Game Boy™ color version of *Tomb Raider* game**

Should you happen to find yourself captivated watching slender *Lara* bound lithely through *Tomb Raider*'s dark, moist-looking caverns, you will do so without quite forgetting that *Lara* is, in a sense, you.[11] The *Lara Croft* figure functions as an avatar (a persona in pixels, a placeholder in cyberspace designating the user's *fiction of presence*)[12] and a body double. Part of why this virtual female is so appealing is that through the player's connection with her, we are invited to imagine escaping the "meat," transcending material limitations of our own embodiment, and experimenting with gender in cyberspace. The *Lara* avatar has physical capabilities that exceed the player's human capabilities, and so she serves to virtually extend their human functions. It seems fair to suggest that the player will be successful in the game to the extent that they can form something of a symbiotic relationship with *Lara*. This involves an imaginary process of shape-shifting, of identifying with a digital character. As cultural critic Mike Ward reminds us, the technodesire that circulates around *Lara Croft* is connected to the fantasy of *having* her sexually but also to the idea of *being* her.

This line of thought has led critics to examine what might be called a virtual transgendering (or "cybertrans") effect: since the majority of gamers are male, might there be some kind of impulse for gender-identity experimentation involved in developing an intimate, computer-mediated relationship to a virtual female, even going so far as to imagine "playing" at *being* a virtual female? In their research into the immensely popular "digital paper dolls" called KISS software that enable *kisekae* (translated as "changing clothes") in Japanese cyberpop culture, Elena Gorfinkel and Eric Zimmerman studied a subcultural activity that is similar to this cross-gendered identification surrounding the *Tomb Raider* game. Although in Japan, *kisekae* is an activity for young girls, the digital form, KISS (*Kisekae Set System*) has a predominantly male adolescent-to-thirty-something audience of consumers/users. With KISS games, clothing is dragged on or off the figures of anime-inspired prepubescent adolescent CGI girls.[13] Gorfinkel and Zimmerman ask, "So why are these guys playing with dolls? In the unforgiving glare of conventional [North American/Western] wisdom, boys who play dress-up with dolls endanger their heterosexual adult masculinity."[14] Rather than offer a definitive answer in this (largely disappointing) cross-cultural study, the authors speculate about how virtuality, interactivity, technodesire, and play network into a pleasurable experience for the audience of KISS games. They conclude that the pleasure of the KISS activity can be accounted for by its ability to encourage play and experimentation, but they do not push the analysis further toward an investigation of how genderBLUR and technodesire are linked.

In research conducted within gaming communities in the US and the UK, adolescent males have largely refused to acknowledge or admit the radical potential of virtual gender experimentation facilitated by the *Tomb Raider* experience. Instead, they explain their attraction to *Lara* and the game by citing her value as eye candy—a virtual sexual object. The sex appeal of this digital siren or fantasy cartoon image is reiterated with such frequency that it becomes intelligible to vote this virtual female one of the sexiest *women* of the year in the US mass media.

To prove undeniably that male gamers play *Tomb Raider* because of the digital "tits and ass," these same fans have applied their considerable artistic talents and imaginations to "upgrading" *Lara* so that she can do some virtual transcendence herself: they have liberated her of her clothing. The first version of *Tomb Raider* was released in November 1996, and within sixty days the first *Nude Raider* sites appeared on the Internet featuring doctored images of a naked *Lara*.[15] Like the design and programming of the KISS software, the *Nude Raider* game patch is the product of considerable technical skill. Freely distributed on the Internet, the patch enables players to manipulate (and inhabit) a fully naked *Lara*-avatar. Core executives feign upset at this development and threaten legal action. But in fact the *Nude Raider* version of *Lara Croft* was reportedly developed in-house at Core, and even if that rumor is untrue, the naked *Lara* hack should not surprise anyone, considering that official publications sanctioned by Core such as *Lara's Book* contain numerous graphical images of her topless or completely naked, but carefully draped over a chair. Moreover, when Eidos developed a record company to produce music for *Lara* with the goal of repurposing the character as a pop star in the spirit of *Kyoko Date,* they called the company Naked Records, and titled the first track released "Getting Naked."[16] Almost as if to counteract the queer cross-gendered identifications that having a female protagonist for a first-person shooter game marketed primarily to men could have, Core has repeatedly and explicitly emphasized, exaggerated, and exploited the presumably heterosexual desirability and virtual seductiveness of *Lara Croft* vis-à-vis her (predominantly male) audience.

To increase their audience, Core hired a nonvirtual avatar to represent their star pixel vixen in the real world. A string of "real" women get paid to pass as *Lara* at trade shows and related promotional media events (Figure 6.2). However, overall, these fleshly avatars were a marketing failure. The young women who appeared as "*Lara*" were not as easily controllable as the virtual version. At least one of them was fired quite publicly because she was too outspoken—she was not hired to be a *Lara* spokesperson, just a silent body double. Reportedly, the *Lara* look-alikes resisted "compromising" their vision of *Lara* as a strong female figure, and thus were immediately replaced, one after the other. In interviews, these models repeatedly voiced their desire not just to resemble *Lara* but to "be" her, for her fans. Interestingly, several of these *Lara*-esque models agreed with Angelina Jolie's admission that a key motivation for "playing" *Lara Croft* was that they were responding to husbands and boyfriends who played the game constantly—ignoring the real women in their lives. "Taking on this part is a woman's revenge isn't it?" Jolie asks rhetorically, with tongue in cheek.[17] Responding predictably, Core opted out of using live models and instead resorted to creating animated *Lara* projections for marketing purposes, to be viewed at trade shows. The lack of virtuality and the

Figure 6.2 *Lara Croft* look-alike human model.

loss of male user's (employer's) control over these *Lara* icons spelled failure for the live *Lara* marketing venture. The fans agreed, as one admitted: "When you see a human *Lara* you realize, if Lar [sic] was real, she'd be crap" (Sawyer).

Was Jolie's human *Lara* also "crap" on Hollywood's silver screen? Despite enormous promotional hype for the *Tomb Raider* film, critics largely panned it, and box office figures were ultimately disappointing. Fans who left their joysticks at home and ventured out to theatres were, for the most part, generally disinterested in a female superhero—virtual or not—whose bust was not as fabulous in real life as it was on the video game ads, and who was stubbornly immune to computer patches that would remove her clothes.[18] In a comment that likely predicted the relatively lukewarm reception of her film, Jolie admitted she was determined to work the part for its feminist potential, commenting that "Lara is a great role model. We're not making her overly sexy, we're taking the breasts down a bit."[19] Again and predictably a profeminist analysis of the *Lara* cyberpop icon is undermined and depoliticized, this time as the Hollywood media-marketing machine opts for sensationalist rhetoric focused on Jolie's personal life, describing her in terms reminiscent of pornography, namely as deviant, dangerous, out of control, into sadomasochistic sex and *(gasp)* bisexual, in transparent attempts to heighten the hype and controversy of the film through hypersexualizing Jolie (Figure 6.3).

POSTFEMINIST ROLE MODEL AND CARICATURE

Lara's, ahem . . . physical arsenal is fully loaded as well. Co-opted by the gaming masses as the late twentieth century's newest pinup girl and sporting a virtual body that owes more to Barbie than to Courtney Love, *Lara*'s popularity may rest less in her kick-ass attitude than in her DD cup size, lending a questionable edge to her feminist positioning.

—Katie Salen[20]

Figure 6.3 *Movieline Magazine* cover story on Angelina Jolie in *Tomb Raider.*

If only it were as easy for them to kick ass in the real world.

—Debbie Stoller, "Faster Pussycat, Click Click"[21]

Can the *Lara Croft* cyberpop icon be a role model for girls and a feminist caricature simultaneously? The question may seem odd, but when the topic is *Lara Croft*, it is not unusual for interested players and critics to comment on her ability to morph from one form to another, fueling an ongoing debate about *Lara*'s position vis-à-vis (third wave) feminism. In order to secure the widest possible appeal for their product, spokespersons at Core Design draw comparisons between their pixel vixen and a vast range of female celebrity figures and icons in popular culture. In interviews, Core designer Adrian Smith has likened *Lara* to the grrl power pop music group the Spice Girls, to the animated character *Jessica Rabbit*, and in an interview for National Public Radio, when reporter Susan Stone asks about the relationship of *Lara* to Barbie, Smith confirms:

(Smith): "Yes, indeed. Yeah. Exactly like that."

(Stone): "A Barbie doll with a gun."

(Smith): "Yes."[22]

Despite the obvious fact that neither Barbie™ nor Jessica Rabbit are generally regarded as feminist role models, Smith maintains that *Lara Croft* is both a feminist and a positive representation of femaleness for her fans (of both genders) and serves as an icon of empowerment to girl gamers. [23] Some feminist critics would agree with Smith to the extent that "tough, and sexy women like *Lara Croft* would be better role models for girls that the few games produced for girls ... like *Barbie-Dress-up*."[24] In this observation, Anne-Marie Schleiner touches on the dilemma that arises for the spectator (or player) of action-adventure heroine figures like *Lara Croft*, *Tank Girl*, and *Xena Warrior Princess*: are these fictional big-boots-wearing, weapons-toting, ass-kicking females breaking down and blowing up stereotypes about gender, or are they simply violent sexist representations of Barbie-with-a-gun inspired by the fantasies of the adolescent male libido? Probably both, and that seeming contradiction might be why *Lara*, like her predecessor *Tank Girl*, has been read as a postfeminist figure, as third-wave feminism celebrates and embraces the contradictions and implications of popculture. [25]

Through a cyberpoetic lens, we see that there is a seductive and essential ambiguity configured into a cyberpop model like *Lara Croft*, not only because she is by "nature" virtual; but also because, like the pixel vixens analyzed previously, *Lara* can be *redescribed* in various ways: as emblematic of a version of femininity[26] that is powerful, active, courageous, independent, adventurous, highly educated,[27] and adept at solving puzzles (i.e., a wizard at logical problems requiring rational solutions rather than emotional sensitivity or compassion), or as stereotypical highly sexualized objects for the titillation of the male gaze. If *Lara* appeals to girls and women it may be somewhat of a bonus, since it is no secret that she was designed for a market of consumers that is predominantly male. However, it is somewhat difficult to recognize *Lara* as simply a prototypical role model for female empowerment, when we consider that she is also a figure that appears to be "an idealized eternally young female automaton, a malleable, well-trained techno-puppet" (Schleiner). This control aspect is not to be ignored, as it may account for a large part of her appeal. As psychologist Oscar Holzberg observes in Eidos' publication *Lara Croft: The Art of Virtual Seduction*:

> We live in a time of lost relationships, and one does not have to psychologically invest a lot in a virtual person; that is comforting. The child in a man can, in this way, calmly play and the man can realize his masculinity with a completely harmless yet concentrated femininity. And when he does not want his virtual playmate anymore, he can simply ignore her, without any feelings of guilt.[28]

We might ask then, what, if any, message does *Lara Croft* transmit about femininity and femaleness? The *Lara* pixel vixen can be read as a model for what will count in digital culture as female beauty, popularizing a misleading and damaging set of ideas about technology, desire, and male control over females. It is equally true that this cyberpop media has little or no effect on "real" men's desire for "real" women, but instead is about the proliferation of a discourse and aesthetic of digital artifice, and the promotion of interactivity—the seductive and intimate connection between user and screen/machine that is a prerequisite for keeping digital capitalism online.

Lara inhabits the virtual landscapes of infotech culture, navigating the labyrinthine caves, metaphorically representing the Web, or matrix that is cyberculture. She is a figure that helps to promote the virtues of a network economy, and her popularity paves the way for the integration, acceptance, even normalization, of other virtual females such as *Ananova* and *Webbie Tookay*. When users engage with *Lara*, they are invited to imagine or *think different* about how virtuality may affect our ideas of ourselves, bodies, gender, and sexuality in both progressive and unforeseen, or regressive and stereotypical, ways. Clearly at the level of the screen, or of simulation, *Lara* performs and popularizes a recognizable stereotypical "heterosexy" femininity, while simultaneously appearing as a mobile, strong, independent, self-reliant female that some would characterize as postfeminist. *Lara* is one step ahead of us, in the game and outside of it, constantly morphing to present an impossibly complex number of readings—an excellent example of cyberpop at its most fascinating, frustrating, and fun.

7

Dangerous Mixtures and Uncanny Flexibility: The Shape-Shifter

Part of the significance of cyberpop lies in the way it reflects the paradoxes and ambiguity that characterize digital culture. Moreover, as a genre cyberpop media plays an important role in the formation of identities and lifestyles by representing modes of technological being and the integration of computer technologies into everyday experience. As Scott Bukatman has argued about cyberpunk, popular cyberpop texts serve as narratives of accommodation to the high-tech order of things—while encouraging a critical discourse on the present, and a self-reflexive awareness of the audience's implication in mainstream technoculture and commerce. A form of *sexy social criticism* (Sterling, *Mirrorshades*) with a didactic function, cyberpop creatively interprets the implications and reverberations of information and computer science on culture and individuals, challenging its audience to *think different*. As an infomediary in the feedback loop of technoscience and popular culture, cyberpop ads, films, novels, and artwork present provocative, creative, and oftentimes critical scenarios about our present and future digital culture by connecting to and sometimes amplifying key conceptual nodes in the network of cyberculture.

THE UNREAL PERSON

> As we move into the era of the Post-Human—replete with genetic engi-
> neering, cosmetic surgery on demand, psychotropic behavioral modi-
> fication, and the unceasing melding of the corporeal, the mechanical
> and the electronic—why should our portraiture not keep pace?

> **—Peter Lunenfeld**[1]

In 1998, Irit Krygier curated *The Unreal Person: Portraiture in the Digital Age*, a show featuring the work of fifteen artists who were considering the impact of information and genomic technoscience on modes of human subjectivity, forms of physical embodiment, and the changing definitions of nature and the human. Commenting on the cultural and historical context for the show, Krygier noted that in popular media, with the airbrush and visual imaging software, "Photographs are routinely retouched digitally to erase any 'unevenness of tone,' wrinkles or lines or other 'imperfections.' These faces and bodies are often resculpted digitally to create ideals of 'beauty' and 'perfection' unattainable in real life at any age."[2] What set the artwork in *The Unreal Person* exhibit apart was the way the artists approached the idea of the portrait, electing to foreground and exaggerate the technological enhancements and digital constructedness of their images (see <http://strikingdistance.com/unreal>). Interestingly, several artists drew attention to this digitized difference by electing to combine elements of animals with humans, or to morph photographs of men and women together, or persons of different races, creating hybrid portraits. In *She with He*, for example, Nancy Burson creates representations of androgyny by combining male and female faces, while in *Hybrid Eyes* Dorit Cypis exhibits only the eyes of her subject, taking one eye from a human face and the other from a cat. In *Self Portraits I, II, III, and IV*, Daniel Lee experimented with remastered photographs of himself, progressively enlarging his forehead and skull, pushing the contours of his facial features outward and upward, until his visage takes on the unmistakable resemblance to an ape. In an artist's statement, Lee comments on the ideas behind his metamorphosis:

> Because technology changes the way we live and the way we create, it
> also changes the way we look. My image, therefore, is an evolutionary
> self-portrait—a look at the distant past and into the far-off future.
> My eyes shrink as electricity eradicates the need to see in the dark.
> My brain and forehead enlarge as information expands my mind.
> And my features blend as communication brings cultures closer and
> closer together—Asian, Caucasian and so on.[3]

This "evolution" or devolution of the informational subject did not go unnoticed by Microsoft Corporation, which immediately commissioned Lee to create additional artworks for their *Evolution* advertising campaign in the UK (1999). According to Lee, "the basic premise was that Microsoft's *Knowledge Management Solutions* would better outfit any company to evolve and thereby survive in the fast-changing world of e-commerce by making them wiser, more agile, faster, and more competitive" (www.daniellee.com). The images started off as photographs of humans, which were then digitally remastered and morphed using Adobe® Photoshop®. Slogans accompanying the portraits included: *The faster you are, the better you'll be,* and *Those who are more flexible will be better able to adapt as the changing e-business environment moves.* Interestingly, rather than pursue Lee's comments about technologically mediated shape-shifting and morphing races, Microsoft elected to use work from Lee that represented the faster, more agile and flexible, connected and competitive wired subject through morphing human images with animals, resulting in science fictional hybrids of *CheetahMan, SnakeWoman, OwlMan, CatGirl, FishSwimmer,* and others (see <www.daniellee.com>).

However, this is not to suggest that race is not present in the *Evolution* images. On closer examination, and considering their juxtaposition to advertising slogans and e-commerce values, a pattern emerges. The only recognizable portrait of a white man is used to signify the idea "wise," while the feminized figures are "flexible" and "agile," and the darker-skinned male figures, who do not have faces and are turned away from the viewer, signify athletic skill and speed, while flanked by unmistakably (and unmorphed) white male figures. Studying this advertising campaign, it is unavoidable to connect white masculinity to intellectual superiority, while masculinity and "racial otherness" is aligned with anonymous objectified brute strength, and all femaleness is relegated to the physical body, but the lithe, tiny, and flexible, partially nude body.

This pattern of representational politics is not unique to the *Evolution* campaign, as is illustrated by examining similar examples of the shape-shifter in popular cybercultural media. What is interesting about this phenomenon is that the shape-shifter is taken up by artists and capitalist corporations as a mascot for digital subjectivity and futural figurings of the human, to signify the breakdown of traditions and boundaries, and the radical connectivity that a networked culture is ushering in. The shape-shifter or morph is adopted to signify the blurring of once distinct categories *visually*, by mixing and remixing recognizable elements of different genders, species, and races into what we might once have called a mosaic, pastiche, or collage.[4]

However, despite these radical remixings and samplings in cyberpop representations of the morph, there is an uncanny durability and inflexibility of the ideologies attached to discourses of race and gender, and these ideologies are *upgraded* rather than *imploded*. The resilience of logic formations that connect whiteness and masculinity to rationality, and femaleness and racial otherness to the physical body, even at a historical moment when boundary blurring is embraced by popular culture as an exciting aesthetic and political maneuver, is evidence not only of the hegemonic metanarratives of sex, gender, and racial dualisms in Western cyberculture (in spite of claims about postmodern "incredulity" and BLUR), but also of the ambiguity and paradox that is at the heart of its popular cultural productions which both reflect and critique the status quo.

ILLUSTRATING TECHNOSCIENCE AND DIGITAL LIFESTYLES

Microsoft's imaginative, fictional images of the computerized subject are playful representations of science fictional futures, yet the markers of race and gender, and their mixtures, are significant elements in what makes the morph or shape-shifter so intriguing. Microsoft and Daniel Lee push the envelope of human subjectivity in the age of informatics into the realm of the fantastic with the "enfreaked," grotesque, and monstrous (but somehow also endearing and beautiful) *OwlMan* and *CatGirl* morphic figures by playing with the concept of "becoming animal." In what was intended to be an equally spectacular and seductive (though not monstrous) advertisement, *TIME* magazine put a morph figure on its cover in 1993, and proclaimed the figure, named "Eve," as "The New Face of America."[5]

Although "Eve" was not created through a mixture of images from different species, she was nevertheless presented as a *hybrid* subject of a multicultural America. As Robert Young and other theorists have argued, the concept of hybridity is inextricably bound up with miscegenation rhetoric and essentialist notions about racial purity—including classification tables that separated the races into different species.[6] Without acknowledging this, or the history of eugenics, degeneration theory, and racial classification sciences in the US, *TIME* reproduced a table of "racial types" and morphed these photographs together to create a composite subject of a networked economy. "Eve," unmistakably a woman of color, became a cover girl who could be interpreted as the offspring of developments in computer imaging technologies, or as an icon signifying trends in interracial breeding, or both, depending on the reader's political perspective.

"Eve's" creator, a digital artist who we are told is of "Asian descent" and dubbed a cybergeneticist, presented his portrait "in the spirit of fun and experiment." And perhaps "Eve" the morph is fun, and playful, and should be interpreted as evidence that racialist discourses and white supremacist logics are being delegitimated and losing their power. However, in her analysis of the "Eve" cover illustration, Evelynn Hammonds argues that *TIME*'s morphic shape-shifter composite is less about the breakdown of boundaries and shifting BLUR culture, than a narrative about "the drama of miscegenation in cyberspace."[7] Hammonds observes, "no woman of color has ever symbolized citizenship in United States history, only the denial of citizenship" (317). This insight points to a pattern in cyperpop representations of the shapeshifter that emerges when we look closer at *which* morphs are used to illustrate *which* technoscientific breakthroughs. Which morph represents agility and flexibility and brute strength, and which one stands in for wisdom? Did the editorial tone of the cover story in *TIME* magazine present multiculturalism and mixed-race breeding as progress, as utopic, playful, experimental, and fun? Or should *TIME*'s choice to feature what appear to be racial classification tables, and a very unlikely candidate for "the generic American subject" (a woman of color) tip us off to the presence of a backlash logic in this publication?

In fact, the patterns of representing digital subjects of the future in cyberpop indicate that the more controversial infotech and biotech becomes, the more far-fetched and imaginative, alien, and monstrous the accompanying illustrations will be. When the technoscience featured in (for example) *Scientific American* (Figure 7.1) or *Popular Science* (Figure 7.2) magazine is perceived to be *challenging*, rather than *extending* or reifying the definition of the human and/or of nature—the more likely it is that we will see feminized and nonwhite representations of the digital or computerized subject. Correspondingly, when the developments in computer, communication, and bioinformatic sciences are presented in the popular science media as *beneficial* to humans, as evidence of scientific *progress*, we begin to see more illustrations of white (or light, or pink) male (or neuter) bodies and figures as cover art.

To consider the cultural context into which "Eve" and the "Evolution" cyberpop figures link, we need to consider that popular science magazines are designed to attract and persuade a large and diverse audience of nonspecialists. Not unlike a cyberpunk novel, these magazines play an infomediary role by translating specialized terms such as bioinformatics and cybernetics for the general reader, filtering technoscience for popular consumption, deciding which data are relevant, what information should be prioritized—much the way an Internet search engine like Yahoo! or Google will sift through the information overload of the Web and return rankings, summaries, and categorizations of the "hits."

These magazines and their cover art and illustrations of technoscientific breakthroughs and developments contribute to what Vivian Sobchack (*Screening*) calls a "visual shorthand" or set of codes that, when repeated from text to text, become recognizable as icons of digital culture, computerized

Figure 7.1 *Scientific American Magazine*, your bionic future.

subjectivity, the genomic revolution, virtual community, and models for the connected lifestyle and computerized subjectivity, among others. The choices made around representing the body of the future *matter* since in our networked culture information is transmitted, downloaded, cut and pasted, cross posted and linked (to) instantaneously. Cyberpop representations are cited and recited, they inform each other intertextually, forming a web of associations that serves as a foundation and lens that is referenced when futural figurations of technoculture and technosubjectivity are envisioned.

Figure 7.2 *Popular Science Magazine*, body of the future.

PORTRAYING THE GENOMIC SUBJECT

Announcing the successful completion of the Human Genome Project (HGP) in 2000 was a media blitz comprising exaggerated claims about genetic science, rhetorics of biological determinism, bioethical debates, eugenic fears, and images of the genomic subject. Computational biologists predicted the dawn of a new age when humans will have read the "book of God" and can eradicate disease, extend life span, genetically engineer future generations, take our heredity in hand, and so forth. This god-like genomic subject experiences better living through technology, and becomes intelligible to itself through its representation in computer databases, by its digital representation of "nature's blueprints" or "the building blocks of life." Since genetic databases

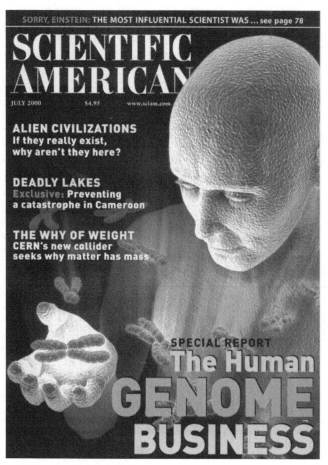

Figure 7.3 *Scientific American Magazine*, the genomic subject.

don't make for good visuals, the popular press and the biotech and bioinformatic industries needed to construct alternative visual rhetorics to communicate the importance of the cracking of the "code of life." The new digital human who holds power over its biological fate in its hand must look the part, and *Scientific American* elected to represent the digital genomic human subject as a hairless, flat-chested, glowing white male (Figure 7.3). Maybe this should come as no surprise considering that for the sake of "diversity" the Human Genome Project screened and mapped a genome that had both a Y and an X chromosome—thus effectively using a male model as the standard for The Human. At the same time, the media blitz proclaimed repeatedly that there is no gene for "race"—an idea taken up by several artists who were commissioned by the Human Genome Project (publicly funded by the US) to interpret the sociocultural implications of the HGP.[8] Politicians, geneticists, religious officials, bioinformatics corporations spokespersons, and a host of other interested expert figures flooded the popular press with statements about the essential sameness that underlies all cultural makers, including ethnic, religious, sexual, gendered, and racial difference—insisting that underneath we all share the same chemical code. And by cracking that code the HGP ushered in a new genomic world order, or so the rhetoric indicated, complete with new pressing ethical dilemmas. A number of controversies were played out on National Public Radio, on television talk shows, the Internet, and in newspapers about the ramifications of playing with "Mother Nature" and the future of transgenic research and human cloning.

A look at the illustration of the generic genomic human on the US Department of Energy Web site's logo shows it to be uncannily similar to the representation chosen for the cover of *Scientific American*.[9] The white, or pink, male or neuter human figure stands in for sameness, and signifies that genetic research is not scary or alien but will benefit EveryOne. In comparison, the cover illustration from *Discover* magazine (Figure 7.4) prefaces a story that emphasizes the connections between genetic science and computer circuitry as controversial; the same bald human figure is present but with important differences, namely, it is recognizably feminized with full eye makeup and dark lipstick. When the female digital human image is used, unlike the previous male (or neuter) figure, she is made to look "new" and different, futuristic by overlaying images of circuitry on her face, and her skin is an inhuman color of greenish-gray. Importantly, her face is not white, pink, or some "neutral/ flesh" tone, signifying the "otherness" of this digital human who is perhaps not fully human at all. A look inside the publication reveals that the story accompanying this illustration is about bioinformatic ALife research, the evolution of silicon computer processors. This female stands in for the cybernetic organism (the cyborg)—a dangerous mixture of organic and inorganic that Haraway describes as "a polychromatic bad girl." When computer programmers are challenging the definition of such concepts as "life," "soul," "nature," and "human"—the logical SF icon is the traditional image of artifice, manipulation, and duplicity—a beautiful woman, with recognizably Caucasian features whether they are set into circuitry or chrome (as is the case with Fritz Lang's Maria in *Metropolis*)—but in this case they have used a woman of color, namely an inhuman green-gray female.

Pushing the concept of experimental biocomputational research even further, *TIME Digital* magazine launched a science fictional spoof issue circa 2026, with an image of the digital subject on the cover (Figure 7.5). The fictional cover stories included one on transgenic experimentation, creating clones from humans and animals, and ALife research. The figure represented is recognizably female, white, and blue eyed, dressed in what appears

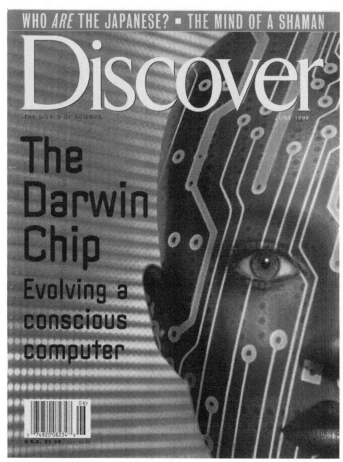

Figure 7.4 *Discover Magazine*, the Darwin chip.

to be latex fetish clothing that reveals her ample cleavage. The jellyfish-robot creature that shares the cover with her represents the alien, which allows the female to be white rather than some inhuman "color"—nevertheless to signify her otherness, she has unnatural orange hair. This choice of hair color would not be remarkable if it were not for the fact that images of digital women are proliferating in cyberpop with hair that is neon blue (*The 6th Day*), iridescent white (*Mya*), or green (*Ananova*). What does it mean for *TIME Digital* to elect to represent the cybercitizen of 2026 in the persona of a cover girl who closely resembles a pixel vixen? *TIME Digital* was marketed as a newsmagazine covering the infotech age, and if the reader were to flip over the fictional 2026 issue to the real issue of the magazine, they would find that cover photo featured a white male surrounded by cell phones, PDAs, and

Figure 7.5 *TIME Digital Magazine,* digital female illustration.

other digital gear designed to extend his reach into cyberspace and secure his node in the connected economy—and to drive the point home this male model is photographed wearing a helmet appropriate for space travel (Figure 7.6). When readers are to be persuaded that digital technology is a positive science, and helpfully augments human functionality in productive ways, the logical choice for an advertisement (according to the pattern of representational politics here) is to select a white male subject as iconic digital human. On the other hand, if the technoscience is being presented as provocative, controversial, or experimental, as this subtle logic goes, a "colorful" female icon will be used to advertise/illustrate it.

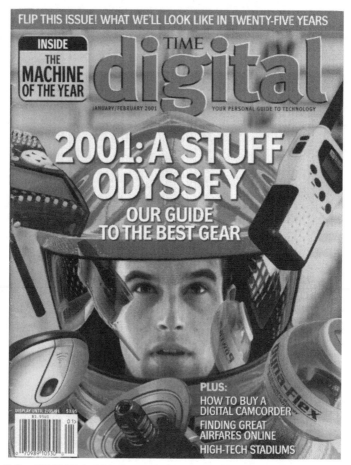

Figure 7.6 *TIME Digital Magazine*, male compusubject illustration.

THE SHAPE-SHIFTER

This detour through selected examples of cyberpop cover art was designed to underscore the point that even at a historical moment when shape-shifters and morphs make sense, when these hybridized figures are regarded as harmless, playful, fun, and appropriate for placement in high-profile advertising campaigns and mass market magazine covers, the underlying logics of the "mix" and of blurring boundaries and imploding dualisms are not necessarily embraced as completely as the proliferation of these figures might suggest. Even in the case of the morph, where at first it appears that identity and the body are hacked, unsecured, edited, and recoded, in a field of radical shift, blur, and play, there are still traces of older, more traditional and hegemonic systems of order in place, foundational discourses about bodies, subjects, genders and races, monsters and freaks, and what counts as normal and healthy or alien and unnatural, which may be challenged by cyberpop media and its figures such as the shape-shifter, but which ultimately get upgraded and reified so as to be compatible with the new digital order of things.

For example, for a polymorph, like the central character in Scott Westerfeld's novel of the same name, to make sense and to be intelligible, a network of associations linking bodies, technologies, and identities, to racial, gendered, and sexual discourses must be in place as part of the discursive formation of cyberculture. What makes the polymorph shape-shifter so intriguing is the way in which this cyberpop character negotiates its implication in the dominant order as a reality hacker, a self-made individual, a flexible, agile, mobile and connected subject, and a human character with whom the reader can identify. The flip side of the popularity of the polymorph, and its close relation, the mutant, is an enduring fascination in popular culture with "enfreakment," exceptional bodies, spectacles of difference and monstrosity, which connects the *fin de siècle* cyberpop culture in a very neat circularity or loop, vis-à-vis the trends of gothicity that numerous historians have mapped as characterizing the close of the 19th century.[10] The question, *why this particular monster, a shape-shifter, now?*, is one that we will return to after considering Westerfeld's work in more detail.

POLYMORPH

Scott Westerfeld's *Polymorph* is the story of a shape-shifter named Lee and a hacker named Freddie. In a set of parallel narratives, one about infiltrating computer databases and virtual worlds, and the other about hacking the physical body itself, *Polymorph* considers the impact of BLURred culture on the individual subjects living in an urban metropolis (New York) in the not-too-distant future. The novel is significant insofar as it illustrates the synergy between developments in communication and information science and new ideas of the human subject that result. Between the covers of this novel we find a dystopian critique of contemporary technoscience, networked into a utopic narrative about the thrill of radical connectivity and the freedom that digital intangibility can deliver. A story about a shape-shifter who morphs from one gender to another, between sexualities, and into mixed-race bodies, *Polymorph* is as much a cyberpop cyberpunk narrative as it is a portrait of the kind of multiculturalism that *TIME* magazine represented with its choice of "Eve" the cover girl as the new face of America. Lee and Freddie travel through various areas of the city, encountering numerous "others" in gay bars, homeless shelters, Mexican coffeehouses, and elite skytop clubs, where the clientele is overrepresented as white and wealthy. With Freddie's skills in cyberspace the couple also venture into chat rooms where users' identities shift with each open window; through virtual worlds filled with avatars; and explorations of sophisticated network architectures that structure the landscape of e-commerce, populated by data bodies and databases.

The central narrative follows Lee, who grew up and continues to reside in a section of New York projects, in the shadow of an industrial zone that spews a fine white toxic dust, coating the neighborhood. Perhaps as a result of this cancerous environment, Lee is born a mutant with the ability to morph from one form to another. Lee is a fully organic human who routinely shape-shifts, incorporating features of faces and bodies from magazine images, anatomy textbook illustrations, and photographs from medical journals. Lee seeks to blend, to live anonymously, invisibly, hiding hir morphic abilities lest zie be institutionalized as a freak (of nature and culture), living on the lam under an assumed name, surviving on federal assistance to the disabled, sleeping through the day and partying in the club scene at night.[11] As the story unfolds, Lee faces disastrous consequences when zie meets up with an evil and violent shape-shifter named Bonita/Bonito. The parallel narrative is about a team of computer nerds led by Freddie, who use their programming talents to become virtually empowered and to aid Lee in escaping from and ultimately destroying her vicious kin. Together the stories complement each other, since they are both about virtuality (identity, embodiment, cyberspace, and community), hacking (the system, the body, community, and the self), and speed (of data transmission, of urban lifestyle, and of "qwerting"—Westerfeld's term for computer-mediated communication, or CMC, in chat rooms).

The book opens in Lee's closet, filled with a jumbled and mismatched collection ("not a wardrobe") of clothing for both genders, varied in size and style, "costumes" for Lee's various personae. After selecting an appropriate ensemble, the small-framed, light-skinned and female Lee begins to morph, an "unpleasant" process involving considerable physiological agony and trauma, requiring intense mental discipline and a "steady vision" of the intended form in the mind's eye. Lee emerges from the closet in a hapa identity, combining the face of a young Chinese girl who lives nearby, with a thin elegant neck modeled after a young Polynesian transvestite and former one-night-stand lover. In this guise, Lee feels sufficiently exotic, extraordinary, and "definitely Asian," which is a plus, since "door workers for the clubs tended to favor Asians, who they assume to be more affluent" than whites. Lee is proud of achieving this "beautiful and statuesque" hybrid form, but to ensure that the look is sufficiently "striking," Lee completes the morph by modeling a set of hands with webbed fingers and opposable thumbs from a medical journal. In this composite form, Lee is outstanding, "not twisted or bizarre, merely alien," definitely a mutant, or in Lee's own words "a hopeful monster."

As *Polymorph* progresses, Lee takes on many forms and identities. Romping through lesbian clubs with female lovers, passing as a black man in an upscale restaurant, morphing into a white female and taking Freddie as a heterosexual lover, and at the end of the book, for only a few pages, morphing into a white gay male. In each version of embodiment, the reader and Lee experience an insider's perspective on the differences of positionality in terms of gender, sexuality, race, and class. The sheer variety of shifts that Lee makes is overwhelming and endlessly intriguing, to the point where it becomes naturalized that there is no connection between Lee's identity and sense of self and hir corporeal form. The mixtures and remixtures seem unlimited; so much so that, closing the book, it is possible to forget that there is one form that Lee does not ever morph into, namely, that of a straight white male. For the majority of the book Lee passes in various mixed-raced female forms, and when Lee does shift to a male persona it is a racial or sexual minority form zie takes on.

Perhaps this is because there is already a stable, solid, heterosexual and Caucasian male in the story, namely, the hacker hero Freddie, Lee's lover and partner in crime. Like the geek chic phenomenon described earlier, Westerfeld's text presents the hacker nerd as a white male, and elevates his talents above that of the racial others and female figures around him—which, in the case of *Polymorph*, are actually embodied by Lee at different times. Freddie's skills at virtual passing and virtual shape-shifting via CMC are ultimately the reason that Lee experiences victory over hir enemy. As Lee watches Freddie in his job as a chat room moderator, zie reflects:

> The organic metamorphosis she used to remold herself [. . .] suddenly seemed crude. Freddie was changing identities from second to second, re-creating himself constantly to play to the weaknesses and imaginations of his conversants. [. . .] Freddie made [. . .] anonymous, exquisite connections through the slender link of text on a screen [. . .] There was a razorlike efficiency to it. He moved [. . .] with a kind of inhuman lightness.[12]

In this scene and others, the author privileges Freddie's proficiency at hacking above Lee's shape-shifting abilities, indicating a kind of net utopia underpinning Westerfeld's book. As Lisa Nakamura (*Cybertypes*), Alondra Nelson, and others have argued, net utopia is the mythification of the flexibility of identity in online culture, and the idea that a user can pass as "virtually" any identity, any gender or race, sexuality, age, or ethnicity, cloaked in the anonymity of glowing icons on a screen, experimenting with difference from the safety and comfort of a computer terminal.[13] The viability of these passing performances has been contested and examined in innumerable studies of online communication, and remains a controversial issue and ongoing debate among theorists, researchers, and online users/participants themselves. Which voices were the loudest and most ecstatic to embrace virtual passing in the popular press during the birth of the Internet and online communities? In fact, it was white men who were interested in promoting net utopia, the hackers who said that the marks of identity should not matter.[14] Virtual passing was championed by white males who felt entitled to power, who wanted to use technology to escape the limits of their bodies (the "meat"), and to expand their networks of influence via cyberspace. In *Polymorph*, as in *Neuromancer, GATTACA,* and *The Matrix,* white male hacker figures slip the bonds of the body while nonwhite male characters and all females remain locked in the realm of the flesh and the organic—or if they do enter the virtual world, they are forced to endure stunning amounts of real physical agony in the process.[15]

Although *Polymorph* initially appears to be a science fiction story about a monstrous creature, in fact Lee's shifts in form seem almost anticlimactic when we consider how much more mobile, networked, inventive, and e-powered the cybersubject can be if zie is armed with a modem and network connection. While Lee writhes and sweats, collapsing in agony and exhaustion from the effort of morphing, the reader cannot help but wonder why zie even bothers, because Freddie the hacker can crack a code and take on an identity, access protected information, and travel to restricted areas, all from the safety of his cubicle and keyboard. Nevertheless, whether it is "high-tech" morphs and hacks (digitalized, CMC, computer avatars, and network infiltration) or "low-tech" morphs and hacks (fleshly, monstrous, fully organic shape-shifting), both activities are considered innovative forays into complicated systems, fraught with risk, promising huge rewards and excellent adventures.

It is no wonder Microsoft® Office picked the shape-shifter as a mascot for its networked Office suite product marketing; by redescribing the morph it is revealed as a cyberpop text that is considerably thicker than it first seems. The technoshape-shifter or polymorph is the only figure that "made sense" in BLUR culture, according to Westerfeld; it is a timely monster, an intriguing and somehow appropriate icon, which effectively reveals some of the ideological undercurrents of cyberculture. For example, Vivian Sobchack insists that there is a connection between the popularity of the shape-shifter and "our morphological imagination"; in other words, in order for the morph to make sense, it must be networked with preexisting ideas about human embodiment as flexible, changeable, transformable, upgradeable—coupled with an idea of the human body as being composed of elements or discrete fragments that can be edited or remixed without risking the integrity of the individual.[16] Moreover, it is not only the body but also the concept of individual identity that is associated with discourses of multiplicity and shift, as Sherry Turkle explains:

> We increasingly live in a world where you wake up as a lover, have breakfast as a mother, and drive to work as a lawyer. In the course

of a day people go through dramatic transitions, and it's apparent to them that they play multiple roles. Well-functioning people, successful people, happy people, have learned to work through all these roles, to cycle through them in productive and joyful ways. On the Internet you can see yourself functioning with seven windows open on your screen, literally assuming different personae in each of those seven windows, having all kinds of relationships, cycling among and being present to all of these roles simultaneously, having pieces of yourself left in these different windows as programs that you've written which represent you while you attend to another window. Your identity is a distributed presence across a series of windows.[17]

The data body—composed of bits and bytes, distributed across windows and databases, commodified and sold back to the BLURred individual—is one node in the conceptual framework that enables a morphological imagination and inspires the popularity of the shape-shifter figure. However, this is not the *central* reason that the figure was selected as a "promising monster" for Microsoft UK; rather, the morph is a logical choice at a moment when e-commerce management and marketing specialists and leadership consultants are stressing the links between adaptation, shift, flexibility, change, innovation, and commercial profit for all kinds of corporations, but specifically for the information and computer technologies sectors. A cursory glance at the business section of any newspaper, or ads in lifestyle and news magazines reveals examples of this rhetoric flourishing:

> Achieving sales and marketing objectives are increasingly difficult in today's rapidly changing business environment. Businesses must have the innovation and flexibility to quickly adapt to opportunities in the marketplace. A Contracted Sales Force® campaign creates the opportunity for sales force expansions without an increase in overhead costs associated with internal sales force expansions.[18]

> In today's business environment, companies are coming to terms with the notion that the business environment isn't changing; it IS change. How a company copes with change may be said to be equivalent of how agile it is—how flexible it is to changing elements in its industry and the economy as a whole, how it keeps functioning optimally in the face of change.[19]

> Today's business economy is fast paced and in constant change [. . .] The PeopleTools™ foundation is inherently flexible making it easy to develop, deploy, and maintain a functionally rich and flexible solution. PeopleTools™ technology can easily adapt and change as the

company's mission, goals, and objectives change in response to competition. The tools also make the applications easily upgradeable for future technology platforms.[20]

In her work *Flexible Bodies,* Emily Martin explains that the reason that contemporary capitalist culture views flexibility so positively and considers it a value in itself is that it complements and is a key concept in a "complex systems" model of culture, economy, and the individual. In a BLUR culture of speed, the rhetoric states, the rate of change is rapid; accordingly, people and corporations are expected to adapt and be flexible and agile, "to shift and to be able to tolerate continuing shifts," so as to increase productivity, respond to fluctuations in market trends and *evolve* or grow.[21] "One of the central attributes of complex systems is that, unlike mechanical systems, they are never in equilibrium," writes Martin, "everything is in flux, continually adjusting to change" (143). In a networked culture, this model makes sense insofar as it explains how to form links between entities (businesses, economic sectors, individuals, and geographic regions), which at base share a common code based on constant morphings, shifts, and blurrings. When Stanley Davis and Christopher Meyer of the *BLUR* e-management guide advise that the way for the individual to succeed in a networked economy is to *node thyself,* they assume the existence and operation of a complex systems network architecture that Martin is describing.

The choice to end this study with a close reading of various examples of the shape-shifter is intended to underscore the ambiguity inherent in popularized cybermedia. Even in the examples above, some of which clearly push the envelope in terms of imagining future digital subjectivities, there is evidence that traditional (and oftentimes stereotypical and inequitable) discourses about race and gender are cited, repurposed, and upgraded—a point made earlier by Anne Balsamo, in her work with cyberpop media, and by Zillah Eisenstein, in her analysis of digital capital. What this discussion has emphasized is the subtle ways that cyberpop media are both innovative and progressive, even while they are obviously opting to simultaneously reproduce some familiar scripts about power, technology, and subjectivities. That newness, seductive and spectacular, is what Donna Haraway might call the radical promise of cyberpop figurations, inviting us to envision forms of identity, social organization, and conceptual architectures outside of binary configurations, tools to help us *think different* about our digital futures.

Notes

INTRODUCTION

1. Evelyn Fox Keller, *Refiguring Life: Metaphors of Twentieth-Century Biology* (New York: Columbia UP, 1996) 85. The prefix "cyber" indicates that these areas of technoscientific research have been influenced by Norbert Wiener's theory of cybernetics, which constructed a model of the human as an information processing system, akin to a computer. Norbert Weiner, *Cybernetics: Or Control and Communication in Animal and the Machine* (Paris: Hermann, 1948) and *The Human Use of Human Beings: Cybernetics and Society* (New York: Doubleday, 1954).

2. These criticisms of cyberpop media are listed by Andrew Darley, *Visual Digital Culture: Surface Play and Spectacle in New Media Genres* (New York: Routledge, 2000) 5-6.

3. Arturo Escobar, "Welcome to Cyberia: Notes on the Anthropology of Cyberculture," *Current Anthropology* 35.3 (1994): 212.

4. Donna Haraway, "A Game of Cat's Cradle: Science Studies, Feminist Theory, Cultural Studies," *Configurations* 2.1 (1994): 60.

5. Richard Coyne, *Technoromanticism: Digital Narrative, Holism, and the Romance of the Real* (Cambridge: MIT P, 1999) 15.

6. William Gibson, *Neuromancer* (New York: Ace, 1984). For a comprehensive and thoroughly readable book-length investigation of William Gibson's work and the impact of *Neuromancer* on cyberculture, see Dani Cavallaro, *Cyberpunk and Cyberculture: Science Fiction and the Work of William Gibson* (London: Athlone, 2000).

7. Sandy Stone, "Will the Real Body Please Stand Up?" in Jenny Wolmark, ed., *Cybersexualities: A Reader on Feminist Theory, Cyborgs, and Cyberspace* (Edinburgh: Edinburgh UP, 1999) 80.

8. Fredric Jameson, *Postmodernism, or, the Cultural Logic of Late Capitalism* (Durham: Duke UP, 1991) 285.

9. Larry Wachowski cited by Jeffrey Wells, "The Keymasters," *Razor* (May 2003) <http://www.reevesdrive.com/newsarchive/2003/razor0503b.htm>.

10. Read Schuchardt, "What is *The Matrix*?: Ancient Wisdom Wrapped in Technological Analogies," *Re:Generation* (1999) <http://www.regenerator. com/5.2/matrix.html>.

11. Scott Bukatman, *Terminal Identity: The Virtual Subject in Postmodern Science Fiction* (London: Duke UP, 1993).

12. Donna Haraway and Thyrza Nichols Goodeve, eds., *How Like A Leaf: An Interview with Donna Haraway* (New York: Routledge, 1999) 108.

13. Judith Butler, *Bodies That Matter: On the Discursive Limits of "Sex"* (New York: Routledge, 1993) 15, 23.

14. Stuart Hall, "Encoding/Decoding" in Simon During, ed., *The Cultural Studies Reader*, 2nd ed. (New York: Routledge, 1999) 514. Rpt. from Stuart Hall, *Culture, Media, Language* (London: Unwin Hyman, 1990).

15. Katherine Hayles, "The Seductions of Cyberspace," in David Trent, ed., *Reading Digital Culture* (n.p.: Blackwell, 2001).

16. Analyzing how the discourse of technomasculinity and the mythos of the hacker converge necessarily includes consideration of how, in the wake of the terrorist bombings in New York City and Washington in 2001, there is a perceived need to get hackers online with American patriotism and cybercapitalism, to change (or "flip") them from "black hats" to "white hats" who will fight the "war" on cyberterrorism. In cyberpop then, we see examples of the "white" male hacker morphing from an infantile and criminalized "script kiddie" to a freedom fighter who can save the world. However, as Jon Katz observes, "a society that desperately needs geeks, does not have to like them," and therefore an analysis of the celebration of technomasculinity must consider how the hacker figure is being upgraded, appropriated, and mainstreamed so as to balance the "considerable wariness and mistrust" that they have generated in popular culture due to the media's manufacturing of the discourse of hacker as public enemy. Jon Katz, *Geeks: How Two Lost Boys Rode the Internet Out of Idaho* (New York: Broadway, 2000) xxiv.

17. Amanda Fernbach, "The Fetishization of Masculinity in Science Fiction: The Cyborg and the Console Cowboy," *Science Fiction Studies* 27 (2000): 248.

18. Lisa Nakamura, *Cybertypes: Race, Ethnicity, and Identity on the Internet* (New York: Routledge, 2002).

19. Andrew Darley, *Visual Digital Culture: Surface Play and Spectacle in New Media Genres* (New York: Routledge, 2000) 7.

CHAPTER 1

1. Donna Haraway, "A Manifesto for Cyborgs: Science, Technology and Socialist Feminism in the 1980s," *Socialist Review* 90 (1985): 149.
2. Donna Haraway, *Modest Witness at Second Millennium, FemaleMan meets OncoMouse: Feminism as Technoscience* (New York: Routledge, 1997).
3. Donna Haraway, "A Game of Cat's Cradle: Science Studies, Feminist Theory, Cultural Studies," *Configurations* 2.1 (1994): 62.
4. This concept is also discussed in "Cyborgs at Large: Interview with Donna Haraway," Constance Penley and Andrew Ross, eds. *Technoculture* (Minneapolis: U of Minnesota P, 1991).
5. Margaret Morse, *Virtualities: Television, Media Art, and Cyberculture*, Bloomington: Indiana UP, 1998) 4.
6. Michael Heim, "The Erotic Ontology of Cyberspace," excerpt from *The Metaphysics of Virtual Reality* (New York: Oxford UP, 1994). Rpt. *Reading Digital Culture*, ed. David Trend (Monneapolis: Blackwell, 2001) 81.
7. Manuel Castells, *The Rise of the Network Society* (New York: Blackwell, 2000).
8. Sherry Turkle, *Life on the Screen: Identity in the Age of the Internet* (New York: Simon, Schuster, 1995) 48.
9. Katherine Hayles, "The Seductions of Cyberspace," *Reading Digital Culture*, ed. David Trent (Cambridge: Blackwell, 2001) 307. Originally in Verena Andermatt Conley, ed., *Rethinking Technologies* (Minneapolis: U of Minnesota P, 1993).
10. Zillah Eisenstein, *Global Obscenities: Patriarchy, Capitalism, and the Lure of Cyberfantasy* (New York: New York UP, 1998) 70.
11. Mark Poster, *The Mode of Information: Poststructuralism and Context* (Chicago: U of Chicago P, 1990) 16.
12. Jean Baudrillard, rev. of "Marshall McLuhan, Understanding Media: The Extensions of Man," *L'homme et la societe* 5 (1967): 227-30, cited and trans. Gary Genosko, *McLuhan and Baudrillard: The Masters of Implosion* (New York: Routledge, 1999) 93.
13. Felix Guattari, "Regimes, Pathways, Subjects," *Incorporations*, ed. Jonathan Crary and Sanford Kwinter (New York: Zone, 1992) 18.
14. Theodore Adorno, *The Culture Industry: Selected Essays on Mass Culture* (New York: Routledge, 1991).
15. Kevin Robins and Frank Webster, *Times of the Technoculture: From the Information Society to the Virtual Life* (New York: Routledge, 1999) 114-15.
16. Hakim Bey, "Notes for CTHEORY," *Digital Delirium*, ed. Arthur Kroker and Marilouise Kroker (New York: St. Martin's, 1997) 153.
17. R. L. Rutsky, *High Technē: Art and Technology from the Machine Aesthetic to the Posthuman* (Minneapolis: U of Minnesota P, 1999).
18. Jean Baudrillard and Claude Thibaut, "Baudrillard on the New Technologies," Trans. Suzanne Falcone 6 Mar. 1996 <www.uta.edu/english/apt/collab/texts/newtech.html>.
19. Jean Baudrillard, *Simulations* (New York: Semiotext(e), 1983) 119-20.

20. Douglas Kellner, "Boundaries and Borderlines: Reflections on Jean Baudrillard and Critical Theory," *Illuminations* <www.gseis.ucla.edu/faculty/kellner>.

21. Guy Debord, *Society of the Spectacle* (Detroit: Black and Red, 1970) 15. Italic in original.

22. Steven Best, "The Commodification of Reality and the Reality of Commodification: Baudrillard, Debord, and Postmodern Theory," *Baudrillard: A Critical Reader*, ed. Douglas Kellner (Cambridge: Blackwell, 1994) 49.

23. Jeremy Rifkin, *The Age of Access: The New Culture of Hypercapitalism Where All of Life is a Paid-for Experience* (New York: Tarcher/Putnam, 2000).

24. Jean Baudrillard, *The Transparency of Evil: Essays on Extreme Phenomena*, Trans. James Benedict (London: Verso, 1993), *La Transparence Du Mal: Essais Sur Les Phenomenes Extremes* (Paris: Editions Galilee, 1990).

25. Mike Gane, *Jean Baudrillard: In Radical Uncertainty* (New York: Pluto, 2000) 43.

26. Peter Lunenfeld, *The Digital Dialectic: New Essays in New Media* (Cambridge: MIT P, 2000) xix.

27. Steven Holtzman, *Digital Mosaics: The Aesthetics of Cyberspace* (New York: Simon, Schuster, 1998) 15.

28. Jay David Bolter and Richard Grusin, *Remediation: Understanding New Media* (Cambridge: MIT P, 1998) 50.

29. Stuart Hall, "Encoding/Decoding," *The Cultural Studies Reader*, ed. Simon During, 2nd ed. (New York: Routledge, 1999) 516. Originally in Stuart Hall, *Culture, Media, Language* (London: Unwin Hyman, 1990).

30. Joseph E. Pelton, *e-Sphere: The Rise of the World-Wide Mind* (London: Quorum, 2000) 13.

31. Charles Bernstein, *A Poetics* (Cambridge: Harvard UP, 1992) 161.

32. Robert Sheppard, "The Necessity of Poetics," August 2000<www.bbk.ac.uk/pores>.

33. Darley describes his project as the design of a "rudimentary poetics" for interpreting the aesthetic of new media and visual digital culture.

34. Loss Pequeño Glazier. *Digital Poetics: The Making of E-Poetics* (Tuscaloosa: U of Alabama P, 2002) 30.

35. Johanna Drucker, *The Visible Word: Experimental Typography and Modern Art, 1909-1923* (Chicago: U of Chicago P, 1994) 43.

CHAPTER 2

1. Peter Forman and Robert W. Saint John, "Creating Convergence," *Scientific American* (Nov. 2000): 50.

2. Edward S. Herman and Robert W. McChesney, *The Global Media: The New Missionaries of Global Capitalism* (London: Cassell, 1997) 107.

3. Stanley M. Davis and Christopher Meyer, *BLUR: The Speed of Change in the Connected Economy* (New York: Little, Brown, 1999).

4. Critical Art Ensemble, "Body Count," 1995 <http://www.nettime.org/desk-mir-ror/zkp/bodycoun.txt>.

5. The networked subject or compu-subject can access information with the click of a mouse, but they are also a source of information to be processed, since the data body is a commodity in the information age, a trail of bits that market researchers follow. Composed of unique identifiers, the data body includes preprogrammed favorite satellite TV channels, subscriptions and membership records, phone numbers, bookmarked Web sites and cookies, Internet downloads and software registrations, telephone numbers, digitalized DNA samples and health, finance, educational and criminal records circulating in the flow of information stored in a web of global databases.

6. Alvin Toffler, *The Third Wave* (New York: Bantam, 1981) 165.

7. Arthur Kroker and David Cook, *The Postmodern Scene: Excremental Culture and Hyper-Aesthetics* (New York: St Martin's, 1986) 279.

8. Jean Baudrillard, *The Ecstasy of Communication* (New York: Semiotext(e), 1988) 103.

9. The commercial was directed by Ridley Scott (famous for his blockbuster science fiction films *Alien* and *Blade Runner*) and produced by TBWA/Chiat/Day. The "1984" spot cost $1.5 million USD to produce—more than any advertisement that had come before it. <Twba.com>

10. For another analysis and image stills from the Macintosh "1984" ad, see Sarah R. Stein's work <www.uiowa.edu/~commstud/adclass/1984_mac_ad.html>.

11. In contrast to IBM products, the Macintosh was marketed as the computer "for the rest of us," part of an effort to represent Apple as a human company, a personal, young, dynamic, innovative alternative. Regis McKenna, *Relationship Marketing: Successful Strategies for the Age of the Customer* (Reading: Addison-Wesley, 1991) <library.stanford.edu/mac/primary/docs/relationmkt.html>.

12. The distinction between computer *operators* and *users* is from Sherry Turkle, *The Second Self*, 32-33.

13. Andrew Shapiro, *The Control Revolution: How the Internet is Putting Individuals in Charge and Changing the World We Know* (New York: Public Affairs, 1999) 27.

14. Bell hooks, "The Oppositional Gaze: Black Female Spectators," Sue Thornham, ed. *Feminist Film Theory: A Reader* (Edinburgh: Edinburgh UP, 1999).

15. Turkle chronicles the red tape around getting the correct tool to open the (hard-drive) box in *Life on the Screen*.

16. Claudia Springer, *Electronic Eros: Bodies and Desire in the Postindustrial Age* (Austin: U of Texas P, 1996).

17. Fredric Jameson, "Progress vs. Utopia or, Can We Imagine the Future?" *Science Fiction Studies* 9.2 (1982): 285.

18. James Gleick, *Faster: The Acceleration of Just About Everything* (New York: Vintage, 2000) 90.

19. Debra Dinnocenzo, *101 Tips for Telecommuters: Successfully Manage Your Work, Team, Technology and Family* (New York: Berrett-Koehler, 1999) 194.

20. Larry Smith, "The Man Who Mistook His Wife for a Palm," *Yahoo! Internet Life Magazine* (Feb. 2001) 99.

21. *Yahoo.com* online news service, "Lost in London Cabs," *Reuters* 31 Aug. 2001 <dailynews.yahoo.com>.

22. Michael Aaron Rockland, "American Mobility," *Dominant Symbols in Popular Culture*, Ray Browne, Marshall Fishwick, Kevin Browne, eds. (Bowling Green: Bowling Green State UP, 1990) 59ff.

23. Stephen Bertman, *Hyperculture: The Human Cost of Speed* (London: Praeger, 1998) 112.

24. Steve Pruitt and Tom Barrett, "Corporate Virtual Workspace," *Cyberspace: First Steps*, Michael Benedikt, ed. (Cambridge: MIT P, 1993) 404.

25. E. Ide Smith and William Tunnel, "Beeper Medicine," *Southern Medical Journal* (July 1988): 816. Cited in Gleick, *Faster*, 85.

26. Tim Jordan. *Cyberpower: The Culture and Politics of Cyberspace and the Internet* (New York: Routledge, 1999), 169-70.

27. Arlie Russell Hochschild, *The Time Bind: When Work Becomes Home and Home Becomes Work* (New York: Owl, 1997, 2001) 129.

28. David Shenk, *Data Smog: Surviving the Information Glut* (New York: HarperEdge, 1997) 21.

29. *WIRED* (March 1997), n.p.

30. Marshall McLuhan, *Understanding Media: The Extensions of Man* (Cambridge: MIT P, 1964) n.p.

31. Marshall McLuhan, "McLuhan Probe," *The Antigonish Review,* ed. George Sanderson, 74-75 3/4 (1988): n.p. Cited in *On McLuhan: Forward through the Rearview Mirror,* ed. Paul Benedetti and Nancy DeHart (Cambridge: MIT P, 1997) 100.

32. McLuhan, *Telescope Revisited*, CBC Television 20 July 1967.

33. Paul Virilio, "Speed and Information: Cyberspace Alarm!" 1995 <www.ctheory.net>.

34. "What is mLife? Ask AT&T Wireless," 1 Feb. 2002 <www.atnewyork.com>.

35. Statistics from C. C. Holland, "mLife Unveiled: How the Marketing Gurus Worked the Web," 2 Feb. 2002 <www.zdnet.com>.

36. Brian McDonough, "AT&T Wireless Pushes mLife with mMode," *Wireless News Factor* 17 Apr. 2002 <www.wirelessnewsfactor.com>.

37. Bukatman, *Terminal*. For more on the discourse of intangibility and the posthuman, see Katherine Hayles, "Life Cycle of Cyborgs."

CHAPTER 3

1. Michael Silver, "Plug Me In Coach," *Business 2.0* (Feb. 2002): 17.

2. MVP = most valuable player.

3. David Whitford, "Curt Shilling Points. He Clicks. He Hits RETURN,"
    Business 2.0 (May 2002): 21.

4. Bruce Sterling's *The Hacker Crackdown: Law and Disorder on the Electronic
    Frontier* (New York: Bantam, 1992); Jon Katz's *Geeks: How Two Lost Boys Rode
    the Internet Out of Idaho* (New York: Broadway, 2000); Steven Levy's *Hackers:
    Heroes of the Computer Revolution* (New York: Penguin, 2001); and Douglas
    Thomas' *Hacker Culture* (Minneapolis: U of Minnesota P, 2002).

5. Allan Freedman interviewed by Chris Seper, "In Nerd Domain, She Hopes
    to Be Sexiest Geek Alive," *Plain Dealer* 2 June 2001, National Sec.: 1A.

6. Casey Kait and Stephen Weiss, *Digital Hustlers: Living Large and Falling
    Hard in Silicon Alley* (New York: Regan/HarperCollins, 2001).

7. Janet Kornblum, "3,000 sexy geeks? You do the math," *USA Today*, 23 Apr. 2001,
    Life Sec.: 3D.

8. For a detailed and personal ethnography of the NASDAQ implosion and its
    devastating effect on the twenty-something entrepreneurs and employees in
    dot-com companies in the US, see Kait and Weiss.

9. Kathryn Balint, "Nerd-do-well; Wise to Their Critics, the Hopelessly Unhip
    Dare to Reprogram, Now They're Cool Jerks," *San Diego Union-Tribune*, 2 May
    2000, Lifestyle Sec.: E-1.

10. John Ciacchella, vice president at A.T. Kearney Inc., the consulting arm of
    Electronic Data Systems Corporation, interviewed by Lisa Baertlein, "Silicon
    Valley seeking better image for geeks," *Houston Chronicle*, 24 May 2001,
    Technology Sec.: 4.

11. Lisa Baertlein, "Silicon Valley Tries to Make Tech Cool to Kids," *High
    Tech Magazine* 22 May 2001<hightechmagazine.com/ManageArticle.
    asp?C=200&A=42>.

12. Julie Hinds, "Revenge of the Nerds: Hollywood Pushes Geek Chic with Sexy,
    Hi-Tech Heroes," *Ottawa Citizen* 19 Feb. 1999: n.p.

13. The concept of *flexing analytical muscles* and the pleasure of critically
    consuming film appears in bell hooks.

14. Jenny Wolmark, *Aliens and Others: Science Fiction, Feminism and
    Postmodernism* (New York: Harvester-Wheatsheaf, 1993) 114.

15. Jay Carr, "Inside the dark, dazzling 'Matrix,' a virtual void," *Boston Globe*, 31
    Mar. 1999, Arts and Film Sec. : F4.

16. Louis Hobson, "*The Matrix:* Plato Thought of It First," *London Free Press*, 31
    Mar. 1999, Entertainment Sec.: C4.

17. Adina Hoffman, "*Matrix*'s Shallow Profundities," *Jerusalem Post*, 19 July 1999,
    Arts Sec.: 7.

18. Steven Rosen, "What is *Matrix*? Too Long, Too Corny, Special Effects Help, but
    Lack of a Story Prevails," *Denver Post*, 31 Mar. 1999, Living Sec.: F-05.

19. Geoff Pevere, "Gothic Cyberpop Thriller Mostly Rocks," *Toronto Star*, 31 Mar.
    1999, Entertainment Sec.

20. For example see William Irwin, ed., *The Matrix and Philosophy: Welcome to the Desert of the Real* (Chicago: Open Court, 2002).

21. Stuart Klawans, "The End of Humanism," *Nation* 268.15 (26 Apr. 1999): 34.

22. Chad Barnett, "Reviving Cyberpunk: (Re)Constructing the Subject and Mapping Cyberspace in the Wachowski Brothers' Film *The Matrix*," *Extrapolation* 41 (2000): 363.

23. In 2000, *The Matrix* won four Academy Awards in the United States, two British Film Academy awards, and a Golden Screen award in Germany.

24. Bill Gates, *What Will Be: How the New World of Information Will Change Our Lives* (San Francisco: Harper, 1997).

25. The term "modern primitives" refers to the (racially diverse) subcultural community in the US that practices ritual body modification, including scarification, tattooing and piercing, etc. In cyberfiction texts when white (male and female) characters execute body modifications, it is far more likely that those procedures will involve the implantation of microchips, sockets, and circuitry, than when racial Others pursue body modification (which will often involve body painting, scarification, tattooing, and piercing). For examples of the "unplugged" see the "Aborigines" in Lisa Mason's *Cyberweb* (New York: Bantam/Spectra, 1995), or the "Rastafarians" in William Gibson's *Neuromancer*.

26. Amanda Fernbach, "The Fetishization of Masculinity in Science Fiction: The Cyborg and the Console Cowboy," *Science Fiction Studies* 27 (2000): 244-45.

27. For detailed consideration of the significance of Reeves' mixed race heritage, see Lisa Nakamura, *Cybertypes: Race, Ethnicity and Identity on the Internet* (New York: Routledge, 2002) and LeiLani Nishime, "The Mulatto Cyborg: Imagining a Multiracial Future," *Cinema Journal* 44.2 (Winter 2005): 34-49.

28. Editorial cited in Vivian Sobchack, "New Age Mutant Ninja Hackers: Reading *Mondo 2000*," <www.rochester.edu/College/FS/Publications/SobchackNinja.html>.

29. Comment by *Mondo 2000* founder R. U. Sirius, Jon Lebkowsky, "It's Better to be Inspired than Wired," Arthur and Marilouise Kroker, eds., *Digital Delirium* (New York: St. Martin's, 1997) 23.

30. Anne Balsamo, *Technologies of the Gendered Body: Reading Cyborg Women* (London: Duke UP, 1996) 223.

31. Brenda Laurel interview with Susie Bright cited in Mark Dery, *Escape Velocity: Cyberculture at the End of the Century* (New York: Grove, 1996) 222.

CHAPTER 4

1. Michel Foucault, *Discipline and Punish: The Birth of the Prison*, trans. Alan Sheridan (New York: Vintage, 1979) 197.

2. *GATTACA*, Written and directed by Andrew M. Niccol, Jersey Films, Sony Pictures, 1997.

3.   Ruby B. Rich, "Dumb Lugs and Femmes Fatales," *Sight and Sound* 5.11 (1995): 8.

4.   Barbara Katz Rothman, *Genetic Maps and Human Imaginations: The Limits of Science in Understanding Who We Are* (New York: Norton, 1998) 13.

5.   Thus the title of the film, G-A-T-T-A-C-A is lifted from a portion of the human genome, located on chromosome 4, where the sequenced nucleotides appear in that order. Niccol makes explicit that his film is a response to the HGP and highlights the connection between the HGP and eugenic science in the following text that is displayed on the screen of the DVD version: "In a few short years, scientists will have completed the Human Genome Project, the mapping of all the genes that make up a human being. We have now evolved to a point where we can direct our own evolution. Had we acquired this knowledge sooner, the following people may never have been born: Abe Lincoln-Marfan's Syndrome; Emily Dickinson-Manic Depression; Vincent Van Gogh-Epilepsy; Albert Einstein-Dyslexia; John F. Kennedy-Addison's Disease; Rita Hayworth-Alzheimer's Disease; Ray Charles-Primary Glaucoma; Stephen Hawking-Amyotrophic Cathedral Sclerosis; Jackie Joyner Kersee-Asthma. Of course the other birth that may have never taken place is your own." Thank you to Jo Thomsen and Katie Kosseff for bringing this text to my attention. For a history of the key breakthroughs and scientists involved in "cracking the code" see Jeff Lyons and Peter Gorner, *Altered Fates: Gene Therapy and the Retooling of Human Life* (New York: Norton, 1995).

6.   For a comprehensive analysis of twentieth-century popular science media representations, rhetorics and corresponding public discourses (and fears) about genetics and eugenics, see Celeste Condit, *The Meanings of the Gene*, (Madison: U of Wisconsin P, 1999).

7.   The rhetoric of coding and uncoding the genome was used in the media and popular science press alongside another popular metaphor: the genome as a text or piece of literature composed of letters that could be read or transcribed into a story (the story of Man). For example, see Matt Ridley, *Genome: The Autobiography of a Species in 23 Chapters* (New York: Perennial, 2000) and Robert Pollack, *Signs of Life: The Language and Meanings of DNA* (Boston: Houghton Mifflin, 1994).

8.   José Van Dijck, *Imagenation: Popular Images of Genetics* (New York: New York UP, 1998).

9.   David Porush, *The Soft Machine: Cybernetic Fiction* (New York: Methuen, 1985) 15.

10.   Elizabeth Grosz, *Volatile Bodies: Toward a Corporeal Feminism* (Bloomington: Indiana UP, 1994) 27.

11.   Many feminist critics, including Barbara Katz Rothman, have commented on the historically consistent choice of using a male subject as the norm for medical and scientific experiments, research, and drug testing. As Rothman observes about the Human Genome Project, "So our representative generic person, with a Y chromosome, will, one more time in our history, be a male. That alone

should make it clear that there is no generic, representative, standard model of the human, and that every choice that is made has political implications" (97). Insofar as the "generic" male model will be used as the archetype for the normal human genome, Richard Lewontin has warned that it will contribute to the pathologizing of any body that deviates from that norm. See Richard C. Lewontin, *Biology as Ideology: The Doctrine of DNA* (New York: Harper Perennial, 1991).

12. For more on the links between eugenic discourse and *GATTACA*, see David A. Kirby, "The New Eugenics in Cinema: Genetic Determination and Gene Therapy in *GATTACA*," *Science Fiction Studies* 2 27 (July 2000): 193-215.

13. Julia Kristeva, *Powers of Horror: An Essay on Abjection* (New York: Columbia UP, 1982) 4.

14. Vivian Sobchack, "The Virginity of Astronauts: Sex and the Science Fiction Film," George Slusser and Eric S. Rabkin, eds., *Shadows of the Magic Lamp: Fantasy and Science Fiction in Film* (Carbondale: Southern Illinois UP, 1985,) 48.

15. For more on the antifeminism in *GATTACA* and other SF genomic and dystopic film see Laura Briggs and Jodi I. Kelber-Kaye, "There is No Unauthorized Breeding in Jurassic Park": Gender and the Uses of Genetics." *NWSA Journal* 12. 3 (October 2000): 92-113.

16. Curtis Edmonds, untitled, rev. of *GATTACA*, The Internet Movie Database (1997) <www.imdb.com>.

17. Official *GATTACA* Web site by Sony Pictures.

18. <http://www.spe.sony.com/Pictures/SonyMovies/movies/GATTACA/home. html>.

19. As Barbara Creed has suggested, the danger of the feminine and its symbolic vagina dentata lies in its duplicity, its ability to bring pleasure and pain to men. Vincent experiences his desire for Irene in exactly these terms. Although the dual nature of the dentata is traditionally symbolic of woman's supposed natural duplicity, in the scene in which Vincent and Irene have sexual intercourse, it is Vincent's duplicity that is at risk of revelation. Perhaps this accounts for the inverted reflection of coitus in the shot, which also suggests that as a result of this weakness, Vincent's world may be turned upside down. See Barbara Creed, *The Monstrous Feminine: Film, Feminism, Psychoanalysis* (New York: Routledge, 1993).

20. Two texts offering current collections of feminist analysis of the controversies and politics of genetic screening and pregnant women's bodies are Robbie Davis-Floyd and Joseph Dumit, eds., *Cyborg Babies: From Techno-Sex to Techno-Tots* (New York: Routledge, 1998), and Janine Marchessault and Kim Sawchuk, eds., *Wild Science: Reading Feminism, Medicine and the Media* (New York: Routledge, 2000).

21. For a detailed discussion of this concept of gender performativity and its intersections with sexuality, see Jackie Stacey, "Masculinity,

Masquerade, and Genetic Impersonation: *Gattaca's* Queer Visions," *Signs* 30. 3 (April 2005): 1851-77.

22. Hannah Kuhlmann, "Escaping Abjection: *GATTACA's* Narratives of Discrimination," unpublished manuscript (2000).

23. David Kirby argues that this scene can be read as a critical commentary on the impact that genetic science has, or can have, on race relations in his essay, "Extrapolating Race in *GATTACA*: Genetic Passing, Identity, and the Science of Race," *Literature and Medicine* 23. 1 (April 2004): 184-200.

24. Lamar the corporate physician seeks to bond with Jerome$_2$ by repeatedly commenting on the remarkable size of Jerome$_2$'s penis. Their relationship is emblematic of the homosociality that ties the narrative together. Vincent, passing as Jerome$_2$, seems uncomfortable with Lamar's attentions, probably due to the fact that he is nervous about the surveillance system of which Lamar is an officer, and the fact that he is reluctant to take pleasure in his own "meatly" but In-Valid endowments because of the risk of revelation involved. Jerome$_2$ "pisses on demand" as Lamar states, but understandably, then immediately rushes away. Through a combination of nerves and self-absorption, Jerome$_2$ is prevented from recognizing that Lamar is an ally who can appreciate the genoistic bind that entraps Vincent. As Lamar reminds Jerome$_2$, and the audience in so many words, having the penis is not tantamount as having phallic power in GATTACian culture, though in the context of this film it might very well be a prerequisite.

CHAPTER 5

1. Mary Ann Doane, "Technophilia: Technology, Representation, and the Feminine," Evelyn Fox Keller, ed., *Body/Politics: Women and the Discourses of Science* (New York: Routledge, 1990). Rpt. ed. Jenny Wolmark, *Cybersexualities: A Reader on Feminist Theory, Cyborgs and Cyberspace* (Edinburgh: Edinburgh UP, 1999) 21.

2. Judith Butler, *Gender Trouble: Feminism and the Subversion of Identity* (New York: Routledge, 1990).

3. For a cinematic critique that considers the social impact of the cybergirl cultural phenomenon, see Andrew Niccols' cautionary tale *S1m0ne* (2002).

4. William Gibson, *Idoru* (New York: Berkeley, 1996) 121.

5. Interview with Julie Roth by Ian Blair, "Say Hello to Motorola's Mya," 28 Apr. 2000 <www.tvindustry.com>.

6. It is imperative for Motorola to develop this voice recognition technology service, since marketing research indicates that the future of e-commerce depends on personalization and interactivity. The information and computer technology industries project that global investment in personalization technologies will reach $2.1 billion (USD) in 2006, up from $500 million (USD) in 2001. (Survey conducted by Datamonitor, 10 Sept. 2001, *Personalization*

Technology Market Booming, source: NUA Internet Reports <www.nua.ie/surveys/>.) Studies suggest that the percentage of e-consumers who spend the most dollars online demand customized content, and resent having to reenter basic data (such as addresses or account numbers) on Web sites (survey conducted by Cyber Dialogue for the Personalization Consortium, 14 May 2001. Source: NAU Internet Reports <www.nua.ie/surveys/>. By developing cyberassistants, Motorola can meet this demand, and will attract partnerships with e-commerce companies looking to direct their advertising demographically, offering
personalized push media, otherwise known as spam.

7. Interview with David Barboza, "Motorola Hopes Mya Will Link the Real World With the Virtual One," *New York Times* 25 Apr. 2000 <www.nytimes.com>.

8. Edward Leida, interviewed in Ruth La Ferla, "The Perfect Model," *New York Times* 8 Feb. 2001 <www.nytimes.com or www.dallasnews.com>.

9. Robert Hamilton, "Virtual Idols and Digital Girls: Artifice and Sexuality in Anime, Kisekae and Kyoko Date," *Bad Subjects* 35 (Nov. 1997) <http://eserver.org/bs/>.

10. Charles Moore, "Ananova Goes Live (So to Speak) on Wednesday," Apr. 2000 <http://www.applelinks.com>.

11. USAToday.com, "Ananova Speaks to Her Adoring Public!" 10 Aug. 2000 <www.clubananova.co.uk/news/interview_august.htm>.

12. Note that it is interesting in all of these pixel vixens whose design evolved from morphing many images of women together, then the result is always a white or very light-skinned complexion with aquiline features and light eyes.

13. "Ananova Speaks to Her Adoring Public!" *USA Today* 10 Aug. 2000 <www.clubananova.co.uk/news/interview_august.htm>.

14. Interview with Luciana Abreu by Rachel Emma Silverman, "Elite Develops Virtual Supermodel—Webbie Tookay," *Financial Express* 23 July 1999) <www.financialexpress.com/fe/daily/19990723/fle23059p.html>.

15. <www.Illusion2K.com>.

16. Miguel Avalos, assistant to John Casablancas (Elite's CEO), interviewed by Silverman, online.

17. Barry Park, "Mya, the virtual face of Motorola," *Fairfax I.T.* 28 Mar. 2000) <http://www.it.fairfax.com.au>.

18. This is my translation of Google.com's translation of the French from an interview with Luciana Abreu, "Webbie Tookay, le top model 100% synthétique de l'agence Elite," *Largeur.com* <http://www.largeur.com>. Here is the original text: "C'est une jeune femme très heureuse qui consomme et s'achète des produits de beauté. . . elle adore le chocolat—ce qui ne pose pas de problème puisqu'elle ne peut pas grossir, la musique disco des années 1970 et les animaux, en particuliers les chiens. Webbie s'intéresse aux problèmes d'environnement et se préoccupe des grandes questions du monde: pauvreté, faim dans le monde, etc." Gabriel Sigrist "Webbie Tookay, le top model 100% synthétique

de l'agence Elite" 20 Sept. 1999. Largeur.com online: <http://largeur.ch/expArt. asp?artID=199>.

19. Steven Stalberg interviewed by Fiona Stewart, "Fantasy Figures," *iVillage.com* <http://www.ivillage.co.uk>.

20. Matt Madden quoted in Laura Schiff, "The Future of Motion-Capture Animation: Building the Perfect Digital Human," *Animation World Magazine* 4.11 (February 2000) <http://www.awn.com/mag/issue4.11>.

21. *Artbyte* 2.3 (Sept./Oct. 1999).

22. Allyson Polsky, "Skins, Patches, and Plug-ins: Becoming Woman in the New Gaming Culture," *Genders* 34 (2001) <http://www.genders.org>.

23. Sandy Stone, "Virtual Systems," Sanford Kwinter and Jonathan Crary, eds., *Incorporations* (New York: Zone, 1992).

24. The concept of a visual iconography was inspired by Vivian Sobchack (1987).

CHAPTER 6

1. Judith Halberstam and Ira Livingston, eds., Introduction to *Posthuman Bodies* (Bloomington: Indiana UP, 1995) 2.

2. Theresa Jenne, "Why is *Lara Croft* So Popular?" <http://www.TombRaiders. com/*Lara*_Croft/Essays/*Lara*Croft/default.htm>.

3. The phrase "beyond Barbie" is from Mary Flanagan, "Mobile Identities, Digital Star, and Post-Cinematic Selves," *Wide Angle* 21.1 (Jan. 1999) 82.

4. Peter Kafka, "Gender Benders," *Forbes* 161.1 (Jan. 1998): 39.

5. A recent survey of the views of adolescent male gamers revealed that they are stimulated by "the cute little grunts and moans and groans" of female characters in games. One survey respondent admits, "I am not proud of this, [but] I like the pain sound." See Kathryn Wright's study "Gender Bending in Games" (1999) <www.womengamers.com>.

6. Comment cited in Miranda Sawyer, "*Lara* Croft: The Bit Girl," *The Face* (1997) <http://www.TombRaider.com/*Lara*_Croft/Essays/face.htm>.

7. Mark, a gamer, cited in Mark Cohen and Eidos Interactive, *Lara Croft: The Art of Virtual Seduction* (New York: Prima, 2000) 106.

8. Rebecca Schneider, *The Explicit Body in Performance* (New York: Routledge, 1997).

9. Toby Guard comments in interview with Katie Salen, "Lock, Stock and Barrel: Sexing the Digital Siren," *Sex Appeal: The Art of Allure in Graphic and Advertising Design,* ed. Steven Heller (New York: Allworth, 2000) 148.

10. Actually there are several hundred *Lara Croft*s if one considers the fan fiction and amateur CGI renditions of the pixel vixen available on the Internet.

11. Mike Ward, "Being *Lara* Croft, Or, We Are All Sci-Fi," *Popmatters.com* 14 Jan. 2000) <http://www.popmatters.com>.

12. The phrase, "fictions of presence," is from Margaret Morse in *Virtualities: Television, Media, Art and Cyberculture* (Bloomington: Indiana UP, 1998).

13. For more on the KISS dolls, see Mary Flanagan, "Mobile Identities, Digital Star, and Post-Cinematic Selves," *Wide Angle* 21.1 (Jan. 1999). For an interesting comparison between KISS software and the *Barbie Fashion Designer* drag-and-drop clothing and virtual dress-up doll computer game in North American markets, see Kaveri Subrahmanyam and Patricia M. Greenfield, "Computer Games for Girls: What Makes them Play?" Justine Cassell and Henry Jenkins, eds., *From Barbie to Mortal Kombat: Gender and Computer Games* (Cambridge: MIT P, 1999) 46.

14. Elena Gorfinkel and Eric Zimmerman, "Technologies of Undressing: The Digital Paper Dolls of KISS," *Sex Appeal: The Art of Allure in Graphic and Advertising Design,* ed. Steven Heller (New York: Allworth, 2000) 162.

15. Missy Kris, "*Lara Croft*: Feminist Media Critique and Audience Response" <http://www.dsuper.net/~miskris/stadium/*Lara*croft/analysis.html>.

16. Stuart Wynne, "Ascension: The Real *Lara Croft*(s)" <http://binky.paragon.co.uk/tombraider/R*Lara*1J.html>.

17. Angelina Jolie cited on official *Tomb Raider* movie Web site <www.tombraiders.com/movie>.

18. Although this chapter suggests that the remediation of the *Lara* cyberpop icon from video game to film was not entirely successful commercially because of the loss of interactive properties (among other factors), Margaret Morse makes a compelling case for considering the continuities between the computer monitor and the film-video screen, the user and the spectator, in her essay "Body and Screen," *Wide Angle* 21.1 (Jan. 1999), 63.

19. Angelina Jolie cited on official *Tomb Raider* movie Web site <www.tombraiders.com/movie>.

20. Katie Salen, "Lock, Stock, and Barrel: Sexing the Digital Siren," *Sex Appeal: The Art of Allure in Graphic and Advertising Design*, ed. Steven Heller (New York: Allworth. 2000), 150.

21. Debbie Stoller, "Faster Pussycat, Click Click," *Shift Magazine* <www.shift.com/shiftstd/html/xx.22.html>.

22. Interview on National Public Radio with Reporter Susan Stone and Adrian Smith of Eidos <http://www.TombRaiders.com/Lara_Croft/Essays/NPR.htm>.

23. The comparison between *Lara* and Barbie is given further weight considering the reaction to the life-sized *Lara* dolls Eidos sent out to stores in Germany as promotional decoration. Evidently, although a very limited supply of these mannequins were produced, Eidos was instantly overwhelmed with purchase requests, as a whirlwind of demands for the figure came in, and the company was forced to "put up extra barricades" around the displays. Admittedly, Eidos "threatened the night watch [security guards] with shooting if the figure was misplaced." See Mark Cohen and Eidos Interactive, *Lara Croft: The Art of Virtual Seduction* (New York: Prima, 2000) 97.

24. Anne-Marie Schleiner, "Does *Lara Croft* Wear Fake Polygons: Gender Analysis of the '1st Person Shooter/Adventure Game with Female Heroine'

and Gender Role Subversion and Production in the Game Patch"
<http://switch.sjsu.edu/web/v4n1/annmarie.html>.

25. For a discussion of how the 1995 film and comic book character *Tank Girl* can
be read as a postfeminist text, see Elyce Rae Helford, "Postfeminism and the
Female Action-Adventure Hero: Positioning *Tank Girl*," *Future Females, The
Next Generation: New Voices and Velocities in Feminist Science Fiction Criticism*
ed. Marleen S. Barr (New York: Roman, Littlefield, 2000).

26. Henry Jenkins, Director of the graduate program in Comparative Media Studies
at MIT commented on National Public Radio *Lara Croft* represents "a new form
of femininity," placing her within "a more aggressive set of images for women,"
which then "becomes a fantasy of empowerment." Jenkins suggested that this
was a positive cultural development, "as long as we don't take those images
overly literally." Cited in interview with Susan Stone (reporting for National
Public Radio) "The *Lara Croft* Phenomenon" transcript available online at
<http://www.TombRaiders.com/Lara_Croft/Essays/NPR.htm>.

27. *Lara Croft* is an interactive fiction in more ways than one; as part of her
background dataset, we learn that *Lara* is a graduate of British Prince Charles'
college, though to date the school does not admit women. See Chris Taylor,
"The Man Behind *Lara Croft*: Adrian Smith's well-endowed computer heroine
is back — better, brainier and busier than ever," *TIME Magazine* 154
(6 Dec. 1999): 78.

28. Oscar Holzberg in Cohen, *Virtual Seduction*, 106.

CHAPTER 7

1. Peter Lunenfeld, "The Alchemical Portrait: Magic, Technology and Digital
Imagery" (Jan. 1998), Huntington Beach Art Center's catalogue,
The Unreal Person: Portraiture in the Digital Age
<www.heise.de/tp/english/inhalt/sa/3218/1.html>.

2. Irit Krygier, Curator's Comment, *The Unreal Person: Portraiture in the Digital
Age* (1998) <http://strikingdistance.com/unreal>.

3. Available online <http://www.daniellee.com>.

4. For a fuller consideration of the progressive and regressive maneuvers in
contemporary representations of mixed-race bodies and cyberpunk film, see
LeiLani Nishime, "The Mulatto Cyborg: Imagining a Multiracial Future,"
Cinema Journal 44.2 (Winter 2005): 34-49.

5. *TIME* Magazine, special issue, *The New Face of America* (2 Dec. 1993). Cover art
is online at <http://www.time.com/time/covers/0,16641,1101931118,00.html>.

6. Robert C. Young, *Colonial Desire: Hybridity in Theory, Culture and Race*
(New York: Routledge, 1995). Also see Anne McClintock, *Imperial Leather:
Race, Gender and Sexuality in the Colonial Closet* (New York: Routledge, 1995),
and Shawn Michelle Smith, *American Archives: Gender, Race, and Class in
Visual Culture* (Princeton, NJ: Princeton UP, 1999).

7. Evelynn M. Hammonds, "New Technologies of Race," ed. Jennifer Terry and Melodie Calvert, *Processed Lives* (New York: Routledge, 1995). Rpt. ed. Gill Kirkup, et al., *The Gendered Cyborg: A Reader* (New York: Routledge, 2000) 315.

8. For example, see the work of Nancy Burson including her piece, "The Human Race Machine," available online as part of *Paradise Now: Picturing the Genetic Revolution* Web site <www.genomicart.org/burson.htm>.

9. See US Department of Energy's Human Genome Web site <www.ornl.gov/sci/techresources/Human_Genome/home.shtml>.

10. Kelly Hurley, *The Gothic Body: Sexuality, Materialism and Degeneration at the Fin de Siècle* (Cambridge: Cambridge UP, 1996). For more on the cybergothic see the very excellent analysis by Dani Cavallaro, *Cyberpunk and Cyberculture* (London: Athlone, 2000).

11. Even though Westerfeld refers to Lee almost exclusively as "she" throughout the novel, I have elected to use gender-neutral pronouns to describe Lee. To this end, "zie" stands in for "he" or "she," and "hir" stands in for "him," "her," "his," or "hers."

12. Scott Westerfeld, *Polymorph* (New Jersey: Penguin, 1997).

13. Alondra Nelson, ed. *Technicolor: Race, Technology and Everyday Life* (New York: New York UP, 2001).

14. The most notorious cases in the history of chat rooms and online communities were white men passing as someone else in order to gain access to exclusive groups. See Sandy Stone, "Will the Real Body Please Stand Up?" in Michael Benedikt, ed., *Cyberspace: First Steps* (Cambridge: MIT P, 1991) <http://www.rochester.edu/College/FS/Publications/StoneBody.html>. Also see Julian Dibble, "My Tiny Life: A Rape in Cyberspace," *The Village Voice*, (23 Dec. 1993) <http://www.levity.com/julian/bungle.html>.

15. For example, Morpheus (*The Matrix*) and Molly (*Neuromancer*) endure torture, while Lee (*Polymorph*) and Molly (*Neuromancer*) survive sexual assault.

16. Vivian Sobchack, *Meta-Morphing: Visual Transformation and the Culture of the Quick-Change* (Minneapolis: U of Minnesota P, 2000) 153.

17. Sherry Turkle, "The Cyberanalyst," John Brockman, ed., *Digerati: Encounters with the Cyberelite* (San Francisco: Hardwired, 1996) 308.

18. <www.mdmco.com/contractedsalesforces.html>.

19. <www.microsoft.com>.

20. <www.peoplesoft.com>.

21. Emily Martin, *Flexible Bodies: Tracking Immunity in American Culture from the Days of Polio to the Age of AIDS* (Boston: Beacon, 1994) 214.

Bibliography

Adorno, Theodor, and Max Horkheimer. *The Culture Industry: Selected Essays on Mass Culture.* New York: Routledge, (1944) 1991.

Anderson, Jim, and Peter Seidler. "Syndi: Your Celebrity Portal." *Artbyte.* 2.3 (September/October 1999): 51-54.

Balint, Kathryn. "Nerd-do-well: Wise to Their Critics, the Hopelessly Unhip Dare to Reprogram, Now They're Cool Jerks." *San Diego Union-Tribune* 2 May 2000, Lifestyle Sec.

—. "Silicon Valley Seeking Better Image for Geeks." *Houston Chronicle* 24 May 2000, Tech Sec.

Ballard, JG Interview with Peter Linnett, *Corridor,* 5 1974. Reprinted in *Re/Search* 8-9. San Francisco: Re/Search Publications, 1984.

Balsamo, Anne. *Technologies of the Gendered Body: Reading Cyborg Women.* Durham: Duke UP, 1996.

Barboza, David. "Motorola Hopes Mya Will Link the Real World with the Virtual One." *New York Times* 25 Apr. 2000.

Barlow, John Perry. "A Declaration of the Independence of Cyberspace." 1991 <www.eff.org/~barlow/Declaration-Final.html>.

Barnett, Chad. "Reviving Cyberpunk: (Re)Constructing the Subject and Mapping Cyberspace in the Wachowski Brothers' Film *The Matrix.*" *Extrapolation* 41 (2000): 359ff.

Barr, Marleen S. *Feminist Fabulation: Space/Postmodern Fiction.* Iowa City: U of Iowa P, 1992.

—. *Lost in Space: Probing Feminist Science Fiction and Beyond.* Chapel Hill: U of North Carolina P, 1993.

—, ed. *Future Females, the Next Generation: New Voices and Velocities in Feminist Science Fiction Criticism.* New York: Rowman, Littlefield, 2000.

Baudrillard, Jean. *The Vital Illusion.* New York: Columbia UP, 2001.

171

—. *Simulations*. New York: Semiotext(e), 1983.

—. *The Transparency of Evil: Essays on Extreme Phenomena*. Trans. James Benedict. London: Verso, 1993.

—. *For a Critique of the Political Economy of the Sign*. Trans. Charles Levin. Telos, 1981.

—. *The Ecstasy of Communication*. New York: Semiotext(e), 1988.

—. Rev. of "Marshall McLuhan, *Understanding Media: The Extensions of Man*." *L'homme et la societe*, 5 (1967). Trans. Gary Genosko in *McLuhan and Baudrillard: The Masters of Implosion*. New York: Routledge, 1999.

Baudrillard, Jean, and Claude Thibaut. *Baudrillard on the New Technologies*. Trans. Suzanne Falcone. 6 Mar. 1996 <www.uta.edu/english/apt/collab/texts/newtech.html>.

Bell, David, and Barbara M. Kennedy, eds. *The Cybercultures Reader*. New York: Routledge, 2000.

Benedetti, Paul, and Nancy DeHart, eds. *On McLuhan: Forward through the Rearview Mirror*. Cambridge: MIT P, 1997.

Benedikt, Michael, ed. *Cyberspace: First Steps*. Cambridge: MIT P, 1994.

Bernstein, Charles. *A Poetics*. Cambridge: Harvard UP, 1992.

Bertman, Stephen. *Hyperculture: The Human Cost of Speed*. London: Praeger, 1998.

Best, Steven. "The Commodification of Reality and the Reality of Commodification: Baudrillard, Debord, and Postmodern Theory." *Baudrillard: A Critical Reader*. Ed. Douglas Kellner. Cambridge: Blackwell, 1994.

Bey, Hakim. "Notes for CTHEORY." *Digital Delirium*. Eds. Marilouise Kroker and Arthur Kroker. New York: St. Martin's, 1997.

Blair, Ian. "Say Hello to Motorola's Mya." 28 Apr. 2000 <www.tvindustry.com>.

Bolter, Jay David, and Richard Grusin. *Remediation: Understanding New Media*. Cambridge: MIT P, 1998.

Brahm, Gabriel, and Mark Driscoll, eds. *Prosthetic Territories: Politics and Hypertechnologies*. San Francisco: Westview, 1995.

Braidotti, Rosi. "Cyberfeminism with a Difference." n.d. <www.let.ruu.nl/womens_studies/rosi/cyberfem.htm>.

—. *Nomadic Subjects*. New York: Columbia UP, 1994.

—. "Meta(l)morphosis." *Theory, Culture, and Society* 14.2 (1997): 67-80.

Braidotti, Rosi, and Nina Lykke, eds. *Between Monsters, Goddesses and Cyborgs: Feminist Confrontations with Science, Medicine and Cyberspace*. London: Zed, 1996.

Bukatman, Scott. *Terminal Identity: The Virtual Subject in Postmodern Science Fiction*. Durham, NC: Duke UP, 1993.

Butler, Judith. *Bodies That Matter: On the Discursive Limits of "Sex."* New York: Routledge, 1993.

—. *Gender Trouble: Feminism and the Subversion of Identity*. New York: Routledge, 1990.

Cadora, Karen. "Feminist Cyberpunk." *Science Fiction Studies* 22.67 (1995): 357-72.

Cairncross, Frances. *The Death of Distance: How the Communications Revolution Will Change Our Lives*. Cambridge: Harvard Business School, 1997.

Carr, Jay. "Inside the Dark, Dazzling *Matrix*, A Virtual Void." *Boston Globe* 31 Mar. 1999, Arts and Film Sec.

Cartwright, Lisa. *Screening the Body: Tracing Medicine's Visual Culture.* Minneapolis: U of Minnesota P, 1995.

Cassell, Justine, and Henry Jenkins, eds. *From Barbie to Mortal Kombat: Gender and Computer Games.* Cambridge: MIT P, 1999.

Castells, Manuel. *The Rise of the Network Society.* New York: Blackwell, 2000.

Cavallaro, Dani. *Cyberpunk and Cyberculture: Science Fiction and the Work of William Gibson.* London: Athlone, 2000.

Cherney, Lynn, and Elizabeth Reba Weise, eds. *Wired_Women: Gender and New Realities in Cyberspace.* Seattle: Seal, 1996.

Cohen, Mark, and Eidos Interactive with Primus Publishing. *Lara Croft: The Art of Virtual Seduction.* New York: Prima, 2000.

Condit, Celeste. *The Meanings of the Gene.* Madison: U of Wisconsin P, 1999.

Conley, Verena Andermatt, ed. *Re-Thinking Technologies.* Minneapolis: U of Minnesota P, 1993.

Coupland, Douglas. *Lara's Book: Lara Croft and the Tomb Raider Phenomenon.* Roseville: Prima, 1998.

Coyne, Richard. *Technoromanticism: Digital Narrative, Holism, and the Romance of the Real.* Cambridge: MIT P, 1999.

Crary, Jonathan, and Sanford Kwinter, eds. *Incorporations.* New York: Zone, 1992.

Creed, Barbara. *The Monstrous Feminine: Film, Feminism, Psychoanalysis.* New York: Routledge, 1993.

Critical Art Ensemble. *Flesh Machine: Cyborgs, Designer Babies, Eugenic Consciousness.* New York: Autonomedia, 1998.

—. *The Electronic Disturbance.* New York: Autonomedia, 2000.

—. "Body Count." 1995 <www.nettime.org>.

Crocker, Elizabeth, and Laura Harris. *Femme: Feminists, Lesbians, and Bad Girls.* New York: Routledge, 1997.

Csicsery-Ronay, Istvan. "Cyberpunk forum/symposium." *Mississippi Review* 16 (1988): 2-3.

—. "The SF of Theory: Baudrillard and Haraway." *Science Fiction Studies* 18 (1991): 387-403.

Curtis, Christy. *Lara Croft: The Art of Virtual Seduction.* Roseville: Prima, 2000.

Darley, Andrew. *Visual Digital Culture: Surface Play and Spectacle in New Media Genres.* New York: Routledge, 2000.

Datamonitor. "Personalization Technology Market Booming." 10 Sept. 2001 <www.nua.ie/surveys>.

Davis, Stanley M., and Christopher Meyer. *BLUR: The Speed of Change in the Connected Economy.* New York: Little, Brown, 1999.

Davis-Floyd, Robbie, and Joseph Dumit, eds. *Cyborg Babies: From Techno-Sex to Techno-Tots.* New York: Routledge, 1998.

Debord, Guy. *Society of the Spectacle.* Detroit: Black, Red, 1970.

Dery, Mark. *Escape Velocity: Cyberculture at the End of the Century.* New York: Grove, 1997.

Dibble, Julian. "My Tiny Life: Crime and Passion in a Virtual World." 1993 <www.levity.com/julian/mytinylife/index.html>.

Dinnocenzo, Debra. *101 Tips for Telecommuters: Successfully Manage Your Work, Team, Technology and Family.* New York: Berrett-Kpehler, 1999.

Doane, Mary Ann. "Technophilia: Technology, Representation and the Feminine."
    Body/Politics: Women, Literature and the Discourse of Science. Eds. Mary
    Jacobus, Evelyn Fox Keller, and Sally Shuttleworth. New York: Routledge, 1990.
    Reprinted in *The Gendered Cyborg.* Ed. Gill Kirkup et. al. New York:
    Routledge, 2000.

—. "Woman's Stake: Filming the Female Body." *Feminism and Film Theory.* Ed.
    Constance Penley. New York: Routledge, 1993.

Drucker, Johanna. *The Visible Word: Experimental Typography and Modern Art,
    1909-1923.* Chicago: U of Chicago P, 1994.

Druckrey, Timothy, ed. *Electronic Culture: Technology and Visual Representation.*
    New York: Aperture, 1996.

Edmonds, Curtis. Untitled, rev. of *GATTACA.* The Internet Movie Database. 1997
    <www.imdb.com>.

Eisenstein, Zillah. *Global Obscenities: Patriarchy, Capitalism, and the Lure of
    Cyberfantasy.* New York: New York UP, 1998.

Escobar, Arturo. "Welcome to Cyberia: Notes on the Anthropology of Cyberculture."
    Current Anthropology 35.3 (1994): 211-31.

Fausto-Sterling, Anne. *Myths of Gender: Biological Theories about Women and Men.*
    New York: Basic, 1992.

Fernbach, Amanda. "The Fetishization of Masculinity in Science Fiction: The
    Cyborg and the Console Cowboy." *Science Fiction Studies* 27 (2000): 234-55.

Flanagan, Mary. "Mobile Identities, Digital Star, and Post-Cinematic Selves." *Wide
    Angle* 21.1 (Jan. 1999): 76-93.

Foreman, Peter, and Robert Saint John. "Creating Convergence." *Scientific American*
    (Nov. 2000).

Foucault, Michel. *Discipline and Punish.* New York: Vintage, 1977.

—. *The History of Sexuality: An Introduction.* New York: Vintage, 1978.

—. *The Archaeology of Knowledge.* Trans. A. M. Sheridan Smith. New York:
    Pantheon, 1972.

Gane, Mike. *Jean Baudrillard: In Radical Uncertainty.* New York: Pluto, 2000.

Gates, Bill. *What Will Be: How the New World of Information Will Change Our Lives.*
    San Francisco: Harper, 1997.

Gauntlett, David, ed. *Web.Studies: Rewiring Media Studies for the Digital Age.*
    London: Arnold, 2000.

Geertz, Clifford. *The Interpretation of Cultures.* New York: Basic, 1973.

Gibson, William. *Neuromancer.* New York: Ace, 1984.

—. *Burning Chrome.* New York: Ace, 1986.

—. *IDORU.* New York: Berkeley, 1996.

Glaser, Rob. "Lost in Futurespace!" *Business 2.0* 26 Sept. 2000.

Glazier, Loss Pequeño. *Digital Poetics: The Making of E-Poetics.* Tuscaloosa: U of
    Alabama P, 2002.

Gleick, James. *Faster: The Acceleration of Just About Everything.* New York: Vintage,
    2000.

González, Jennifer. "Envisioning Cyborg Bodies." *The Cyborg Handbook.* Ed. Chris
    Hables Gray. New York: Routledge, 1995. Rpt. in *The Gendered Cyborg.* Ed. Gill
    Kirkup, et al. New York: Routledge, 2000.

Gorfinkel, Elena, and Eric Zimmerman. "Technologies of Undressing: The Digital Paper Dolls of KISS." *Sex Appeal: The Art of Allure in Graphic and Advertising Design.* Ed. Steven Heller. New York: Allworth, 2000.

Gray, Chris Hables, ed. *The Cyborg Handbook.* New York: Routledge, 1995.

Grosz, Elizabeth. *Volatile Bodies: Toward a Corporeal Feminism.* Bloomington: Indiana UP, 1994.

Guattari, Felix. "Regimes, Pathways, Subjects." *Incorporations.* Ed. Sanford Kwinter and Jonathan Crary. New York: Zone, 1992.

Halberstam, Judith, and Ira Livingston, eds. *Posthuman Bodies.* Bloomington: Indiana UP, 1995.

Hall, Stuart. "Encoding/Decoding." *The Cultural Studies Reader.* Ed. Simon During. 2nd ed. New York: Routledge, 1999. Rpt. from *Culture, Media, Language.* London: Unwin Hyman, 1990.

Hall, Stuart, and Jessica Evans, eds. *Visual Culture: The Reader.* Thousand Oaks, CA: Corwin, 1999.

Hamilton, Robert. "Virtual Idols and Digital Girls: Artifice and Sexuality in Anime, Kisekae and Kyoko Date." *Bad Subjects.* Issue 35 (Nov. 1997) <eserver.org/bs>.

Hammonds, Evelynn M. "New Technologies of Race." *Processed Lives: Gender and Technology in Everyday Life.* Ed. Jennifer Terry and Melodie Calvert. New York: Routledge, 1997. Rpt. in *The Gendered Cyborg.* Ed. Gill Kirkup et al. New York: Routledge, 2000.

Haraway, Donna J. "A Manifesto for Cyborgs: Science, Technology and Socialist Feminism in the 1980s." *Socialist Review* 90 (1985): 65-107.

—. *Simians, Cyborgs, and Women: The Reinvention of Nature.* New York: Routledge, 1991.

—. *Modest-Witness, Second-Millennium: FemaleMan Meets OncoMouse: Feminism and Technoscience.* New York: Routledge, 1996.

—. *How Like a Leaf: An Interview with Donna Haraway.* Ed. Thyrza Nichols Goodeve. New York: Routledge, 1999.

—. "A Game of Cat's Cradle: Science Studies, Feminist Theory, Cultural Studies." *Configurations* 2.1 (1994): 59-71.

—. "Cyborgs at Large." Interview with Constance Penley and Andrew Ross. *Technoculture.* Ed. Andrew Ross and Constance Penley. Minneapolis: U of Minnesota P, 1991. 1-20.

Hayles, N. Katherine. "The Life Cycle of Cyborgs: Writing the Posthuman." *A Question of Identity.* Ed. M. Benjamin. New Jersey: Rutgers UP, 1993. Rpt. in *Cybersexualities.* Ed. Jenny Wolmark. Edinburgh: Edinburgh UP, 1999.

—. "The Materiality of Informatics." *Configurations* 1.1 (1993): 147-70.

—. *How We Became Posthuman: Virtual Bodies in Cybernetics, Literature, and Informatics.* Chicago: U of Chicago P, 1999.

—. "The Seductions of Cyberspace." *Reading Digital Culture.* Ed. David Trent. Oxford: Blackwell, 2001.

Heim, Michael. *The Metaphysics of Virtual Reality.* New York: Oxford UP, 1994.

Helford, Elyce Rae. "Postfeminism and the Female Action-Adventure Hero: Positioning *Tank Girl.*" *Future Females, The Next Generation: New Voices and Velocities in Feminist Science Fiction Criticism.* Ed. Marleen S. Barr. New York: Roman, Littlefield, 2000.

Herman, Edward S., and Robert W. McChesney. *The Global Media: The New Missionaries of Global Capitalism*. London: Cassell, 1997.

Himanen, Pekka. *The Hacker Ethic*. New York: Random, 2001.

Hinds, Julie. "Revenge of the Nerds: Hollywood Pushes Geek with Sexy, Hi-Tech Heroes." *Ottawa Citizen* 19 Feb. 1999.

Hobson, Louis. "*The Matrix*: Plato Thought of It First." *London Free Press* 31 Mar. 1999. Entertainment Section.

Hochschild, Arlie Russell. *The Time Bind: When Work Becomes Home and Home Becomes Work*. 1997. New York: Owl, 2001.

Hoffman, Adina. "*Matrix*'s Shallow Profundities." *Jerusalem Post* 19 July 1999, Arts Sec.

Holland, C. C. "mLife Unveiled: How the Marketing Gurus Worked the Web." 2 Feb. 2002 <www.zdnet.com>.

Holtzman, Steven. *Digital Mosaics: The Aesthetics of Cyberspace*. New York: Simon, Schuster, 1998.

hooks, bell. "The Oppositional Gaze: Black Female Spectators." *Feminist Film Theory: A Reader*. Ed. Sue Thornham. Edinburgh: Edinburgh UP, 1999.

Hopkins, Patrick, ed. *Sex/Machine: Readings in Culture, Gender and Technology*. Bloomington: Indiana UP, 1999.

Hurley, Kelly. *The Gothic Body: Sexuality, Materialism and Degeneration at the Fin de Siècle*. Cambridge: Cambridge UP, 1996.

Irwin, William, ed. *The Matrix and Philosophy: Welcome to the Desert of the Real*. Chicago: Open Court, 2002.

Jameson, Fredric. *Postmodernism, or, the Cultural Logic of Late Capitalism*. Durham: Duke UP, 1991.

—. "Progress vs. Utopia or, Can We Imagine the Future?" *Science Fiction Studies* 9.2 (1982): 147-58.

Jenks, Chris, ed. *Visual Culture*. New York: Routledge, 1995.

Johnson, Steven. *Interface Culture: How New Technology Transforms the Way We Create & Communicate*. New York: Basic, 1997.

Jordan, Tim. *Cyberpower: The Culture and Politics of Cyberspace and the Internet*. New York: Routledge, 1999.

Kait, Casey, and Stephen Weiss. *Digital Hustlers: Living Large and Falling Hard in Silicon Alley*. New York: HarperCollins, 2001.

Katz, John. *Geeks: How Two Lost Boys Rode the Internet Out of Idaho*. New York: Broadway, 2000.

Keller, Evelyn Fox. *Refiguring Life*. New York: Columbia UP, 1996.

—. *The Century of the Gene*. Cambridge: Harvard UP, 2001.

Kellner, Douglas, ed. *Baudrillard: A Critical Reader*. Cambridge: Blackwell, 1994.

Kevles, Daniel J., and Leroy Hood, eds. *The Code of Codes: Scientific and Social Issues in the Human Genome Project*. Cambridge: Harvard UP, 1992.

Kirby, David. "The New Eugenics in Cinema: Genetic Determinism and Gene Therapy in *GATTACA*." *Science Fiction Studies* 27 (2000): 193-215.

Kirkup, Gill, et al., eds. *The Gendered Cyborg: A Reader*. New York: Routledge, 2000.

Kolko, Beth, et al., eds. *Race in Cyberspace*. New York: Routledge, 2000.

Kornblum, Janet. "3,000 Sexy Geeks? You Do the Math." *USA Today* 23 Apr. 2001, Life Sec.

Kris, Missy. "Lara Croft: Feminist Media Critique and Audience Response." <www.dsuper.net/~miskris/stadium/laracroft/analysis.html>.

Kristeva, Julia. *Powers of Horror: An Essay on Abjection.* New York: Columbia UP, 1982.

Kroker, Arthur, and David Cook. *The Postmodern Scene.* New York: St. Martin's, 1986.

Kroker, Arthur, and Marilouise Kroker, eds. *Digital Delirium.* New York: St. Martin's, 1997.

Krygier, Irit. Curator's Comment. *The Unreal Person: Portraiture in the Digital Age.* 1998 <strikingdistance.com/unreal>.

Kuhlmann, Hannah. "Escaping Abjection: *GATTACA*'s Narratives of Discrimination." Unpublished manuscript, 1999. U of Minnesota.

La Ferla, Ruth. "The Perfect Model: Gorgeous, No Complaints, Made of Pixels." *New York Times* 8 Feb. 2001, Section 9, p. 1.

Lebkowsky, Jon. "It's Better to be Inspired than Wired." *Digital Delirium.* Ed. Arthur Kroker and Marilouise Kroker. New York: St. Martin's, 1997.

Levy, Steven. *Hackers: Heroes of the Computer Revolution.* New York: Penguin, 2001.

Lewontin, Richard C. *Biology as Ideology: The Doctrine of DNA.* New York: Harper Perennial, 1991.

Lunenfeld, Peter. "The Alchemical Portrait: Magic, Technology and Digital Imagery." *The Unreal Person: Portraiture in the Digital Age.* Huntington Beach Art Center catalogue. Jan. 1998 <www.heise.de/tp/english/inhalt/sa/3218/1.html>.

—. *The Digital Dialectic: New Essays in New Media.* Cambridge: MIT P, 2000.

Lyons, Jeff, and Peter Gorner. *Altered Fates: Gene Therapy and the Retooling of Human Life.* New York: Norton, 1995.

Marchessault, Janine, and Kim Sawchuk, eds. *Wild Science: Reading Feminism, Medicine and the Media.* New York: Routledge, 2000.

Martin, Emily. *Flexible Bodies: Tracking Immunity in American Culture from the Days of Polio to the Age of AIDS.* Boston: Beacon, 1994.

McCaffery, Larry, ed. *Storming the Reality Studio: A Casebook of Cyberpunk and Postmodern Fiction.* Durham: Duke UP, 1991.

McClintock, Anne. *Imperial Leather: Race, Gender and Sexuality in the Colonial Closet.* New York: Routledge, 1995.

McCorduck, Pamela. "Sex, Lies, and Avatars," *WIRED* 4.04 (Apr. 1996) <www.wired.com/wired/archive/4.04/turkle_pr.html>.

McDonough, Brian. "AT&T Wireless Pushes mLife with mMode." *Wireless News Factor* 17 Apr. 2002 <www.wirelessnewsfactor.com>.

McKenna, Regis. "Relationship Marketing: Successful Strategies for the Age of the Consumer." Reading: Addison-Wesley, 1991. <library.stanford.edu/mac/primary/docs/relationmkt.html>.

McLuhan, Marshall. *Understanding Media: The Extensions of Man.* Cambridge: MIT P, 1964.

—. "McLuhan Probe." *The Antigonish Review.* Ed. George Sanderson. 74-75, 3/4 (1988).

—. *Telescope Revisited.* CBC Television, 20 July 1967.

Microsoft Press Computer Dictionary. 3rd Edition. Richmond: Microsoft, 1997.

Mirzoeff, Nicholas, ed. *The Visual Culture Reader.* New York: Routledge, 1998.

—, ed. *An Introduction to Visual Culture*. New York: Routledge, 1999.

Moore, Charles. "Ananova Goes Live (So to Speak) on Wednesday." Apr. 2000 <www.applelinks.com>.

Morse, Margaret. *Virtualities: Television, Media Art, and Cyberculture*. Bloomington: Indiana UP, 1998.

(1988). "Body and Screen." *Wide Angle* 21.1 (Jan. 1999): 63-75.

Moser, Mary Anne, and Douglas MacLeod, eds. *Immersed in Technology: Art and Virtual Environments*. Cambridge: MIT P, 1996.

Nakamura, Lisa. "Head Hunting in Cyberspace." *The Women's Review of Books*. XVIII, . 5 (Feb. 2001): 10-11.

(1988). *Cybertypes: Race, Ethnicity, and Identity on the Internet*. New York: Routledge, 2002.

Nakamura, Lisa, Beth Kolko, and Gilbert Rodman, eds. *Race in Cyberspace*. New York: Routledge, 2000.

Negroponte, Nicolas. *Being Digital*. New York: Vintage, 1995.

Nelkin, Dorothy, and M. Susan Lindee. *The DNA Mystique: The Gene As a Cultural Icon*. New York:Freeman, 1996.

Nelson, Alondra, ed. *Technicolor: Race, Technology and Everyday Life*. New York: New York UP, 2001.

Newman, Leslea, ed. *The Femme Mystique*. Boston: Alyson, 1995.

O'Farrell, Mary Ann, and Lynne Vallone, eds. *Virtual Gender: Fantasies of Subjectivity and Embodiment*. Ann Arbor: Michigan UP, 1999.

Park, Barry. "Mya, The Virtual Face of Motorola." *Fairfax I.T.* 28 Mar 2000 <www.it.fairfax.com.au>.

Pelton, Joseph E. *e-Sphere: The Rise of the World-Wide Mind*. Westport: Quorum, 1990.

Penley, Constance, and Andrew Ross. "Cyborgs at Large: Interview with Donna Haraway." *Social Text* 25-26 (1990): 8-23. Rpt. in *Technoculture*. Ed. Andrew Ross and Constance Penley. Minneapolis: U of Minnesota P, 1991: 1-20.

Pevere, Geoff. "Gothic Cyberpop Thriller Mostly Rocks." *Toronto Star* 31 Mar. 1999, Entertainment Sec.

Pollack, Robert. *Signs of Life: The Language and Meanings of DNA*. Boston: Houghton Mifflin, 1994.

Polsky, Allyson. "Skins, Patches, and Plug-ins: Becoming Woman in the New Gaming Culture." *Genders* 34 (2001). <www.genders.org>.

Porter, David, ed. *Internet Culture*. New York: Routledge, 1996.

Porush, David. *The Soft Machine: Cybernetic Fiction*. New York: Methuen, 1985.

Poster, Mark. *The Mode of Information: Poststructuralism and Context*. Chicago: U of Chicago P, 1990.

(1988). *The Information Subject*. New York: Routledge, 2001.

Pruitt, Steve, and Tom Barrett. "Corporate Virtual Workspace." *Cyberspace: First Steps*. Ed. Michael Benedikt. Cambridge: MIT P, 1993.

Rich, Ruby B. "Dumb Lugs and Femmes Fatales." *Sight and Sound* 5.11 (1995): 6-10.

Ridley, Matt. *Genome: The Autobiography of a Species in 23 Chapters*. New York: Perennial, 2000.

Rifkin, Jeremy. *The Biotech Century: Harnessing the Gene and Remaking the World*. Los Angeles: Tarcher, 1998.

—. *The Age of Access: The New Culture of Hypercapitalism Where All of Life is a Paid-for Experience*. New York: Putnam, 2000.

Robins, Kevin, and Frank Webster. *Times of the Technoculture: From the Information Society to the Virtual Life*. New York: Routledge, 1999.

Rockland, Michael Aaron. "American Mobility." *Dominant Symbols in Popular Culture*. Ed. Ray Browne, Marshall Fishwick, and Kevin Browne. Bowling Green: Bowling Green State UP, 1990.

Rosen, Steven. "What is *Matrix*? Too long, too corny, special effects help, but lack of a story prevails," *The Denver Post*, Living Section, (March 31, 1999): F-05.

Ross, Andrew. *Strange Weather: Culture, Science and Technology in the Age of Limits*. London: Verso, 1991.

Ross, Andrew, and Constance Penley, eds. *Technoculture*. Minneapolis: U of Minnesota P, 1991.

Rothman, Barbara Katz. *Genetic Maps and Human Imaginations: The Limits of Science in Understanding Who We Are*. New York: Norton, 1998.

Rutsky, R. L. *High Technē: Art and Technology from the Machine Aesthetic to the Posthuman*. Minneapolis: U of Minnesota P, 1999.

Salen, Katie. "Lock, Stock, and Barrel: Sexing the Digital Siren." *Sex Appeal: The Art of Allure in Graphic and Advertising Design*. Ed. Steven Heller. New York: Allworth, 2000.

Samuelson, Robert J. "Puzzles of the 'New Economy.'" *Newsweek* 17 Apr. 2000: 49ff.

Sandoval, Chela. "New Sciences: Cyborg Feminism and the Methodology of the Oppressed." *The Cyborg Handbook*. Ed. Chris Hables Gray. New York: Routledge, 1995. Rpt. in *Cybersexualities: A Reader on Feminist Theory, Cyborgs and Cyberspace*. Ed. Jenny Wolmark. Edinburgh: Edinburgh UP, 1999.

Sawyer, Miranda. "Lara hit in *The Face*" *The Croft Times*. (June 5, 1997) <www.cubeit.com/ctimes/news0007b.htm>.

Schenk, David. *Data Smog: Surviving the Information Glut*. New York: HarperCollins, 1997.

Schiff, Laura. "The Future of Motion-Capture Animation: Building the Perfect Digital Human." *Animation World Magazine* 4.11 (Feb. 2000). <www.awn.com/mag/issue4.11>.

Schleiner, Anne-Marie. "Does Lara Croft Wear Fake Polygons?: Gender Analysis of the '1st Person Shooter/Adventure Game with Female Heroine' and Gender Role Subversion and Production in the Game Patch." *Switch* 4.1 <switch.sjsu.edu/web/v4n1/annmarie.html>.

Schneider, Rebecca. *The Explicit Body in Performance*. New York: Routledge, 1997.

Schuchardt, Read. "What is *The Matrix*? Ancient Wisdom Wrapped in Technological Analogies." *Re:Generation*. <www.regenerator.com/5.2/matrix.html>.

Seeper, Chris. "In Nerd Domain, She Hopes to be the Sexiest Geek Alive." *Plain Dealer* 2 June 2001, National Sec.

Shapiro, Andrew. *The Control Revolution: How the Internet is Putting Individuals in Charge and Changing the World We Know*. New York: Public Affairs, 1999.

Shenk, David. *Data Smog: Surviving the Information Age*. New York: HarperCollins, 1997.

Sheppard, Robert. "The Necessity of Poetics." Aug. 2000 <www.bbk.ac.uk/pores>.

Shiner, Larry. "Confessions of an Ex-Cyberpunk." *New York Times* 7 Jan. 1991: A17.

Sigrist, Gabriel. "Webbie Tookay: Le Top Model 100% Synthetique de l'Agence Elite." <www.largeur.com>.

Silver, David. "Looking Backwards, Looking Forwards: Cybercultural Studies 1990-2000." *Web.Studies: Rewiring Media Studies for the Digital Age.* Ed. David Gauntlett. New York: Oxford UP, 2000.

Silver, Michael. "Plug Me In, Coach." *Business 2.0,* 3.2 (Feb. 2002): 17-20.

Silverman, Rachel Emma. "Elite Develops Virtual Supermodel—Webbie Tookay." *Financial Express.* 23 July 1999 <www.financialexpress.com/fe/daily>.

Slataslla, Michelle, and Joshua Quittner. *Masters of Deception: The Gang That Ruled Cyberspace.* New York: Harper Perennial, 1995.

Smith, Ide, and William Tunnel. "Beeper Medicine." *Southern Medical Journal* 81.7 (July 1988): 816-17.

Smith, Larry. "The Man Who Mistook His Wife for a Palm." *Yahoo! Internet Life Magazine* (Feb. 2001).

Smith, Shawn Michelle. *American Archives: Gender, Race and Class in Visual Culture.* Princeton, NJ: Princeton UP, 1999.

Sobchack, Vivian. *Screening Space: The American Science Fiction Film.* Piscataway, NJ: Rutgers UP, 1987.

—. "The Virginity of Astronauts: Sex and the Science Fiction Film." *Shadows of the Magic Lamp: Fantasy and Science Fiction in Film.* Ed. George Slusser and Eric S. Rabkin. Carbondale: Southern Illinois UP, 1985.

—. "New Age Mutant Ninja Hackers: Reading *Mondo 2000.*" <www.rochester.edu/College/FS/Publications/SobchackNinja.html>.

—, ed. *Meta-Morphing: Visual Transformation and the Culture of the Quick-Change.* Minneapolis: U of Minnesota P, 2000.

Springer, Claudia. *Electronic Eros: Bodies and Desire in the Postindustrial Age.* Austin: U of Texas P, 1996.

Sterling, Bruce. *The Hacker Crackdown: Law and Disorder on the Electronic Frontier.* New York: Bantam, 1992.

—, ed. *Mirrorshades: The Cyberpunk Anthology.* New York: Ace, 1998.

Stewart, Fiona. "Fantasy Figures." *iVillage.* <www.ivillage.co.uk>.

Stone, Sandy. *The War of Desire and Technology at the Close of the Mechanical Age.* Cambridge: MIT P, 1991.

—. "Virtual Systems." *Incorporations.* Ed. Jonathan Crary and Sanford Kwinter. New York: Zone, 1992.

—. "Will the Real Body Please Stand Up?" *Cybersexualities: A Reader on Feminist Theory, Cyborgs and Cyberspace.* Ed. Jenny Wolmark. Edinburgh: Edinburgh UP, 1999.

Stone, Susan. Interview with Adrian Smith of Eidos. NPR. <www.TombRaiders.com/Lara_Croft/Essays/NPR.htm>.

Stromberg, Johnathan. "Rethinking the Basis of Technology." <www.vegan.swinternet.co.uk/articles/science/Rethinking_technology.html>.

Taylor, Chris. "The Man behind Lara Croft: Adrian Smith's well-endowed computer heroine is back—better, brainier and busier than ever." *TIME Magazine* 6 Dec. 1999: 154.

Terry, Jennifer, and Melodie Calvert, eds. *Processed Lives: Gender and Technology in Everyday Life.* New York: Routledge, 1997.

—. *Deviant Bodies: Critical Perspectives on Difference in Science and Popular Culture.* Bloomington: Indiana UP, 1995.

"The New Face of America." *TIME* Special Issue 2 Dec. 1993.

Thewleitt, Klaus. "Circles, Lines and Bits." *Incorporations.* Ed. Jonathan Crary and Sanford Kwinter. New York: Zone, 1992.

Thibaut, Claude. "Baudrillard on the New Technologies: An Interview with Claude Thibaut" Trans. Suzanne Falcone. 6 Mar. 1996 <www.uta.edu/english/apt/collab/texts/newtech.html>.

Thomas, Douglas. *Hacker Culture.* Minneapolis: U of Minnesota P, 2002.

Thomsen, Rosemarie Garland, ed. *Freakery: Cultural Spectacles of the Extraordinary Body.* New York: New York UP, 1996.

—. *Extraordinary Bodies.* New York: Columbia UP, 1996.

Toffler, Alvin. *The Third Wave.* New York: Bantam, 1981.

Treichler, Paula, ed. *The Visible Woman: Imaging Technologies, Gender, and Science.* New York: New York UP, 1998.

Trend, David, ed. *Reading Digital Culture.* Cambridge: Blackwell, 2001.

Turkle, Sherry. *The Second Self: Computers and the Human Spirit.* New York: Touchstone, 1995.

—. *Life on the Screen: Identity in the Age of the Internet.* New York: Touchstone, 1997.

—. "The Cyberanalyst." *Digerati: Encounters with the Cyberelite.* Ed. John Brockman. San Francisco: Hardwired, 1996.

USA Today. "Ananova Speaks to Her Adoring Public!" 10 Aug. 2000 <www.clubananova.co.uk/news/interview_august.htm>.

US Department of Commerce, National Telecommunications and Information Administration. Report "Falling through the Cracks." 2000 <www.ntia.doc.gov/ntiahome/digitaldivide/>.

Van Dijck, José. *Imagenation: Popular Images of Genetics.* New York: New York UP, 1998.

Virilio, Paul. "Speed and Information: Cyberspace Alarm!" *CTHEORY.* <www.ctheory.com/a30-cyberspace_alarm.html>.

Waldby, Catherine. *The Visible Human Project: Informatic Bodies and Posthuman Medicine.* New York: Routledge, 2000.

Ward, Mike. "Being Lara Croft, Or, We Are All Sci-Fi." *Popmatters.* 14 Jan. 2000 <www.popmatters.com>.

Watson, James D. *The Double Helix.* New York: New American Library, 1991.

Weiner, Norbert. *Cybernetics: Or Control and Communication in Animal and the Machine.* Paris: Hermann, 1948.

—. *The Human Use of Human Beings: Cybernetics and Society.* New York: Doubleday, 1954.

Westerfeld, Scott. *Polymorph.* New York: ROC, 1997.

"What is mLife? Ask AT&T Wireless." 1 Feb. 2002 <www.atnewyork.com>.

Wingerson, Lois. *Unnatural Selection: The Promise and the Power of Human Gene Research.* New York: Bantam, 1998.

Woesler, Christine de Panafeiu. "Automata—A Masculine Utopia." *Nineteen Eighty-Four: Science between Utopia and Distopia*. Ed. Everett Mendeksohn. Dordrecht: Reidel, 1984.

Wolmark, Jenny, ed. *Cybersexualtiies: A Reader on Feminist Theory, Cyborgs and Cyberspace*. Edinburgh: Edinburgh UP, 1999.

—. *Aliens and Others: Science Fiction, Feminism and Postmodernism*. New York: Harvester-Wheatsheaf, 1993.

Wynne, Stuart. "Ascension: The Real Lara Croft(s)." <binky.paragon.co.uk/tom-braider/Rlara1J.html>.

Yahoo.com. "Lost in London Cabs." *Reuters* 31 Aug. 2001 <dailynews.yahoo.com>.

Young, Robert. *Colonial Desire: Hybridity in Theory, Culture and Race*. New York: Routledge, 1995.

Index

An environmentally friendly book printed and bound in England by www.printondemand-worldwide.com

PEFC Certified

This product is
from sustainably
managed forests
and controlled
sources

www.pefc.org

PEFC/16-33-415

FSC
www.fsc.org

MIX
Paper from
responsible sources
FSC® C004959

This book is made entirely of chain-of-custody materials

#0222 - - C0 - 229/152/11 - PB